People and organizational management in construction

People and organizational management in construction

Shamil Naoum

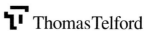

Published by Thomas Telford Publishing, Thomas Telford Ltd,
1 Heron Quay, London E14 4JD.
URL: http://www.thomastelford.com

Distributors for Thomas Telford books are
USA: ASCE Press, 1801 Alexander Bell Drive, Reston, VA 20191-4400, USA
Japan: Maruzen Co. Ltd, Book Department, 3–10 Nihonbashi 2-chome, Chuo-ku,
Tokyo 103
Australia: DA Books and Journals, 648 Whitehorse Road, Mitcham 3132,
Victoria

Learning Resources
Centre

12 55256 9

First published 2001

Also available from Thomas Telford Books
The Decision makers: ethics for engineers. James Armstrong, Ross Dixon &
Simon Robinson. ISBN: 0 7277 2598 X
Management decisions for engineers. James Parkin. ISBN: 0 7277 2501 7

A catalogue record for this book is available from the British Library

ISBN: 0 7277 2874 1

Typeset by Academic + Technical Typesetting, Bristol
Printed and bound in Great Britain by MPG Books, Bodmin, Cornwall

Contents

Contents

Preface

The importance of the construction industry is highlighted by the fact that it is very labour intensive and provides work for about 6–7% of the total work force in the UK. Despite its importance, there seems to have been a limited amount of research conducted on the behavioural aspects of the construction industry. Moreover, the texts that are available on the management of organizations and people in construction are also limited. The aim of this book is therefore to fill this important gap by applying general principles of management specifically to the construction industry.

The idea of writing this book grew out of my belief that people are the heart of any successful organization and can be regarded as the building blocks of its structure. Throughout my career as a project manager and as a lecturer in construction management, I became convinced that practitioners, as well as construction students, needed a book that could offer an applied approach to people and organizational management in order to help them understand human and organizational behaviour as well as to assist in the search for the most appropriate ways of improving organizational performance and effectiveness. In this book, this will be achieved through the study of the management concepts and theories and the application of these concepts and theories in construction-related case studies. It is the blending of theory with practice that is at the heart of good management of people and organization and the study of the subject should reflect that experiential learning, as in the case studies and examples presented in this book.

The key issues which will be discussed in this book are evolution of management theories, environmental forces, strategy, organization structure, work groups, organizational culture, leadership, motivation and personnel management.

About the author

Dr Shamil Naoum is a senior lecturer at South Bank University. He received a BSc in Building and Construction Engineering from the University of Technology in Baghdad, an MSc in Construction Management and Economics from Aston University in Birmingham, and a PhD in Construction Management from Brunel University in Middlesex.

Before beginning his academic career he worked in the construction industry as a site engineer and project manager. He is a full member of the Chartered Institute of Building and the American Society of Civil Engineers.

Dr Naoum has considerable research experience in construction management related areas such as Human Resources Management, Procurement Methods and Information Technology. Dr Naoum also supervises PhD students researching into construction management problems. He wrote the well known book *Dissertation Research and Writing for Construction Students*, which was published by Butterworth-Heinemann in 1998.

During his academic career, Dr Naoum has presented papers at many international conferences and for publication in a diverse group of scholarly journals, including *Construction Engineering and Management* by the American Society of Civil Engineers (USA), *International Journal of Project Management* (UK), *Journal of Engineering Construction and Architectural Management* (UK) and *Occasional Papers No. 45* by the Chartered Institute of Building (UK).

Acknowledgments

This book builds on the thoughts and ideas of earlier writers on the subject of organization and human behaviour. I would like to give special credit to previous contributors in the field. In particular, I wish to record my acknowledgments to the work of the following writers.

- Laurie Mullins for his book, *Management and Organizational Behaviour*, published by Pitman (1999), fifth edition.
- Fremont Kast and James Rosenzweig for their book, *Organization and Management – A System and Contingency Approach*, published by McGraw-Hill (1985), fourth edition.
- David Langford, Mick Hancock, Richard Fellows and Andy Gale for their book, *Human Resources Management in the Construction Industry*, published by Longman (1995).
- Garry Johnson and Kevan Scholes for their book, *Exploring Corporate Strategy*, published by Prentice-Hall (1999), fifth edition.
- Henry Mintzberg for his book, *The Structuring of Organizations*, published by Prentice-Hall (1998).
- Jan Drucker and Geoff White for their book, *People Management in Construction*, published by the London Institute of Personnel Management (1996).
- Charles Handy for his book, *Understanding Organizations*, published by Penguin (1998), fifth edition.
- Fred Luthans for his book, *Organizational Behaviour*, published by McGraw-Hill (1998), eighth edition.
- John Kotter and James Herskett for their research book, *Corporate Culture and Performance*, published by Macmillan (1992).
- Joseph Litterer for his book, *The Analysis of Organisations*, published by Wiley (1967).
- John Child for his book, *Organisation – A Guide to Problems and Practice*, published by Harper and Row (1984).
- Richard Fellows, David Langford, Robert Newcombe and Sydney Urry for their book, *Construction Management in Practice*, published by Longman (1998), seventh edition.

- Robert Newcombe and Mike Hancock for their workbook 1 and 2 on *Concepts of Management*, MSc in Construction Management by distance learning, produced by the University of Bath (1996).
- Antony Sidwell for his notes on *Organizational Theory*, MSc in Construction Management and Economics, University of Aston (1980), unpublished notes.
- Andrew Brown for his book, *Organisational Culture*, published by Pitman (1998), second edition.

References to sources of information and material are given as accurately as possible throughout this book. Apologies are expressed if any acknowledgment has inadvertently not been recorded.

Acknowledgments for permission to reproduce copyright material

Chapter 2

McGraw-Hill for Fig. 2.3 from *Organization and Management* by F. Kast and J. Rosenzweig (1985).

Chapter 3

McGraw-Hill for Fig. 3.1 from *Organization and Management* by F. Kast and J. Rosenzweig (1985).
Prentice-Hall for Table 3.1 from *Exploring Corporate Strategy* by G. Johnson and K. Scholes (1999).

Chapter 4

Routledge for Fig. 4.2 from *Strategic Human Resource Management* by O. Lundy and A. Cowling (1996).
Professor D. Langford and S. Male for Fig. 4.5 and case studies 1 and 2 from *Strategic Management in Construction*, originally published by Gower 1991 (out of print).
Harvard Business School Press for Table 4.1 from *Competing for the Future* by G. Hamel and C. Prahalad (1994).

Chapter 5

Prentice-Hall for Fig. 5.2 and Fig. 5.8 from *The Structuring of Organizations* by H. Mintzberg (1998).
Harvard Business Review for Fig. 5.7 from 'Evolution and Revolution as Organisations Grow' by L. Greiner (1972).
Longman for Fig. 5.9 from *Construction Management in Practice* by R. Fellows, D. Langford, R. Newcombe and S. Urry (1991).
Paul Chapman Publishing Ltd (part of Sage Publishing) for the case study from *Case Studies in Organisational Behaviour and Human Resources Management*, written by Fiona Mills and edited by D. Gowler, K. Legge and C. Clegg (1998).

Acknowledgments

Chapter 6

McGraw-Hill for Fig. 6.2 from *The Human Organisation* by R. Likert (1967).
Harcourt, Brace and World for Fig. 6.3 from *Human Behaviour* by B. Berelson and G. Steiner (1964).
McGraw-Hill for Fig. 6.6 from *Organization and Management* by F. Kast and J. Rosenzweig (1985).
McGraw-Hill for Fig. 6.7 from *Organizational Behaviour* by F. Luthans (1998).

Chapter 7

Penguin Books for Fig. 7.3 from *Understanding Organizations* by C. Handy (1998).
Institute of Personnel Management for Fig. 7.5 from *Changing Culture – New Organisational Approach* by A. Williams, P. Dobson and M. Wilters (1993).
Pitman for Fig. 7.7 from *Organisational Culture* by A. Brown (1998).
Harper and Row for Fig. 7.8 from *Search for Excellence* by T. Peters and R. Waterman (1982).
Paul Chapman Publishing Ltd (part of Sage publishing) for case study from *Case Studies in Organisational Behaviour and Human Resources Management*, written by D. Guest, R. Peccei and A. Fulcher and edited by D. Gowler, K. Legge and C. Clegg (1998).

Chapter 8

Harvard Business Review for Fig. 8.3 from 'How to Choose a Leadership Pattern' by R. Tannenbaum and H. Schmidt (1958).
Gulf Publishing for Fig. 8.4 from *Leadership Dilemmas* by R. Blake and A. MacCanse (1964).
McGraw-Hill for Table 8.2 from *Theory of Leadership Effectiveness* by F. Fiedler (1967).
The University of Bath for the case study from *Concepts of Management*, MSc in Construction Management by distance learning. Management in construction module by R. Newcombe and M. Hancock (1996).

Chapter 9

Macmillan for Fig. 9.3 from *Existence, Relatedness and Growth* by C. Alderfer (1972).
Wiley for Fig. 9.4 from *The Motivation to Work* by C. Herzberg (1959).
Wiley for Fig. 9.6 from *Work and Motivation* by V. Vroom (1964).
McGraw-Hill for Fig. 9.7 from *Organizational Behaviour* by J. Luthans (1998).
Addison-Wesley for Fig. 9.10 from *Work Redesign* by J. Hackman and G. Oldham (1980).
Pearson Education for Fig. 9.11 from *Management and Organizational Behaviour* by L. Mullins (1999).

Chapter 10

Institute of Personnel Management for the case study from *Managing People in Construction* by J. Drucker and G. White (1996).

Further acknowledgements

I also wish to record my acknowledgement to the following authors who, despite numerous efforts, I have been unable to trace.

L. Fahey and V. Narayanan for adapting Fig. 3.2 from *Macro-environmental Analysis for Strategic Management*, cited in Gary Johnson and Kevin Scholes, *Exploring Corporate Strategy* (1999).

West for Fig. 3.2 from *Macro-environmental Analysis for Strategic Management* by L. Fahey and V. Narayanan (1986).

A. Dalbecq and A. Filley for modifying Fig. 5.5 from *Program and project management in a matrix organisation: A case study*. (Monograph No. 9, Graduate School of Business, Bureau of Business Research and Service, University of Wisconsin, Madison (1974)).

Raymond H. Van Zelst for Fig. 6.5 from *Sociometrically Selected Work Teams Increase Productivity*, cited in Joseph Litterer, *The Analysis of Organisations* (1967).

Psychological Review for Fig. 9.2. from 'A Theory of human motivation' by A. Maslou (1943).

Personnel Psychology for Fig. 6.5 from *The Analysis of Organisations* by J. Litterer (1967).

D. Hall for adapting Fig. 9.9 from *Career stage model* (1989), cited in Fred Luttans, *Organizational Behaviour* (1998).

Organisational Behaviour and Human Performance, for Fig. 9.9 from 'An examination of Maslow's need hierarchy in an organisational setting' by D. Hall (1968).

Finally, I wish to express my gratitude to the staff of Thomas Telford who masterfully crafted the production of this book.

Dr Shamil Naoum
School of Construction, South Bank University, UK

Chapter 1

Introduction

The meaning of organization

Organizations come in various sizes and shapes to perform specific functions. The function of the organization can be classified as 'formal' and 'informal'. A formal function produces a visible product, such as a car or a building, that is usually consumed by portions of society that are outside the organization. An informal function, on the other hand, does not necessarily produce a result immediately visible to the outside society; examples are organizing a conference or arranging a social activity. Within the context of formal and informal functions, the meaning of organization is to achieve certain objectives through a collection of people and other resources. These resources are co-ordinated by a set of procedures and integrated by a form of organizational structure. The ways in which the objectives are planned and the manner in which people are co-ordinated and managed differ considerably among organizations.

In general, most 'formal' organizations have six common elements within their boundaries:

(*a*) the operation (task and technology)
(*b*) objective (visible and invisible products)
(*c*) resources (human and non-human)
(*d*) structure (formal and informal)
(*e*) management (strategic and operational)
(*f*) environment (internal and external).

The success or failure of the organization is dependent upon the clarity of the operation and the objective, the quality of the people employed, the availability of the resources and the appropriateness of the structure and the management system adopted.

Each organization consists of many interdependent parts. For example, a building firm may consist of a commercial department, contract department, planning department and a purchasing department. No one department within the organization can achieve success in isolation.

1

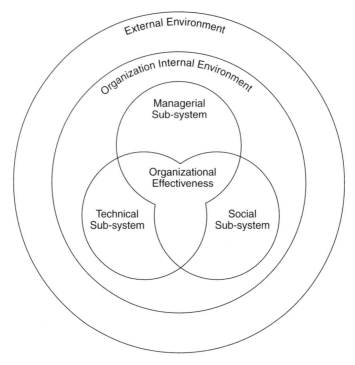

Fig. 1.1.   Organizational sub-systems

All departments are interrelated and dependent on one another. What affects one part of the organization at a particular time will also affect others. These parts are functioned and administrated by a collection of 'systems' and 'sub-systems'.

There are three main sub-systems that integrate the operation and resources within the organization, these are:

(a)   *the managerial sub-system* – including setting goals, planning a strategy, structuring, co-ordinating and administrating

(b)   *the technical sub-system* – including planning and control techniques, production methods, facilities and equipment

(c)   *the social sub-system* – including leadership, personnel management, work groups, motivation and culture.

Figure 1.1 illustrates the overlap between the three sub-systems of the organization, which are presented in the form of a 'conceptual' model. The term 'model' will be referred to frequently throughout this book. The technique of using a model is applied to represent or explain phenomena and theories in the real world. It has been used in the formal sciences and is now being adopted more and more by the social sciences. The theoretical model in Fig. 1.1 shows that organizational effectiveness is dependent upon the interaction between the managerial, the technical and the social sub-systems. It has to be said, however, that the possibilities of drawing a conceptual model to illustrate a particular phenomenon are endless. In other words, other writers may draw Fig. 1.1 with a different shape or details. Chapter 2 provides further discussion on the system approach of management and the concept of models, with special reference to the building industry.

The essential elements of formal organizations will be 'changed' and/or 'modified' over the years. For example, the people that are currently running a large construction company are not the same as those who ran the corporation ten or twenty years ago and, more likely, the employees in the organization today are largely different from those who were there forty of fifty years ago. If we examine what happened to the organization, we see that, for the most part, the new organizational member does the same things that his/her predecessor did. However, probably there is a new set of values and beliefs (i.e. culture) that govern the organization. There could also be a new structure and management style used to co-ordinate the people and the tasks. All of these changes are determined by the complex and dynamic nature of the 'environment', discussed in chapter 3.

Aim and learning objectives of the book

This book provides a system approach to people and organizational management with special reference to the construction industry. It is concerned with interactions among the external environment and the corporate management of the organization, the process of management and the behaviour of people at work. The underlying aim of the book is to highlight the importance of the managerial and social functions in affecting the attitude and behaviour of people at work which, in turn, influences organizational effectiveness.

The learning objectives of this book are to:

- ➢ understand the nature of the external environment and the forces that affect the strategic decisions of the organization
- ➢ understand the nature of organizations and essential features which affect the leadership style and functions of an organization
- ➢ evaluate the design of organizational structures and groups that accompany the allocation of work and responsibilities
- ➢ distinguish between various organizational cultures which are reflected in a structure and a set of systems
- ➢ develop a fundamental understanding of theories relating to motivation and job satisfaction

> understand the role of the personnel function in management of people at work
> relate the various theoretical frameworks that serve as a foundation for a model of organizational behaviour.

Need for the book

This book fulfils a need in the construction industry by providing managers and students with an understanding of the interrelated processes between people and the organization. There are a number of texts available on 'organizational behaviour' and 'human behaviour' but few authors have concentrated their attention on these aspects in the construction industry. This book is specifically designed to assist:

(*a*) executive managers (such as corporate managers and human resource managers) who wish to expand their knowledge of the key management issues
(*b*) practising managers such as project managers and site managers
(*c*) students on Direct Membership Exam (DMX) courses.

This book will also assist:

(*a*) MSc (taught masters) students on Built Environment courses such as construction management, construction project management, quantity surveying, facility management, architecture and civil engineering
(*b*) honours undergraduate students in Built Environment courses
(*c*) Chartered Institute of Building (CIOB) (member) new Educational Framework course programmes offered by universities/colleges of higher educational, etc.
(*d*) students undertaking distance learning courses.

Approach to the book

As mentioned above, the system view of organizations and their management serves as the basic conceptual framework for this book. The key concept of organization systems is that the whole organization is composed of a set of independent but interacting sub-systems (e.g. strategic, technical, social and managerial), and these sub-systems are in continuous interaction with the external environment. Naturally, no one book can cover all of these sub-systems, as their complete study would involve most of the units of a major course or indeed all the courses within a whole university. Therefore, in this book, I will be concentrating on a narrower subset of systems – part of the strategic and social management system.

The style of writing the book reflects my previous experience as a project manager and my current profession as a lecturer and researcher in construction management. It is the blending of theory with practice which is at the heart of good management of people and organization and the study of the subject should reflect that experiential learning, such as the use of case studies, is of great benefit in the study of organization, for it allows managers and students both to apply concepts and theories, and, just as important, to build their own. Moreover, it is also the case that research and theory can help in stimulating a deep understanding of organization and its people. This book builds in substantial parts of such research and theory.

The plan of the book

Figure 1.2 illustrates the theoretical framework of the interrelated process of people and organizational management which will be used as a guided model for this book. The reason for presenting this theoretical framework is to understand, predict and control the complex phenomena of what are commonly called 'organizational behaviour' and 'human behaviour'.

The design of the model is based on the following propositions.

(*a*) The external environment influences corporate strategy.
(*b*) Corporate strategy influences structure, culture and leadership style.
(*c*) Leadership style influences structure, culture and human resources.
(*d*) Structure influences leadership style, work groups and culture.
(*e*) Culture influences the structure and the work environment.
(*f*) Motivation and job satisfaction are influenced by leadership style, structure, personnel management, work groups and the work environment.
(*g*) Culture and work environment influence organizational effectiveness and development.
(*h*) Motivation and job satisfaction influence organizational effectiveness and development.
(*i*) Organizational effectiveness and development reversibly influence the strategy and the leadership style of the organization.

Chapter 1: Introduction

This chapter provides a general introduction to people and organizational management and outlines the main aim and learning objectives of the book.

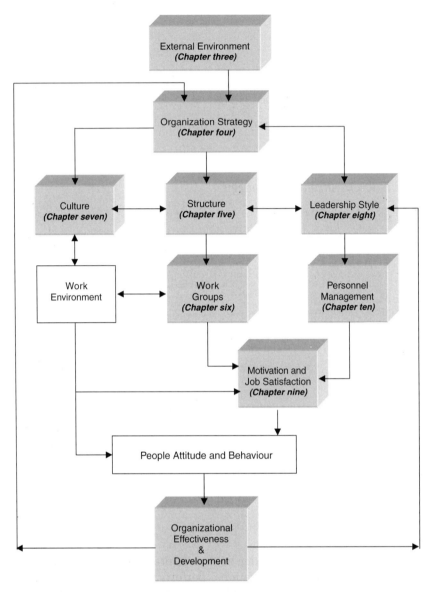

Fig. 1.2. People and organizational management model

Chapter 2: Management theory

This chapter looks at the evolution of organization and management theory in four stages: (1) the classical view; (2) the human relation view; (3) the development of the modern systems concept; and (4) the contingency concept.

Chapter 3: The environment

This chapter looks in detail at the nature of the environmental system and how it affects organizations. The first part of the chapter relates the concept of environment to work organization and identifies the perceived boundary between an organization and its environment. The second part explains the relationship between an organization and its environment. The effects of social, economical, political and technological factors on organizations are discussed.

Chapter 4: Organizational strategy

This chapter is concerned with managing the organization at its corporate and business level. It will define the meaning of strategy, strategic decision and strategic management. It will also illustrate the activities involved in the process of formulating a business strategy. These activities include organizational analysis, strategy formulation, strategy evaluation, strategic choice, action plan, strategy implementation and control.

Chapter 5: Organizational structure

This chapter provides an understanding of the importance of organizational structure and its effects on the organization's effectiveness. The first part of the chapter discusses subjects that are associated with organizational structure. The nature and typology of organization structure, including the traditional (simple) structure, divisional (functional) structure and matrix (project management) structure are then explained. The second part discusses the factors that affect the design or choice of the appropriate structure supplemented with empirical research findings.

Chapter 6: Work groups

This chapter provides the reader with an appreciation of the importance of groups for effective organizational performance. The first part of the chapter explains the meaning and nature of groups, as well as distinguishing between formal and informal groups. The second part of the chapter examines the factors that influence group cohesiveness and performance. References will be made to construction-related research that links group cohesiveness with organizational factors. These organizational factors include organization structure and leadership style, which are discussed in chapters 5 and 8. The final part analyses the nature of role relationships and role conflict.

Chapter 7: Organizational culture

This chapter provides an understanding of the concept of culture and how culture can affect people's values and behaviour towards achieving organizational goals. The first part of the chapter defines the term culture and determines its main characteristics. It also examines various types of organization cultures and explains their link with organizational structure, discussed in chapter 5. The second part looks into the factors that influence the choice of culture. The third part addresses the relationship between the issue of culture, strategy and performance. It links organizational goals with the human resources dimension of the organization, in terms of the transmission of required values and behaviour.

Chapter 8: Leadership

This chapter provides an understanding of the nature of leadership and the factors that determine the effectiveness of the leadership style. The first part of the chapter explains the meaning and importance of leadership in work organization. It also highlights the relationship between the terms 'leadership' and 'management' as they are sometimes seen as synonymous. The second part of the chapter reviews three approaches to the problem of leadership, namely trait, style and situational approaches. Each of these approaches will be reviewed within the context that explains the difference between effective and ineffective leadership. Models for understanding leadership situations in construction will also be discussed together with their implications. The third part of the chapter deals with the relationship between leadership style and the type of power that the leader can exercise over the followers. Various sources of power will also be described together with their implications. The difference between power and authority will also be explained.

Chapter 9: Motivation and job satisfaction

This chapter provides an understanding and appreciation of the complex nature of work motivation and its impact in achieving the goals and objectives of the organization. The first part of the chapter explains the meaning and underlying concept of motivation, together with emphasis on the relationship between motivation, job satisfaction and performance. The second part examines the main theories of motivation and evaluates their relevance to construction work situations. The third part establishes the factors that affect workers' motivation and job satisfaction in the construction industry. Particular attention is drawn to the impact of organization structure and design.

Chapter 10: Personnel management

This chapter provides the reader with an appreciation of the function of the personnel department and recognizes its importance for improving organizational effectiveness. The first part of this chapter explains the nature of the personnel function and analyses personnel policies and activities. The second part deals with the 'soft' issues of personnel or human resources management (HRM), namely interviewing, recruitment, training, management development and health and safety at work.

Chapter 2

Evolution of organization and management theory

A journey of a thousand miles begins with one step (Japanese proverb).

People are social animals with a propensity for organizing and managing their own affairs in an increasingly complex and dynamic environment. Modern concepts of organization and management theory are not completely distinct and unrelated. They evolved from earlier views which came from practising executives, administrators, scientists, sociologists and economists who recorded their observations and experiences and set them forth as general guidelines for others. Many current management practices are influenced and guided, either consciously or subconsciously, by these traditional concepts. This chapter looks at the evolution of organization and management theory in four stages: (1) the classical view; (2) the human relation view; (3) the development of modern system theory; and (4) the contingency concept.

Learning objectives

To:

> ➤ explain the nature of organizations and the meaning of management
> ➤ contrast main features of various approaches of organization and management theories
> ➤ evaluate the relevance of these various approaches to the construction industry.

The meaning of management

Chapter 1 introduced six main elements that are associated with modern organizations, these are:

(*a*) the operation (task and technology)
(*b*) objective (visible and invisible products)
(*c*) resources (human and non-human)
(*d*) structure (formal and informal)
(*e*) management (strategic and operational)
(*f*) environment (internal and external)

At the heart of these factors is the element of management. Since the 19th century, the meaning of the word management was often questioned – what is it? who needs it? why and how to manage? In short, the answer to these questions is that everyone needs management in order to achieve certain individual and collective objectives, through a faculty of techniques, systems and approaches.

The first major contribution to defining management was made by a well-known French mining engineer called Henri Fayol (1841–1925) (see Fayol 1949). His definition of management was in terms of five functions:

- to forecast and plan – examining the future and drawing up the plan of action
- to organize – building the structural, material and human aspects of the undertaking
- to command – maintaining activity among the personnel
- to co-ordinate – binding together, unifying and harmonizing all activity and effort
- to control – seeing that everything occurs in conformity with established rules and expressed commands

Subsequent writers on organization and management studies added other social and cultural factors to Fayol's definition of management, these are:

- relating the organization to the external environment and responding to society needs
- developing an organizational climate where people can accomplish their individual and collective goals.

Achieving individual and organization objectives is the key element in modern management and sums up the results of the management techniques aimed at achieving a high level of performance. Performance is commonly represented by the following relationship:

Performance = effectiveness, efficiency and participant satisfaction

- *Effectiveness* is the achievement of productivity through efficient management of human and technical resources. In other words, 'doing the right thing'.
- *Productivity and efficiency* refer to the ratio of output (product) to input (resources). In other words, 'doing things right'.

- *Participant satisfaction* is the human satisfaction of those people involved in the production/building process, such as clients, shareholders, middle managers, site managers, professionals, contractors, sub-contractors and operatives.

Evolution of management theory

Approaches of management theory can be traced back to the late 19th century, about the same time as the start of the industrial revolution. Figure 2.1 shows the evolution of management theories. There are four main approaches of management theory:

- classical
- human relations
- system
- contingency.

Each is now discussed in turn.

Classical theory (1850s–1930s)

Classical theory looked into organizational management in terms of its purpose and formal structure. There are three distinctive pillars to classical theory, these are:

- traditional universal management (also known as administrative management)

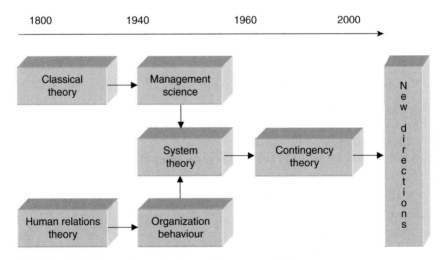

Fig. 2.1. Evolution of organization and management theory

- quantitative management (also known as scientific management)
- formal structuring (also known as the bureaucratic model).

Traditional universal management

The traditional universal management approach began with the work of Henri Fayol on improving efficiency in French industry. As mentioned above, in 1916, Fayol identified five functions of management, namely *planning, organizing, commanding, co-ordinating* and *controlling*. At that time, the identification of these five functions was unique. He also described the following fourteen principles.

(a) *Division of work.* The principle of specialization of labour in order to concentrate activities for more efficiency.

(b) *Authority and responsibility.* Authority is the right to give orders and the power to exact opinion.

(c) *Discipline.* Discipline is absolutely essential for the smooth running of business, and without discipline no enterprise could prosper.

(d) *Unity of command.* An employee should receive orders from one superior only.

(e) *Unity of direction.* One head and one plan for a group of activities have the same objectives.

(f) *Subordination of individual interest to general interest.* The interest of one employee or a group should not prevail over that of the organization.

(g) *Remuneration of personnel.* Compensation should be fair and, as far as possible, afford satisfaction to both personnel and the firm.

(h) *Centralization and decentralization.* Centralization is essential to the organization and is a natural consequence of organization.

(i) *Scalar chain.* The scalar chain is the chain of superiors ranging from the ultimate authority to the lowest tank.

(j) *Order.* The organization should provide an orderly place for every individual. A place for everyone and everyone in their place.

(k) *Equity.* Equity and a sense of justice should pervade the organization.

(l) *Stability of tenure of personnel.* Time is needed for the employee to adapt to their work and to perform effectively.

(m) *Initiative.* At all levels of the organizational ladder, zeal and energy are augmented by initiative.

(n) *Esprit de corps.* This principle emphasizes the need for teamwork and the maintenance of interpersonal relationships.

According to Luthans (1998), Fayol's work on the functions and principles of traditional universal management did not become part of mainstream management theory in the UK until the 1950s. Since that time there have been many other process theories, but they have not added much to Fayol's original conception of management theory.

Many of the terminologies have changed. For example, Fayol's commanding is now known as directing or leading. Also the meaning of Fayol's functions have become broader. For example, planning incorporates communication, motivation and leadership. Yet, despite these changes, the universal assumption is still made, and the traditional universal approach of management remains basically the same as that proposed by Fayol over eighty years ago.

Quantitative management

The second major pillar of classical theory was the development of the quantitative management approach. At the same time that Fayol identified the traditional universal approach for management, Frederick Taylor, Frank Gilbreth and Henry Gantt were tackling the problem of efficiency in a scientific way. In 1916, Taylor developed two principles of management. The first principle was that there is a 'one best way' of performing a task. Taylor argued that, by applying scientific methods of analysis, it is possible to break down the work into tasks and sub-tasks and then rearrange them into the most efficient method of working (this was named method study). Taylor's second principle was that, by separating the actual execution of the work from its management, there will be a more efficient method and procedure for coordinating and controlling the work. These two principles were then set forth into new duties of management:

- the development of a true science for each person's work and not the old rule-of-thumb
- the scientific selection, training and development of workers, unlike in the past when they chose their own work and trained themselves as best they could
- co-operation with the workers to ensure work is carried out in the prescribed way
- the division of work and responsibility between management and the workers.

Around 1915, Gilbreth took Taylor's work further and developed a technique on work measurement, named 'work study'. It all began while he was an apprentice bricklayer and noticed that the bricklayers who taught him worked in three distinct ways – one when they were demonstrating the job to him, one working normally and yet another when working on bonus. The end result was the same in each case, bricks were laid, but this illustrated a maxim that every manager should remember – it is the way in which it is done that is important. This is the concept of work study, which eliminates the ineffective movements and inefficient tools from the operation in order to increase efficiency and productivity without changing the work load of the operator.

The work of Gilbreth and Taylor was carried on forward throughout the 20th century and, in about 1960, the quantitative management approach achieved autonomy from the traditional universal approach and established its formal root. During the 1960s the quantitative approach was characterized by the techniques of operational research. At that time, various mathematical models were developed to solve decisional problems such as CPM (Critical Path Method), PERT (Project Evaluation and Review Technique) and linear programming.

By the 1960s, the quantitative approach turned away from emphasis on narrow operational research techniques toward a broader perspective of 'management science'. The management science approach incorporates quantitative decision techniques and model building as in operational research, but it also incorporates computerized information systems and operations management. This latter emphasis in the quantitative approach marked the return toward a more broadly based management theory.

Formal structuring

The third major pillar of classical theory was the development of the 'bureaucratic model structure' by a German sociologist, Max Weber (1864–1920). This marked the beginning of the formal organization where rules and procedures were designed to co-ordinate and direct people towards organizational goals. Weber was concerned with the way in which authority and power were exercised. He defined power as 'the probability that one actor within a social relationship will be in a position to force people to obey his own will despite resistance, perhaps through a treat of unwilling to comply'. On the other hand, persuasion (closely linked with power) was described as 'allowing the arguments or opinion of another to influence decisions.'

Authority, however, was defined as 'the probability that certain specific commands from a given source will be voluntarily obeyed with legitimate commands, by a given group of persons'. Under this definition, Weber described three types of authority – traditional, charismatic and legal.

(a) *Traditional.* In this type of organization, authority is recognized by tradition or custom vested, most usually in the position of the individual and not his/her expertise. For example, society and/ or group accept the authority of monarchies and parents because it is hereditary or has always been so. In construction, a builder may give his son authority to lead the firm in order to take over the business in the future; this is an example of a traditionally vested authority. If authority is exercised on the basis of heritage alone and without consideration of expertise, it will result in failure.

(b) *Charismatic.* In this form of organization, leadership and authority are given because of personal ability and aura. This depends greatly on personal qualities and the willingness of the group to follow. In a business world this may be seen in owner/managers and in an entrepreneur flair, although entrepreneur in an economic context means something else.

(c) *Legal authority.* This third type is legitimatized by an acceptance of the principle of law – the acceptance by a group that some order and structure is necessary for it to function properly. This type of authority is vested in the position and not the incumbent forming 'bureaucracy'.

According to Sidwell (1980), the decisive reason for the advance of bureaucratic organization has always been its pure technical superiority over any other form of organization. Blau and Scott (1966) summarized the characteristics of Weber's bureaucratic organization in the following way.

(a) Organization tasks are distributed in the clear cut division of labour, creating specialisms and expertise of staff emphasizing technical qualifications.

(b) Job roles are organized hierarchically, in most cases in a pyramid structure where authority and subordination are clearly seen.

(c) A formal set of rules exists to govern decisions and actions.

(d) Officials are accepted to assume impersonal organization to clients and individuals as cases. Here, formal behaviour is encouraged.

(e) An employment and career structure using qualifications, experience, seniority, etc. as a rational basis for advancement is in operation.

Around 1940, Merton acknowledged that the bureaucratic model proposed by Weber will provide control and predictability of behaviour within an organization. However, the techniques used to achieve this rely heavily on a 'machine model' of human behaviour involving standard practices and procedures. Merton's thesis predicted three consequences.

(a) There will be a reduction in the amount of personal relationships. Bureaucracy is a set of relationships between functions, roles and offices, ignoring personal ability and achievements.

(b) Internalization of the rules of the organization by the participants will increase, that is rules originally conceived to achieve goals become rigid and an end in themselves even if the goals change or are not best served by these atrophied procedures. In some cases the organization becomes an end to itself.

(c) There will be an increased use of categorization as a decision making technique and this may seriously reduce the search for alternatives such as innovation.

These three results combine, first, to make the behaviour of the participants/organization predictable and rigid which serves to provide reliability and predictability of behaviour. Second, defensibility of individual action is attained (in group defensiveness) and, third, it has the disadvantage that it produces a rigidity of behaviour towards third parties which may cause difficulty and dissatisfaction. This is important where there are clients of the organization requiring individual treatment, such as the National Health Service.

Human relations theory

At about the same time the classical theory took its path, the human relations approach (also known as behavioural approach) branched out on its own (see Fig. 2.1). Here, simplistic assumptions were made about human beings, and equally simplistic solutions to behavioural problems were offered.

At around 1960, about the same time the quantitative approach moved from emphasis on narrow operational research to a management science perespective, the human relations approach had a parallel development. This path veered toward a more broadly based 'organizational behaviour', and now relies heavily on the behavioural sciences and makes more complex assumptions. More direct attention devoted to organizational behaviour is the result of the interaction between the human being and the formal organization (Luthans 1998).

The starting point in the development of the human relations approach were the famous Hawthorne experiments, led by Elton Mayo at the Western Electricity Company in America (1924–1932). The four main phases of the Hawthorne experiments were illumination experiments, telephone relay study, interviewing programme and bank wiring observation room.

The illumination experiments

The first experiment was somewhat in line with the scientific management approach where two groups of people were selected, one to act as a test group and the other as a control group. The researchers began by increasing the level of lighting in the test group's work area, arguing that if lighting was improved, output should similarly improve. The control group's lighting was not changed. The results of this experiment were inconclusive as output in the test group varied with no apparent relationship to the level of lighting. Output also increased in the control group although the lighting remained unchanged. With this confusion, the scientific experts requested Mayo's assistance. Mayo, an Australian carrying out research at Harvard University, was a psychologist. Nevertheless, he viewed individual workers in the same mechanistic way as did Taylor.

The telephone relay study

In this experiment, the work was boring and repetitive. For the purpose of this study, Mayo selected six women and separated them from the normal production line. Before transferring them, the output of each woman was recorded without her knowledge and was around 2500 relays in a 48 hour week, including Saturday, and with no rest pauses. The test was to measure whether a series of planned and controlled changes, such as increased payment, hours of work, rest breaks and the provision of refreshment, would have an effect on the level of output. During the experiment, the researchers adopted a friendly manner with the workers, listening to their problems and keeping them informed of the experiment. The outcome of the research showed a continuous increase in output, reaching an average of around 3000 relays for each girl as a result of the extra attention given to the workers and the apparent interest in them by the management.

After this experiment Mayo arrived at a new conclusion – that productivity and work satisfaction are to a very large extent dependent on the social relationships between workers and between workers and their supervisors.

The interviewing programme

The two experiments described above drew attention to the form of supervision as a contributing factor to the workers' level of production. As a result, the research team conducted a large interviewing programme asking workers about their feelings towards their supervisors. The methodology adopted led to a rather interesting outcome. In the first questionnaire, the workers regarded a number of questions as irrelevant and they also wanted to talk about other issues than just supervision and immediate working conditions. The interview questionnaire was then modified to include more open-ended questions.

Arising from this approach, the interviewers found out far more about the workers' true feelings and attitudes towards factors such as the company itself, management, group relationships, family life and society in general. The interview programme was significant in giving an impetus to present day personnel management and the use of counselling interviews, and highlighting the need for management to listen to workers' feelings and problems.

The bank wiring observation room

In a later study, Mayo attempted to learn more about the nature of the social relationship that appeared in the telephone relay study. In order to achieve this, he observed the behaviour of 14 men in a part of the work area known as the bank wiring room. Despite a financial incentive scheme, it soon became apparent that the group never produced more or less than 6000 units per day, although more could have been produced if they wished. Instead, a group norm had been established to which all were required to adhere. If a worker produced too much, he was a 'rate-buster'; too little and he was a 'chiseler'. In this experiment, it was concluded that group pressures on individual workers were stronger than financial incentives offered by management.

System theory

While the classical and human relations approaches were going their separate ways, the system approach to management evolved, which attempted to integrate these two earlier approaches (see Fig. 2.1). It came about as a result of the increasing complexity of organizations and as a response to a rapidly changing environment (technical, economic, social and governmental).

The premise of the system approach is to encourage managers to inter-relate the organization with its people and to view the organization both as a whole and as part of a larger environment. At the highest level, system theory considers the universe as a suprasystem with our own solar system a sub-system within it. Getting down to Earth, the nations of the world form a political economic and social system interacting with each other with inputs and outputs. Industries, including the construction industry, are sub-systems within the nation's economy. Changes in population growth and demographic characteristics induce changes in needs for buildings, as do pressures for reduction in government expenditure. All these changes represent outputs from their systems which in turn affect the input to the construction industry sub-system.

Cleland and King (1983) provide the following definition of the system approach:

A system approach by its very nature is made up of interdependent elements, as such actions which affect one element must affect others also, and actions of one

element cause reactions on the part of others. The recognition of such interactions and interdependencies both within and without the organization is
the essence of the system theory.

In taking this approach into consideration, projects, organizations and
the environment can be viewed as two main systems, open and closed.

Open system

In an open system, the organization is highly affected by the external
environment and four factors are at play (see Fig. 2.2):

- *inputs* – the resources required to initiate the project or to operate the
  organization
- *process* – the activities involved in transforming or converting the
  inputs into outputs
- *outputs* – the completed products such as buildings and/or successful organizations
- *feedback* – the measures for achieving the aims and objective of the
  project and/or organization.

The environmental influences on an organization are discussed in
detail in chapter 3. In short, they are:

- *economical* – interest rates, inflation rates, taxation, the market and
  unemployment level
- *social* – the construction industry culture towards work, business
  and training
- *technical* – availability of resources
- *political* – laws and regulations regarding employment, industrial
  relations, health and safety.

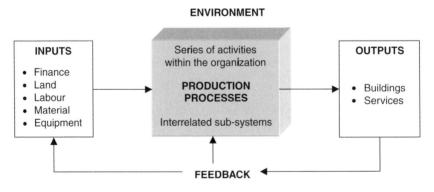

Fig. 2.2. The organization as an input–process–output system

Closed system

In a closed system, the environment does not play an important part in the business processes, such as construction methods and ways of contracting. A closed system focuses on optimizing the internal efficiency of the operation rather than looking outside the organization for effective actions.

Systems interaction

There is interaction between the systems and there is a hierarchy of systems and sub-systems. Kast and Rosenzweig (1985) viewed the organization as an open, socio-technical system composed of a number of sub-systems, as illustrated in Fig. 2.3. Under this view, an organization is not simply a technical or a social system. Rather, it is the structuring and

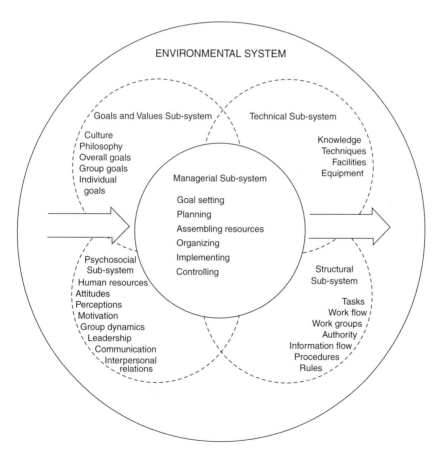

Fig. 2.3. Interactions of organizational sub-systems (from Kast and Rosenzweig (1985, p. 114))

integrating of human activities around various technologies. The technologies affect the types of inputs into the organization, the nature of the transformation processes, and the outputs from the system. However, the social system determines the effectiveness and efficiency of the utilization of the technology

The internal organization can be viewed as being composed of several major sub-systems. The organizational goals and values are one of the more important of these sub-systems. The organization takes many of its values from the broader socio-cultural environment. A basic premise is that the organization as a sub-system of the society must accomplish certain goals that are determined by the broader system. The organization performs a function for society, and if it is to be successful in receiving inputs, it must conform to social requirements.

The technical sub-system refers to the knowledge required for the performance of tasks, including the techniques used in the transformation of inputs into outputs. It is determined by the task requirements of the organization and varies depending on the particular activities. The technology for manufacturing automobiles differs significantly from that used in an oil refinery or an electronics company. Similarly, the task requirements and technology in a hospital are different from those in a university. The technical sub-system is shaped by the specialization of knowledge and skills required, the types of machinery and equipment involved, and the layout of facilities. The technology affects the organization's structure as well as its psychosocial sub-system.

Every organization has a psychosocial sub-system that is composed of individuals and groups in interaction. It consists of individual behaviour and motivation, status and role relationships, group dynamics, and influence systems. It is also affected by sentiments, values, attitudes, expectations and aspirations of the people in the organization. These forces set the 'organizational climate' within which the human participants perform their roles and activities. We would therefore expect psychosocial systems to differ significantly among various organizations. Certainly the climate for the person on the assembly line is different from that of the scientist in the laboratory or the doctor in the hospital.

Structure involves the ways in which the tasks of the organization are divided (differentiation) and co-ordinated (integration). In the formal sense, structure is set forth by organization charts, by position and job descriptions, and by rules and procedures. It is also concerned with patterns of authority, communication and work flow. The organization's structure provides for formalization of relationships between the technical and the psychosocial sub-systems. However, it should be emphasized that this linkage is by no means complete and that many interactions and relationships occur between the technical and psychosocial sub-systems that bypass the formal structure.

The managerial sub-system spans the entire organization by relating the organization to its environment, setting the goals, developing comprehensive, strategic and operational plans, designing the structure, and establishing control processes.

Kast and Rosenzweig went on to state that Fig. 2.3 provides one way of viewing the organization. The goals and values, as well as the technical, structural, psychosocial and managerial sub-systems, are shown as integral parts of the overall organization. This figure is an aid to understanding the evolution of organization theory. Traditional management theory emphasized the structural and managerial sub-systems and was concerned with developing principles. The human relation and behavioural scientists emphasized the psychosocial sub-system and focused their attention on motivation, group dynamics and other related factors. The management science school emphasized the technical sub-system and methods for quantifying decision making and control processes. Thus each approach to organization and management has tended to emphasize particular sub-systems, with little recognition of the importance of the others. The modern approach views the organization as an open, socio-technical system and considers all the primary sub-systems and their interactions.

As Handy (1998) put it:

If the structure [of an organization] is its skeleton, the jobs, perhaps, its muscles, the people its blood and guts and its physical perspectives its flesh, then there still remains the nervous system, the respiratory system, the circulation system, the digestive system, etc. As with the body, the systems of an organization overlap and interline the parts, the structure and its members. They are of a different logical order from the structure or the component pieces, for they are defined by their purpose, and are concerned with flows or processes through the structure They are in fact 'systems' – it remains the best, if the vaguest, word meaning at its broadest only an interdependent set of elements.

This provides an argument for having a hierarchy in the management function because to manage an organization totally requires someone at the top able to oversee the whole problem (using system theory) and to ensure that the organization operates in a balanced and controlled manner. Further down the hierarchy, there is lower and middle management who tend to be concerned with detailed skills and techniques, work study, planning computer programming etc., in order to solve individual problems and in an attempt to increase efficiency by cutting unnecessary operations and creating optimum methods and procedures. This is done under the direction of a supervisor who makes use of other conceptual thought disciplines attempting to view the whole picture providing a balanced programme, monitoring and controlling the application of these techniques applied by his/her management staff. System theory provides the manager with a useful framework to examine the markets, economics, finance and labour resources (Sidwell 1980).

Contingency theory

While interaction between the organization system and its environment is essential for survival, a firm's chances of success depend more on the ability of management to achieve an optimum degree of 'fit' between the complex and sometimes conflicting organizational objectives and culture, culture and structure, structure and strategy, individual employee's ability and expectations, type of work and external environment. This is the premise of the contingency theory which states that 'there is no one best way to structure the organization, to lead a team, to design a system. All depend or are contingent upon the situation or problem at hand'. Some of the situational variables that might influence a company's actions in designing an organization structure are as follows.

- *Nature of the operation.* Task and technology in an organization are the centre point of concern in any type of organization design and analysis. The nature of the task will have an important influence on how the organization is designed. The work of Joan Woodward in the 1950s clearly showed that organization structure and human relationships were largely a function of the existing technological situation (see chapter 5).
- *Strategy.* Chandler's study (1962) showed a strong relationship between the strategy a business adopts and the structure of its organization. He states that different kinds of organization structure are necessary for coping effectively with different strategies. The choice of corporate purpose and the design and administration of organizational processes for accomplishing the purpose are by no means impersonal procedures, unaffected by the characteristics of managers.
- *Subordinates' characteristics.* Some research evidence seems to suggest that a major contribution to organizational effectiveness is derived from adapting the structure to accommodate more adequately the psychological needs of organizational members. For example, Herzberg *et al.* (1959) drew attention to the conflict that is likely to prevail between a traditional definition of formal organization structure and the needs of psychologically mature individuals.
- *Environment.* Rapidly changing environments impose great pressure on organizations to design flexible structures. Lawrence and Lorsch (1967) found that bureaucracy was not able to cope with a highly dynamic situation; decentralization did not work well in a highly cybernated situation; and free-form, matrix designs were not adaptable to a situation demanding cutbacks and stability.

However, Lawrence and Lorch also argued that:

Contingency theory suggests that organizational variables are in a complex inter-relationship with one another and with conditions in the environment and that environmental contingencies act as constraints and opportunities and influence the organisation's internal structures and processes.

Another example of a contingency situation can be related to leadership styles. Here, the works of Fred Fiedler, Blake and Mouton, Vroom and Yetton, Hersey and Blanchard (see chapter 8) are of significance. In short, these works showed that there is a continuum of leadership styles ranging from 'task-oriented' to 'people-oriented' styles and there is no one best style to lead a group or an organization. Effective leadership depends upon matching the leadership style to the situational variables such as goals and strategy, subordinates' characteristics, and nature of the task and technology.

The concept of models

The system and contingency theories discussed above aim to establish relationships between the sub-systems and try to explain causality. The design of a model (such as the one presented in Fig. 2.3) becomes useful here. Such a model provides a framework for the problem and should consist of components (i.e. sub-systems) which represent discrete and identifiable components in the physical reality to be studied. It shows the linkages between the sub-systems that are under investigation.

There are three types of variables that are commonly used to construct a model, as follows.

(a) *Independent variable (inputs)*. This is the component or sub-system that does the causing and which, when varied, appears to induce change in another variable (or sub-system).
(b) *Dependent variable (outputs)*. This is the component or sub-system which is acted upon or caused by the independent variable. It is usually related to effectiveness and performance.
(c) *Intervening/moderating variable (process)*. This is the transformation or conversion process that explains linkages between the dependent and independent variables and can cause the relationship between them to change.

Figure 2.4 shows an example of a system model applied to a building project. Here, the characteristics of both the client and the project are seen as independent variables (i.e. inputs). Procurement method, contractual arrangement, leadership style, etc., are intervening (moderating) variables (i.e. moderate) which are selected to achieve the optimum

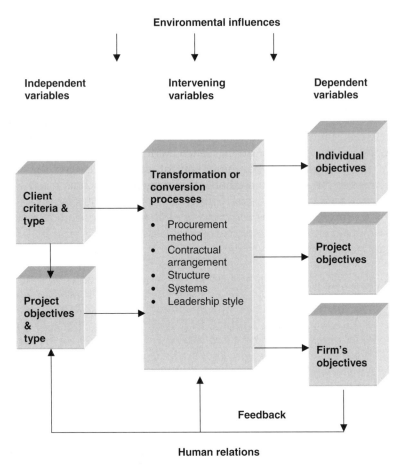

Fig. 2.4. *An example of input–process–output model of projects*

level of the dependent variable, project performance (i.e. output). This model suggests the following.

(a) The characteristics of the client organization, the project type and procurement method are each a sub-system of the building process and they are interrelated to one another to produce a building project. A change in one part of the system will affect the system as a whole. This is the essence of system theory.

(b) Project performance depends on the appropriateness of the selected conversion processes, such as the procurement method and the leadership style for the project, and there is no one best method or style. The selection of the type of procurement method depends on the characteristics of the client and the nature of the project. This is the essence of the contingency theory.

Summary and conclusion

Research and writing on organization and management, in some form or another, can be traced back thousands of years. However, around the late 19th century, three distinctive approaches to management had emerged. The first approach, known as classical theory, suggests that there are mechanical and technical aspects of management that can affect organizational effectiveness. This embraces a wide field of activity such as straightforward administration, letter writing, arranging meetings, specifications, drawings, planning, control, etc. The classical approach also refers to the scientific methods of management such as the work of Taylor on method study and Gilbreth's work on work study which marked a new era in the concept of scientific management.

The second approach suggests that there is the human aspect of management which involves the intuitive flair required when organizing and motivating human resources or inventing and developing new ways of doing things. In this approach, other management skills were recognized alongside management techniques such as human resource management (also known as behaviour science), for example, leadership style, the structure of power and authority, delegation, personnel management, conflict resolution and motivation.

These approaches into management concepts (i.e. technique, scientific management and behavioural science) are regarded as sub-systems of the overall suprasystem of the environment. In order to achieve a high level of performance, these three systems should be interrelated and should not be looked into in isolation from one another. This is the concept of the third approach, known as system theory. System theory suggests that managers should consider the whole problem, look at the system as a whole and try to tackle the problem in holistic terms.

In addition to charting the interrelationship between the sub-systems and organizational goals, there is also the fourth approach known as contingency theory, which recognizes the complexity involved in managing modern organizations. It is seen as an extension of system theory and states that there is no one best form of organizational structure and management system. The design of structures and systems depends upon the nature of the task and the nature of the environmental influences.

References

BLAU, P. and SCOTT, W. *Formal Organizations.* London, Routledge, 1966.
CHANDLER, A. *Strategy and Structure.* Cambridge, MA, MIT Press, 1962.
CLELAND, D. and KING, W. *Systems Analysis and Project Management.* New York, McGraw-Hill, 1983, 3rd edn.

FAYOL, H. *General and Industrial Management.* Boston, MA, Pitman, 1949.

HANDY, C. *Understanding Organizations.* London, Penguin, 1998, 5th edn.

HERZBERG, F., MAUSNER, B. and SYNDERMAN, B. *The Motivation to Work.* Chapman and Hall, 1959, 2nd edn.

KAST, F. and ROSENZWEIG, J. *Organization and Management.* Chapters 4 and 5, New York, McGraw-Hill, 1985, 5th edn.

LAWRENCE, P. and LORSCH, J. *Organization and Environment.* Cambridge, MA, Harvard Business School, 1967.

LUTHANS, F. *Organizational Behaviour.* New York, McGraw-Hill, 1998, 8th edn.

SHETTY, Y. and LUTHANS, F. Contingency Theory of Management – A Path Out of the Jungle. Reading. *Academic of Management Review*, 1979.

SIDWELL, A. *Notes on Organizational Theory.* MSc Construction Management and Economics, University of Aston, 1980, unpublished notes.

Chapter 3

The environment

Organizations often manipulate events and people within their internal and external environment. Environmental forces, being economical, political, social and technical, impose a great pressure on organizations to look for opportunities and plan or react to threats.

The term environment describes the circumstances and the external conditions that surround the organization and the project at a particular period of time. The project and its organization are separated by a boundary and they are regarded as sub-systems of the overall suprasystem of the environment. The project, organization and the external environment continuously interact with each other, generating dynamic input and output processes. This is the essence of the open system theory which was discussed in chapter 2 (see Fig. 2.2). Therefore, the understanding of environmental impacts on organizations is vital to managers in order to analyse their organization and the people that are working within it. This chapter examines the nature of the environment together with its interaction with the organization.

Learning objectives

To:

> ➤ discuss the term 'environment' within the context of the work organization
> ➤ explain the characteristics of the external environment
> ➤ examine the nature of the external environmental forces and the character of its interaction with the organization.

The environment, boundaries and organizations as an open system

The term environment describes the circumstances and the external conditions that surround the organization and its projects at a particular period of time. These circumstances and conditions are separated by a 'boundary'. The word boundary in conceptual terms is important to define in the study of organization. It is at the boundary level that the input–transformation–output processes take place and where the most rapid exchanges, such as jobs and contracts, have to be handled. For example, the boundary of the contracting firm can be defined by establishing what is outside the system (i.e. the firm), or is not part of the system, because it does not share the goals of the system. Therefore, outside the boundaries of the contracting firm there is the client, the professional consultants, the material and plant suppliers and the sub-contractors. The client and professional team do not share the contractor's goal of making a profit from the contract. Equally, the contractor may not share the architect's ambitions for the aesthetic performance of the building (Newcombe and Hancock 1996).

In general, there are three types of boundaries: physical, sociological and psychological boundaries. The physical boundaries are relatively easy to define – tangible assets which the firm has inside its boundary, including its people and its operating assets such as buildings, plants, land and the like. The sociological and psychological boundaries of human behaviour are rather difficult to describe because the activities that are necessary for the organization's transformation process are very rapid. Therefore, the boundary is not a simple line drawn between two objects. It is also not a hypothetical fence but more like a 'zone'.

Boundaries provide the following functions.

- Boundaries act as a filter between the organization and the environment. For instance, the organization filters inputs, such as new staff, selection and introduction procedures, and outputs by, for example, limiting the range of products or services it will offer.
- Boundaries act as a buffer between the zones (i.e. between the organization and its environment and between the project and its organization). Figure 3.1 shows that there are three environmental zones separated by line boundaries. These zones are known as:
  - the external environment (macro level – zone 1)
  - the organizational environment (micro level – zone 2), including strategic and co-ordinative levels
  - the project environment (site/operation level – zone 3)

The zones shown in Fig. 3.1 correspond closely to the management levels of the organization. At the core there is the operating or site management

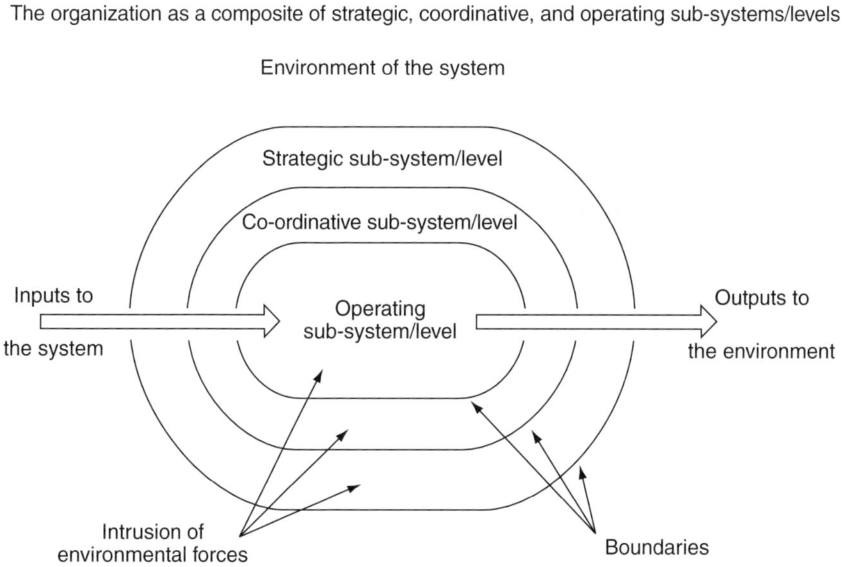

The organization as a composite of strategic, coordinative, and operating sub-systems/levels

Environment of the system

Fig. 3.1.   An organization and its boundaries (from Kast and Rosenzweig (1985, p. 133))

function. This is surrounded by layers of co-ordinative and strategic management sub-systems, both providing 'lines of defence' and acting as 'buffers', each seeking to prevent the intrusion of environmental forces, protecting the central operating sub-system from any unwanted intrusions that might upset the efficient functioning of the operation core.

Characteristics of the external environment

Before discussing environmental forces and their effect on an organization, it is important to understand the four commonly known characteristics of the environment as a whole. These characteristics are commonly described by: (1) stability; (2) sophistication; (3) market diversity; and (4) hostility.

Stability

An organization's environment can range from stable and static to fluctuating and dynamic. In a stable condition, the environment is relatively straightforward to understand and not undergoing significant changes. For instance, a contractor operating within a local market, dealing with clients who require the same type of building, with an expected rate of demand, decade after decade, is an example of an organization operating in a stable environment. Here, the technical processes may be fairly simple, and the market is to a certain extent fixed over time. In such circumstances, if change does occur, it is likely to be predictable and, therefore, the contractor can be in position to analyse historical data in order to forecast future conditions.

On the other hand, in dynamic conditions, the environment is unpredictable due to a variety of factors, e.g. an unstable government or unexpected shifts in the economy. Moreover, there are changes in client criteria, fluctuations in construction work, changes in project characteristics, changes in contractual arrangements and a rapid change in advanced technology. Therefore, firms that operate under a dynamic environment must be prepared to cope with environmental forces, otherwise they risk being out of business. This is what actually happened in the 1980s and 1990s, when firms failed to recognize the need for change. The term 'change' implies changes in:

(*a*) the strategy of the firm (chapter 4)
(*b*) the design of the organizational structure (chapter 5)
(*c*) organizational culture (chapter 7)
(*d*) people and organizational behaviour (chapters 5–10)

Sophistication

An organization's external environment can also range from less sophisticated (simple) to highly sophisticated (complex). The level of sophistication depends upon the characteristics of the firm, such as the type of products that it builds, the size of the company and the geographical location where it operates. In a simple environment, knowledge can be rationalized and the building process can be broken down into comprehensively simple components. For instance, a self-employed bricklayer or a constructor who builds straightforward dwellings, utilizing simple tools, equipment and construction methods will most likely face a simple environment. On the other hand, a large multi-national contractor or a speculative developer undertaking multi-million pound complex contracts, scattered all over the country, will face a complex environment. A complex environment requires a great deal of sophisticated knowledge about clients and their projects, the technology involved, the market, competition and much more.

Firms that are operating in a complex environment will find it difficult to handle complexity just by analysis of historical data. Complexity as a result of diversity might be dealt with by ensuring that different parts of the organization that are responsible for different aspects of diversity are separate, and given the resources and authority to handle their own part of the environment. Therefore, organizational strategy and structure are very essential to be revisited regularly in order to ensure that the company is steered towards the right direction (see chapters 4 and 5). On the other hand, there are organizations who have learned to cope with complexity, and their adopted strategy is based on experience which may provide competitive advantage. However, coping with complexity on experience alone is not the best approach to manage the organization.

Market diversification

Naturally, all contractors (small or large) have their own market. There are two types of markets, integrated and diversified. An integrated market is that in which a contractor offers specialized services or products to certain types of clients and, perhaps, locally, for example a bricklayer or local house builder.

On the other hand, market diversity may result from a broad range of clients, products, services and geographical areas. Therefore, market diversity can affect organizational structure through an enforced change in strategy.

Hostility

An organization's environment can range from munificent to hostile. As Mintzberg (1979) described it, it can range from that of a prestige surgeon who picks and chooses his/her patients, through that of a construction firm that must bid on all its contracts. Hostility is influenced by fierce competition, by the organization's relationships with other organizations, government, as well as by the availability of adequate resources to it. The construction environment can be regarded as hostile because of the highly competitive market. However, some construction firms managed to decrease the extent of hostility by diversifying their services by, for example, offering alternative contractual arrangements to remove the element of competition and foster a long-term relationships with clients.

Forces of the external environment on organizations

The external environment comprises the national and geographical conditions under which all organizations are operating. All organizations (irrespective of size) operate within the same culture and climate, and share the same environmental forces. These forces are commonly known as: (1) economical; (2) social; (3) political; and (4) technological. Figure 3.2 demonstrates some examples of such environmental forces.

Government action and restructuring
- By the mid-1990s, pressures for cost containment from governments had become a priority issue within public health services around the world. This pressure required pharmaceutical companies to ensure that new drugs were safe, efficient and cost-effective in order to obtain a licence.
- The introduction of market-based economies in eastern Europe had led to a new imperative for profit. This and the transfer of western technology and work practices led to great productivity gains, but also higher unemployment and job insecurity.

Capital markets
During 1996, Eurotunnel, the operator of the Channel Tunnel, was negotiating to restructure its debts, having suspended interest payments in autumn 1995. The bank consortium — not wishing to see Eurotunnel declared bankrupt — considered a debt-for-equity swap as part of the deal to keep the company in business. However, other shareholders did not wish to see their equity further diluted. Eurotunnel was caught in the middle, needing to placate shareholders with very different interests.

Demographics
By the mid-1990s, the trend of an ageing population was well established in the western economies. This provided many companies with an easily identifiable target market for their goods/services.

Other markets, such as Asia, however, were experiencing a population explosion and a resulting reduction in the average age of their population, giving these markets their own particular needs and opportunities.

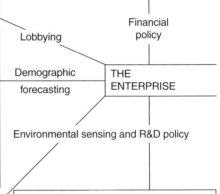

Socio-cultural
Growing health consciousness, sophisticated and social pressures on smokers in western countries has affected the sales of tobacco products in these markets. This situation led to controversial advertising campaigns by tobacco companies such as Philip Morris, which attempted to play down the risks of passive smoking in an attempt to protect their market, and a switch by the tobacco companies into concentrating their efforts on the developing world.

Technology
- The high costs of R&D, the long lead times and the critical need for new products to treat *antibiotic-resistant drugs* led Glaxo Wellcome and SmithKline Beecham to announce their first scientific collaboration in 1996.
- The development of 3D graphic accelerator chips has enabled computer games companies to create PC-based games which match those found in arcades in terms of graphics quality and realistic 3D effects, leading to increased sales of computer games.

Fig. 3.2.   Examples of environmental influences (from Fahey and Narayanan (1986) cited in Johnson and Scholes (1999))

The influence of the economy on organizations

The relationship between the construction industry and the general economy is very important because of three main characteristics that are associated with the construction industry. Hillebrandt (1979, pp. 10–12)

Labour markets
High levels of unemployment combined with continued 'downsizing' of workforces and the automation of many processes changed the face of the UK labour market.

The labour force had to become more flexible as there was an increasingly high demand for labour on short-term contracts and for part-time working — especially in the service sector.

Competition
Deregulation of the UK financial services sector led to intense competition in the industry. Building societies began to compete directly with domestic banks in the early 1980s. By the mid-1990s, many had shed their mutual ownership status and converted into public companies.

In response, many banks merged or acquired other financial service providers to obtain the critical mass required to be successful in an increasingly competitive industry.

Labour policy and industrial relations

Marketing policy

THE ENTERPRISE

Economic forecasting

Purchasing

Environmental sensing and R&D policy

Economic conditions
By 1996, Japan had witnessed four years of economic stagnation, exchange rate pressure, financial crisis and political upheaval. This forced many Japanese companies to restructure, shifting production overseas and reducing their workforce in Japan.

The change in corporate fortunes enabled Ford to take management control of Mazda, and News Corporation to buy a stake in a Japanese television station — both unprecedented investments which would have been unthinkable before the recession.

Ecology
Widespread concern and anger caused by the failure of UK water companies to plug water leaks — in some cases as high as 30 per cent — while introducing bans on the use of water helped companies which produce hazard detection and measurement equipment to increase their sales as the water companies were forced by Ofwat, the industry's regulator, to address the problem and reduce leakage rates.

Suppliers
- Brazil is the world's largest coffee producer. In 1994, severe frosts cut the yield of the 1995 coffee bean harvest to less than half that predicted. This disruption to supplies forced Brazil's coffee-roasting industry to import coffee for domestic consumption for the first time ever.
- In mid-1996 the price of platinum surged on the world's markets as threatened strike action led to concerns over the metal's availability.

identified them as follows.

- First, its size. The value of the final product of the construction industry in the UK, including materials, amounts to about 12% of the gross domestic product. The total employment is about 6% of the labour force. These significant figures are not only applicable in the UK but they are also internationally acceptable. As a result of construction serving many parts of the economy, it is therefore vulnerable to overall economic trends. The characteristics of building activity (i.e. long lead–lag times, large value contracts and heterogeneous organization and markets) mean that, although individual projects or sectors may be severally influenced by fluctuations in the market, the influence on the industry as a whole is dampened. The total picture for the industry may remain fairly constant because there is often time and the opportunity for firms to move into other markets. Clearly, however, a general depression will drag the industry down with it.

- Second, construction is regarded as creating investment products, i.e. the new products which it creates are wanted, not for their own sake, but on account of the goods or services which they can create or help to create. So, by virtue of the long life of construction products, the stock of products is large in relation to the annual production. Therefore, small fluctuations in the demand for the stock of buildings and works will have very large repercussions on the demand for the buildings and works created by the industry. For example, most public and private building activities are financed from capital revenue or loans, very largely as a form of investment. As the availability of funds is regulated by dependable revenue, in optimistic periods clients may anticipate a need for constructed facilities. Conversely, periods of recession may adversely affect the need or ability to fund building works. On the other hand, inflation offers some incentive for capital investment in buildings.

- Third, the government is the main client for most of the construction work carried out in the industry as a whole. This has an important and far-reaching effect on the industry and the economy because government has a means of very direct control over the demand on the industry.

Therefore, changes in the economic climate can have rather significant consequences on the corporate strategy and organizational development of construction firms.

The influence of social and political factors on organizations

At the social and political level, decisions by the government on the priorities of investments. Programmes will affect the construction market, directly where expenditure cuts or changes in emphasis affect specific projects, and indirectly by influencing the level of demand for, labour, materials and other resources. This influence may also occur at local government level and will affect both public and private sectors.

Changes in the structure and needs of the community will create different demand for building. Moreover, demographic changes can alter the need for housing, schools and jobs. Alterations in the structure and tastes of society can also influence the type of facilities required. Detailed prediction and analysis of these influences are essential but far from easy.

Strategic response to the environment

Over the past decade or so there have been a number of studies which have investigated the relationship between environmental forces and strategy. Two of the most well known studies in this field are the works of Chandler (1967) and Miles and Snow (1978). Chandler investigated large firms (including construction companies) and found that the most successful companies were those who developed new strategies to fit the changing environment and then established internal structures and processes to implement these strategies.

The subject of strategy is discussed in great detail in chapter 4, but below is a summary of the work of Miles and Snow (1978). They described four major types of organization in relation to their strategies and steps in environmental analysis.

- *Defenders* are organizations that have narrow product–market domains. Top managers in this type of organization are highly expert in their organization's limited area of operation but do not tend to search outside of their domains for new opportunities. As a result of this narrow focus, these organizations seldom need to make major adjustments in their technology, structure or methods of operation. Instead, they devote primary attention to improving the efficiency of their existing operations.
- *Prospectors* are organizations that almost continually search for market opportunities, and they regularly experiment with potential responses to emerging environmental trends. Thus, these organizations often are creators of change and uncertainty to which their competitors must respond. However, because of their strong concern for product and market innovation, these organizations are not usually completely efficient.
- *Analysers* are organizations that operate in two types of product-market domains, one relatively stable, the other changing. In their stable areas, these organizations operate routinely and efficiently through the use of formalized structures and processes. In their more turbulent areas, top managers watch their competitors closely for new ideas, and then they rapidly adopt those which appear to be the most promising.

- *Reactors* are organizations in which top managers frequently perceive change and uncertainty occurring in their organizational environments but are unable to respond effectively. Because this type of organization lacks a consistent strategy–structure relationship, it seldom makes adjustment of any sort until forced to do so by environmental pressures.

Johnson and Scholes (1999, p. 98) identified the following four steps for organizational analysis.

(a) As a first step, it is useful to take all initial views of how uncertain the environment is. Is it relatively static or does it show signs of change? In what ways? Is it simple or complex to understand? This helps in deciding what focus the rest of the analysis is to take.

(b) The second step might be to identify which macro environmental influences are likely to affect the organization's development or performance This can be done by considering the way in which political, economical, social and technological influences impinge on organizations (known as a PEST analysis). Table 3.1 shows an example of a PEST analysis of environmental forces.

Table 3.1.   PEST analysis (adapted from Johnson and Scholes (1999, p. 105))

What environmental factors are affecting the organization?
Which of these are the most important at the present time? In the next few years?

Political/legal	**Economical factors**
Monopolies legislations	Business cycles
Environmental protection laws	GNP trends
Taxation policies	Interest rates
Foreign trade regulations	Money supply
Employment law	Inflation
Government stability	Unemployment
	Disposable income
	Energy availability and cost
Socio-cultural factors	**Technological**
Population demographics	Government spending on research
Income distribution	Government and industry focus on
Social mobility	techological effort
Lifestyle changes	New discoveries/development
Attitudes to work and leisure	Speed of technology transfer
Commission	Rates of obsoleteness
Levels of education	

(*c*) The third step focuses towards an explicit consideration of the immediate environment of the organization – for example the competitive arena in which the organization operates.

From these three steps should emerge a view of the really important developments taking place around the organization. It may be that there are relatively few of outstanding significance or it could be that there are many interconnected developments.

(*d*) The fourth step is to analyse the organization's competitive position: that is, how it stands in relation to other organizations competing for the same resources or customers. This can be done in a number of ways and chapter 4 discusses this in more detail.

The aim of such analysis is to develop an understanding of opportunities that can be built upon and threats that have to be overcome as shown in Table 3.1.

Structural response to the environment

Similarly to strategic responses to the environment, there have also been important studies dealing with structural responses of managers to environmental forces. Among the most well known is the study of Mintzberg (1979) on the structuring of organizations. The subject of organizational structure is discussed in some detail in chapter 5, but below is a summary of the main organizational structures and the five hypotheses presented by Mintzberg concerning the relationship between structure and the environment. In general, there are three types of structure.

(*a*) *The simple structure (craftsman).* A simple or a craft structure organization has an informal line relationship among its members. It is the type of organization which is common to most businesses at their development stage. It consists of an owner who starts the business and who undertakes most of the management responsibilities, perhaps with a partner.

(*b*) *The functional.* A functional structure is based on a grouping of all the specialists in autonomous departments. Thus each specialist department provides a common service throughout the organization. In this structure, line managers and the staff (who provide the service) exercise a formal authority over their subordinates only, not across the structure.

(*c*) *The matrix.* With the continuous growth of organizations and as a result of projects becoming larger and technologically complex, it has become necessary for organizations to add a horizontal dimension to the traditional functional structure in order to

improve co-ordination and functional integration among individuals and groups. The matrix structure can facilitate this integration
whereby the normal vertical hierarchy is overlaid by some form of
lateral authority, influence and communication.

Within these structures, there are two kind of systems (see chapter 5,
pp. 84–86).

(a) The *mechanistic* system, which is defined as a rigid structure with
     specialized functionally. Here, co-ordination is done through
     successive hierarchical levels of superior authority.
(b) The *organic* system, which has less formalized definitions of jobs,
     with more flexibility and adaptability, and communication net-
     works involving consultation rather than command.

Based on the above types of structures and systems, Mintzberg
proposed the following five hypotheses (see chapter 5, pp. 106–107).

- Hypothesis 1. The more dynamic the environment, the more
  organic the structure.
- Hypothesis 2. The more complex the environment, the more
  decentralized the structure.
- Hypothesis 3. The more diversified the organization's markets,
  the greater the propensity to split it into market-based units.
- Hypothesis 4. Extreme hostility in its environment drives any
  organization to centralize its structure temporarily.
- Hypothesis 5. Disparities in the environment encourage the
  organization to decentralize selectively to differentiated work
  constellations.

Summary and conclusion

This chapter has dealt with environmental forces and their effect upon
organizations. The term environment is defined as the external conditions
that surround the organization and its projects, separated by some kind of
'boundary'. It is through the boundary where the input–transformation–
output processes take place and where the most rapid exchanges (such as
jobs and contracts) have to be handled.

The nature of the environment, being stable, sophisticated, diversified
or hostile, will determine what course of action (i.e. strategy) the organization should take in order to survive or take advantages of opportunities.
There are four major environmental forces that require close attention;
these are political, economical, social and technical forces. The PEST
technique helps analyse these environmental factors and their effects. In
this technique, the analyser asks three fundamental questions: (1) What

environmental factors are affecting the organization? (2) Which of these are the most important at the present time? (3) Which of these are likely to be the most important in the next few years. The following chapter deals with these issues in some detail.

References

CHANDLER, A. *Strategy and Structure*. Cambridge, MA, MIT Press, 1967.

FAHEY, L. and NARAYANAN, V. *Macro-environmental Analysis for Strategic Management*. West, 1986.

HILLEBRANDT, P. *Economic Theory and the Construction Industry*. London, Macmillan Press, 1979.

JOHNSON, G. and SCHOLES, K. *Exploring Corporate Strategy*. Englewood Cliffs, NJ, Prentice-Hall, 1999, 5th edn.

KAST, F. and ROSENZWEIG, J. *Organization and Management*. New York, McGraw-Hill, 1985, 5th edn.

MILES, R. and SNOW, C. *Organizational Strategy, Structure and Process*. Tokyo, McGraw-Hill, 1978.

MINTZBERG, H. *The Structuring of Organizations*. Prentice-Hall, 1979.

MULLINS, L. *Management and Organizational Behaviour*. Boston, MA, Pitman, 1999, 5th edn.

NEWCOMBE, R. and HANCOCK, M. *Concepts of Management*. MSc in Construction Management by distance learning. Management in construction module. University of Bath, 1996.

Chapter 4

Organizational strategy

In order for the organization to survive, it requires a business strategy to link its operational and administrative activities with the external environment. The anticipated outcome of the strategic process is to win in the face of the competition and to be able to deal effectively with the forces which represent opportunities and threats to the organization.

This chapter is concerned with managing the organization at its corporate and business level. It will define the meaning of strategy, strategic decision and strategic management. It will also illustrate the activities involved in the process of formulating a business strategy. These activities include the identification of opportunities and threats, the setting up of organizational objectives, organizational appraisals, evaluation of alternative strategies, strategic choice, action plan, and strategy implementation and control. Figure 4.1 summarizes the overall principles of the chapter (also see Fig. 1.1).

Learning outcomes

To:

- ➢ understand the concept and importance of a corporate and business strategy
- ➢ understand the meaning of strategic management
- ➢ identify the various types of strategies
- ➢ recognize the process of a business strategy.

The concept of strategy

The term 'strategy' originally came about to represent a planned framework for achieving a military mission. The Oxford dictionary defines

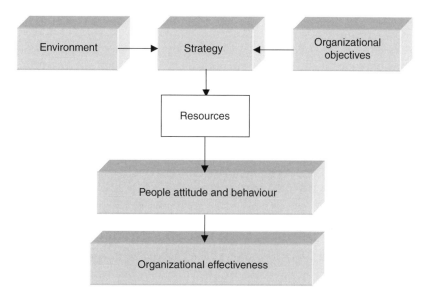

Fig. 4.1. Overall principles of chapter 4

strategy as 'the art of planning operations in war, especially of the movements of armies and navies into favourable positions for fighting'.

While the roots of strategy, in its military sense, reach far back into history, its study, in a business sense, has been more prolific in the past thirty years or so. Organizational strategy was acknowledged in the construction industry in the 1960s following increasing pressures from the environment (such as technological advances and government legislation) which demanded a change in the way organizations had to run their business. Organizations have to be effective in strategic terms, to be strategically aware and appreciate the ongoings and nature of change. A comprehensive set of skills and competencies is required in order to be able to deal effectively with the forces that represent opportunities and threats to the organization.

At the outset, there are three fundamental questions related to corporate strategy which require attention:

What is the organization best at?
Where does the organization stand now in relation to the external environment?
Where should the organization be in a few years' time?

In order to answer these questions, there needs to be a thorough analysis of the strengths and weaknesses of the organization and the effects of environmental forces on the internal affairs of the organization. This is known as strategic 'fitting' or 'stretching' of the organization. The notion of 'strategic

Table 4.1. Differences between strategic fit and stretch (adapted from Hamel and Prahalad (1994))

Aspect of strategy	Environment-led 'fit'	Resource-led 'stretch'
Underlying basis of strategy	Strategic fit between market opportunities and organization's resources	Leverage of resources to improve value for money
Competitive advantage through...	'Correct' positioning Differentiation directed by market need	Differentiation based on competences suited to or creating market need
How small players survive...	Find and defend a niche	Change the 'rules of the game'
Risk reduction through...	Portfolio of products/ businesses	Portfolio of competences
Corporate centres invest in...	Strategies of divisions or subsidiaries	Core competences

fit' is that mangers attempt to develop a business strategy based on opportunities arising from an understanding of the environmental forces which are influencing the organization and adapting the resources accordingly. Table 3.1 in chapter 3 provided examples of environmental factors that need to be analysed, known as the PEST analysis. The notion of 'strategic stretch', on the other hand, is the identification and leverage of the resources and competencies of the organization which yield or provide competitive advantage. In other words, organizational effectiveness is not all about the conditions of the market or the general state of the industry. It is also about a manager's ability to identify strategies for growth on the basis of stretching competencies unique to the organization. Table 4.1 summarizes some of the differences between strategic fit and stretch.

The aspects of strategic fit and stretch will lead to 'strategic decisions', which form one of several sets of decision making rules for linking the organization with its environment. Johnson and Scholes (1999, pp. 4–10) identified several characteristics which are usually associated with the term 'strategy' and 'strategic decisions'. The following is a summary of these characteristics:

(a) Strategic decisions are likely to be concerned with or affect the long-term direction of an organization.

(b) Strategic decisions are normally about trying to achieve some advantage for the organization. Strategic advantage could be thought of as providing higher quality, value for money services than other competitors in the market.

(c) Strategic decisions are likely to be concerned with the scope of an organization's activities. In other words, does (and should) the organization concentrate on one area of activity, or should it have many? Organizations should clearly define the boundaries of their business in terms of the type of products and modes of service.

(d) Strategy can be seen as the matching of activities of an organization to the environment in which it operates. This notion is sometimes known as the search for strategic fit.

(e) Strategy can also be seen as building on an organization's resources and competence to create opportunities or to capitalize on them. For example, designing and developing buildings that are not only of low cost but also unique in the market.

(f) Strategies may require major resource changes for an organization.

(g) The strategy of an organization will be affected not only by environmental forces and resource availability, but also by the value and expectations of those who have power in and around the organization. In some respects, strategy can be thought of as a reflection of the attitudes and beliefs of those who have most influence on the organizational culture.

The following are examples of strategic decisions in construction:

- diversification of building types
- expanding or shrinking the market, by type of client or/and location
- differentiation of building product (uniqueness)
- producing better value for money buildings
- ownership
- a merger or company takeover
- a partnership
- contracts bidding.

Strategic decisions can be diffused throughout the organization over time and therefore can have an impact on the operational decisions and the administrative decisions within the organization, as follows.

- *Operational decisions* (also known as tactical decisions) provide the means of transforming inputs into outputs. The bulk of a firm's time will be devoted to the operational decisions such as estimating, buying, selling and accounting.
- *Administrative decisions* are concerned with organizational structuring and resource allocation.

The impact of the strategic decision on the administrative decision is one of the primary concerns of this book. This is known as strategic human resource management. The model presented in Fig. 4.2 (Lundy

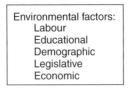

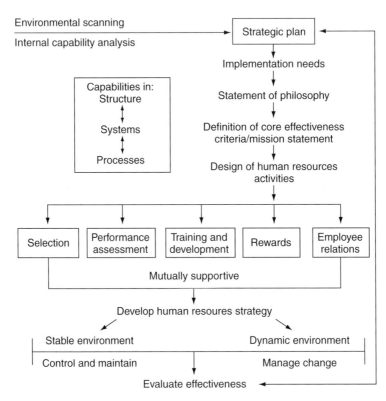

Fig. 4.2. Strategic human resource management (from Lundy and Cowling (1996, p. 5))

and Cowling 1996, p. 5), is built on the assumption that strategy can affect the personnel management of the organization and that in turn it will influence human behaviour and performance. The model incorporates important areas of attention intended to further the understanding and development of the concept of strategic human resource management. These are capability analysis and planning, development of core effectiveness criteria, design of sub-activities of human resource management in support of strategy and development of organizational change strategies. Figure 4.2 consists of four main parts:

- environmental analysis (both external and internal) in which a human resource perspective is introduced into the strategic process
- implementation, in which attention is devoted to the interpretation of strategic aims in terms of specification of philosophy, culture and resultant required human resource effectiveness criteria, which, when combined with task-specific effectiveness criteria provide the basis for the design of a co-ordinated set of activities such as selection and employee rewards
- consideration of approaches to the management of change
- evaluation of effectiveness focusing on human resource outputs.

Strategic management

Strategic management is the process in which strategic decision makers determine objectives and make choices to achieve these objectives within the constraints of the resources available and firm's mission. The nature of strategic management is, however, different from other aspects of management. For example, a project manager is most often required to deal with problems of operation control on site, such as the efficient production of buildings, the management of people and the monitoring of the cash flow of the project. Similarly, the managing director of the firm may be focusing on the installation of a new technological system to improve the efficiency of the operation. Of course, all these activities are very important, but they are essentially concerned with effectively managing resources already deployed, often in a limited part of the organization, within the context and guidance of an existing strategy. This is called operational control. It is vital to the effective implementation of strategy, but it is not the same as strategic management. According to Johnson and Scholes (1999), the scope of strategic management is greater than that of any one area of operational management. Strategic management is concerned with complexity arising out of ambiguous and non-routine situations with organization-wide rather than operation-specific implications.

Strategic management is therefore concerned with taking the right decision, at the right time and using the right reform to make the strategy work effectively. Effective strategic management creates a productive alliance between the nature and the demands of the environment, the organization's culture and values, and the resources that the organization has at its disposal. Broadly speaking, there are four modes in which strategic management can be carried out:

- internally by individuals
- internally by teams
- employing a full-time or a part-time corporate planner
- employing an external strategic consultant.

Each of these modes has its own advantages and disadvantages. For instance, if strategic management is conducted by internal individuals, it can be cheaper but riskier than if carried out by internal teams that can produce a better quality decision but slower. The advantage of employing an external consultant is that decisions will be non-biased and a macro viewpoint of the situation should be provided. However, the disadvantages of the use of an external consultant are that it can be an expensive method and the consultants employed may not fully understand the business. The answer as to which mode to choose depends on the following:

- type of management (entrepreneur or family business)
- size of the organization
- complexity and uncertainty of the market
- speed of making a decision
- financial stand
- leadership style (democratic or autocratic – see chapter 8).

For example, small construction companies will probably prefer to use individual employees. The style of corporate leadership is a key factor in such a decision. An autocratic leader will most likely make the decision by himself or herself. On the other hand, a more democratic leader will prefer to involve teams of people. Before discussing the process involved in conducting a strategic management, it is important to know the types of strategies that are available to organizations.

Types of strategies

In general, there are two types of strategies: the planned approach and the reactor approach (also see chapter 3, p. 37).

The planned approach

This is a formal and systematic approach to strategic management, where firms look ahead for opportunities and threats and plan and work out in advance the long-term future of the company. This approach is more likely to be adopted by large and sophisticated construction firms. The term 'systematic' implies that the business strategy is combined with interrelated activities and there is a right way and a wrong way to make business decisions. Moreover, better decisions will be obtained with less effort if certain steps in the decision making process are completed in their sequence. Ansoff (1987) asserts that:

> *a strategic management is a systematic approach to a major and increasingly important responsibility of general management: to position and relate the*

firm to its environment in a way which will ensure its continued success and make it secure from surprises.

Langford and Male (1991) reported that a comprehensive, systematic approach to strategic planning (the planning mode) can challenge and reformulate the strategic logic of the firm's future development. Strategic management literature differentiates between first- and second-generation strategic planning. In first-generation planning strategists will only look at one set of alternatives whereas in second-generation or contingency planning multiple sets of alternatives will be considered, perhaps with a series of strategies worked out to allow for anticipated changes in the environment. First-generation planning leads to a programmed strategy where the strategy is worked out in such detail that it becomes difficult to alter once implemented. A contingency strategy, on the other hand, requires the strategist to choose the best strategy under a given set of circumstances but to have the flexibility inherent within it to be able to adapt to changing environmental circumstances. This requires careful environmental scanning, monitoring and evaluation. Second-generation planning leads to contingency strategy formation where 'what if' situations are created for decision makers.

The reactor approach

This is an informal and unsystematic approach, where firms adopt a flexible 'wait and see' strategy to respond to the environmental changes. Such an approach is adopted by a relatively small firms, although the reactor approach can still be applied in large firms. This can have some advantages over the planned strategy, including the following.

(*a*) The company will save executive time, cost and talent by not engaging in formal planned strategy.

(*b*) The opportunities of the firm will not be restricted to those included in the strategic plan.

(*c*) The business will gain the advantages of the delay in decision making – fuller information, for example.

However, the advantages of having a planned business strategy outweigh those of reactor strategy. These advantages are discussed in the following section.

Advantages of a planned business strategy

Organizational objectives and polices are formulated within the framework of a business strategy. Ansoff (1987) summarized the need for a planned business strategy as follows:

(*a*) The firm's management will take time to consider the important strategic issues rather than just react to the urgent tactical matters which often seem more important.

(*b*) The process of formulating a business strategy will force the firm to identify its strengths and weaknesses and build up a business 'capability profile'.

(*c*) Opportunities in the market place will be identified before they arise, allowing the firm time to prepare to exploit a market leadership position.

(*d*) This analysis of market opportunities will also highlight the risks involved in pursuing particular strategies and thus provide a basis for ranking those opportunities.

(*e*) The credentials of competitors will be subject to a much more searching analysis than previously conducted, which will enable the business to take advantage of any foibles thus revealed.

(*f*) The firm will better be able to anticipate changes in markets and prepare offensive or defensive action to cope with these changes.

(*g*) A corollary of this last point is that such sophisticated market intelligence will also reveal trends which are occurring in the firm's environment – trends which are often obscured until it is too late for the company to react.

(*h*) Continual crisis management will also be avoided, the firm's executives may actually enjoy this situation.

(*i*) Necessary changes in the structure and operating procedures of the business in response to strategic changes can be introduced over a much longer timescale with less disruption to existing operations. This is particularly important to large corporations and even medium-sized firms with long established infrastructures which make it difficult for them to change quickly. Smaller firms are of a more organic nature and are able to adapt more readily.

(*j*) A well defined business strategy will focus the efforts of all those involved in the enterprise and thus enhance corporate harmony.

(*k*) The systematic development of all the resources of the business, both physical and human, will result from the formulation of a strategy for the whole business and the subsequent tactical plans. The sense of security which this engenders in staff should improve motivation.

(*l*) Last, but not least, will be the effect on the strategic decision makers themselves. First, in presenting them with the opportunity to review strategic matters and to make genuine strategic decisions and, second, in creating a climate of strategic thinking in which managers can exercise their judgement on the broader organizational aspects of the business. It has been argued that regardless of the value of the strategic plan which is produced, the process of strategy formulation is beneficial in itself in stimulating executive thought.

There is evidence to suggest that corporate planning can lead to significant improvements in performance. For example, the work of Taylor and Sparkes (1977) showed that companies with corporate planning performed around 30–40 per cent better in terms of earnings per share, earnings on common equity, and earnings on total capital employed.

In construction, despite the fact that the industry is fragmented in nature and faces intense competition with fluctuating demand, the planned approach has also proved to be advantageous for construction firms. There is evidence to suggest that firms which adopted a systematic and sophisticated approach to planning during the volatile decade of the 1970s were more successful in riding the storm and even developing their businesses than those construction firms whose planned effort was underdeveloped. Research by Lansley (1981) showed that the level of sophistication of a firm's corporate planning is one of the surest indicators of a firm's ability to perform well in the future. Of 26 (construction) firms studied during the mid-1970s recession, eight had adopted sophisticated methods of planning (relative to firms of a similar size and type of business) and eight had adopted fairly unsophisticated planning methods. All the firms entered the recession in a good state of health, but those with relatively unsophisticated methods fared very badly indeed. All suffered substantial reductions in their business and several went into liquidation. Of the relatively sophisticated firms, five fared extremely well, growing and developing substantially throughout the recession – only one performed poorly.

It is evident from the above that construction firms can benefit from the introduction of an explicit form of business strategy. Below is a discussion on how to formulate a business strategy.

The business strategy process

The rationale as to why organizations go through the process of developing a strategy can be due to one or more of the following reasons:

- to increase productivity or efficiency of the operation
- to overcome or solve a business problem, such as quality or reputation
- concern for the future market
- to improve contract bidding
- to grow

- to create a highly motivated work environment
- to provide a high job satisfaction to employees
- to create a new culture.

The process of developing a business strategy can take seven stages (see Fig. 4.3).

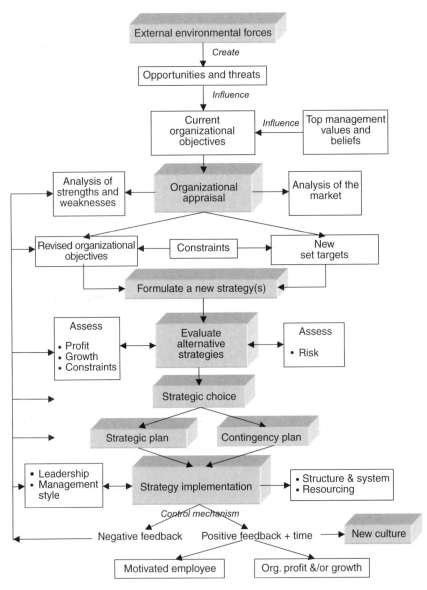

Fig. 4.3. The business strategy process

Stage 1. Strategic analysis
Stage 2. Strategy formulation
Stage 3. Evaluation of alternative strategies
Stage 4. Strategic choice
Stage 5. Action plan
Stage 6. Strategy implementation
Stage 7. Strategic control and feedback

It has to be stressed here that, although the diagram in Fig. 4.3 is drawn in a linear form, the elements within the model are interlinked and they may overlap with each other. For example, while evaluating a particular strategy, management may decide to implement part of it, so strategic choice and strategic implementation may overlap. Therefore, the business strategy process does not necessarily follow the linear path as neatly and as tidily as shown in Fig. 4.3.

Stage 1. Strategic analysis

This is the first step of developing a business strategy where the mission of the organization will be clearly defined. At this stage, a contingency view of strategic formulation can be set in terms of three major elements:

(*a*) analysis of environmental forces
(*b*) organizational objectives
(*c*) organizational appraisal.

Analysis of the environmental forces – what are the opportunities and threats to the organization resulting from the environmental analysis?

This aspect of strategic analysis, which leads to strategy formulation, is discussed in some detail in chapter 3. Briefly, the environmental forces (political, economical, social and technical) impose a great pressure on managers of organizations to keep their fingers on the pulse, in order not to miss opportunities, and to plan or react to threats. Due to the nature of construction products and services, the construction industry is very volatile/vulnerable to environmental forces.

Organizational goal and objectives – what does the organization want to do?

The goals and objectives of the organization are very much influenced by the environmental forces and expectations of the top managers and their values and beliefs. Which views prevail will depend on which group has the greatest power and understanding. This can be of great importance in recognizing why an organization follows the strategy it does. Cultural influences from within the organization and from the world around it also influence the strategy an organization follows, not least because the environmental and resource influences on the organization are likely to be interpreted in terms of the assumptions inherent in that culture (cultural issues are discussed in some details in chapter 7). Organizational objectives can take two forms, economic and non-economic objectives.

Economic objectives. With this kind of objective, the aim of most enterprises starting a business is to achieve maximum profit with an attractive return on the investment over the long term. However, as the organization grows in size, profit maximization may not be the only long-term objective of the firm. Other objectives such as growth, employee satisfaction and company reputation, become more important. There is evidence to suggest that the spectacular growth of the largest UK construction corporations between 1919 and 1939, and especially since 1945, has often been accomplished by modest profit performance which seems to point to a preference for growth rather than profitability. To this effect, Barnard (1981) provided typical economic objectives for a contracting firm; he stated:

> *the economic objectives of the firm include: growth of turnover, earnings, market share in existing markets and number of markets in which the firm operates (types of construction clients, localities, etc.); stability of annual gross turnover, gross profit return on investments (ratio of gross profit to total assets, fixed assets or shareholders equity) and in utilisation of scarce physical or human resources held by the firm.*

Non-economic objectives. With this kind of objective, the aim of the organization is to fulfil the need and expectations of the firm's participants. Barnard (1981) provided typical non-economic objectives for a contracting firm, stating:

> *the non-economic objectives of the firm include: internal politics, e.g. retention of control by the existing owners or board, external politics, e.g. to avoid intervention by central, local or other government bodies; to meet reasonable aspiration of employees and develop them to their full potential; to serve clients and the general community well; to maintain a good reputation within the industry.*

Organizational appraisal

Analysis of the market. Which market should the organization enter? Should it diversify or remain specialized? Should it expand or stay local? The analysis of market segments seeks to answer these questions and establishes the segments of markets which might be most attractive and appropriate. Newcombe (1976) defined strategy in terms of market diversification and geographical expansion for the following reasons.

(a) Market diversification was chosen in recognition of the distinct nature of the different markets which exist within the overall building market. General contracting, civil engineering, speculative house building, property development, building products, plant hire, etc. are all within the construction market but each requires a different set of resources, skills and management expertise. A successful general contractor may fail miserably in speculative house building (as many have) or in civil engineering. Conversely, a civil engineering contractor may undertake a building contract at his peril. On a specialization/diversification continuum, a firm operating in a single market could be termed a specialist firm, while at the other extreme a firm operating in many markets may be called diversified. Four market diversification strategies were identified:

(i) *single market* – firms that grew by expansion within one market

(ii) *dominant market* – firms that grew by expansion within one main market but in addition had entered secondary markets

(iii) *related market* – firms that grew by expansion by means of entry into related markets, by offering related services or products, by use of related technology, by related vertical activities, or some combination of these

(iv) *unrelated market* – firms that grew by expansion into new markets, offering new services and products and using new technologies unrelated to the original market scope.

(b) geographical expansion, that is, geographic centralization or decentralization, was seen as a critical element in the analysis of construction firms whose task, by the very nature of the building industry, is geographically dispersed. The importance of geographical expansion as a definite strategy for construction firms has been highlighted by several studies of the industry and this was selected as a second dimension of strategy. Four degrees of geographic expansion were identified by Newcombe: local, regional, national and international.

Analysis of weaknesses and strengths.   What can the organization realistically do and what can it not do? This includes analysis of the physical resources, human resources and financial resources that make up the organization's strategic capability.

Just as there are outside influences on the organization and its choice of strategy, so there are internal influences. One way of thinking about the strategic capability of an organization is to consider its strengths and weaknesses (what it is good or not so good at doing, or where it is at a competitive advantage or disadvantage. This is known as a SWOT analysis (strengths, weaknesses, opportunities and threats). Table 4.2

Table 4.2.   Typical strengths and weaknesses of contracting firms

Strengths	Weaknesses
• Good location	• Poor location
• Workload flexibility	• Workload rigidity
• Diversity of products	• Very specialized
• Good reputation and successful track record	• Bad reputation
• Good financial standing	• Smaller budget than competitors
• Appropriate information technology	• Lack of information technology
• Good project management skills	• Lack of project management skills
• Efficient management of the resources	• Poor management of the resources
• Skilled employees	• Basic or shortage of skilled employees
• Appropriate resources	• Lack of appropriate resources
• Enthusiastic employees	• Demoralized employees

illustrates an example of a typical assessment of the strengths and weaknesses of contracting firms. These strengths and weaknesses might be identified by considering the resource areas of a business, such as its physical plant, its management, its financial structure and its products. Here, the aim is to form a view of the internal influences – and constraints – on strategic choice.

However, it is also important to consider the particular competencies of the organization and the way in which they may yield opportunities. On occasions, specific resources – for example, the particular location of an organization – can provide it with a competitive advantage.

Analysis of each and all of the above components will result in modified organizational objectives and a new set of targets should lead to a strategy formulation and a viable strategic plan – one that has a reasonable probability of success. This approach reflects system concepts and a contingency view because it recognizes the interrelationship among the various components. An organization may not be able to capitalize on an environmental opportunity (e.g. market demand) if in fact it does not have the competence or resources to do so. Similarly, an organization is unlikely to succeed if its strategic plan is based on managerial interests, without reference to competence, opportunity or societal responsibilities. Integrating these three components of strategy formulation is a delicate and complex task. Being aware of them is an important first step; reconciling their implications and combining them into a viable strategy are considerably more difficult.

Obviously, some managers and some organizations are successful without explicit time-consuming attention to strategy formulation. Their intuitive what to do and when to do it may fit the situation. They may be lucky. On the other hand, it is more likely that they have gone through some unconscious strategy formulation process that leads to an appropriate response, even though they cannot articulate their rationale. While such success stories are evident, the long-term probability of success is enhanced with a more careful, explicit approach to thinking through the various factors involved.

According to Kast and Rosenzweig (1985), explicit strategy formulation has a proactive factor that suggests innovation rather than merely reaction and adaptation. It provides the means for an organization to influence its environment and carve out a 'niche' that is suited to its particular strengths and interests. Some managers shy away from explicit strategy formulation because they are apprehensive about the rigidity that may be applied. However, long range and comprehensive are not synonymous with singleness of purpose or rigidity. Organization strategy can be firm and resilient without being brittle or cast in concrete. Strategy formulation is a continuous process of refinement based on past trends, current conditions, and estimates of the future. A visible strategy serves to focus organizational effort, to facilitate commitment on the part of the participants (and perhaps motivate them), and to increase the probability of self-control in sub-units and individuals.

Stage 2. Strategy formulation

This stage is basically to take all the above components into consideration and work out alternative ways to achieve organizational objectives: What should the organization do? Where? How? and When? At this stage it is important to formulate a strategic plan where the objectives and the strategic plan are clearly defined.

Stage 3. Evaluation of alternative strategies

Having analysed the organization in terms of objectives, the market, weaknesses and strengths, the next step is to evaluate the 'feasibility' of each alternative strategy proposed. At this stage, the corporate planner or the strategic manager needs to make an 'initial' assessment of the following resources:

- *financing* – how much is each strategy going to cost?
- *human resources* – how many people are needed? which administrative staff?
- *administrative resources* – What equipment? What marketing? What accommodation? etc.

Based on the above resources, each strategy will then be evaluated with respect to: (1) profit; (2) growth; (3) risk.

Profit

The principal analysis here is to evaluate the profit that will be generated from the alternative strategies. Profitability is usually measured in terms of the return on the capital invested. The element of 'time' is a crucial factor in determining the feasibility of the organization strategy. For example, major public sector ventures such as bridges and highways may well be assessed on the basis of 'payback period' and 'cost–benefit analysis'. Detailed discussions on the payback period and cost–benefit analysis of investments are outside the scope of this book but can be reviewed in many other texts that deal with financial venture analysis (see Grundy *et al.* (1998) on profit and Williams and Giardina (1993) on cost-benefit analysis).

Growth

Another important criteria for assessing alternative strategies is growth. According to Langford and Male (1991), growth for contractors can be achieved in the following ways.

- *Efficiency only.* This requires no additional resources, turnover is maintained but there is a better use of inputs to achieve efficiency. Managers are concerned therefore with managing the internal dynamics of the contracting organization. This is called a defender strategy, especially if contractors operate efficiently in 'niche markets'.
- *Growth in size only.* This is a strategy of expansion where the attention of managers is directed more to the external environment in order to pursue opportunities rather than necessarily directing attention inwards to improve efficiency at the same time. This is called a prospector's strategy.
- *Growth in size and efficiency.* This requires attention to be directed first, outwards to the opportunities presented in the environment and second, internally to increase efficiency. This is called analyser strategy.
- *No growth in size.* A no growth or minimum growth strategy is essentially unstable. This has close similarities to the reactor strategy.

Risk

Having assessed profit and growth, it is then crucial to assess the element of risk associated with each strategy. The risk that the organization faces depends greatly on the type of product it constructs and the level of uncertainty that exists about key issues in the environment. Any kind of strategy involves an element of risk. For example, expanding within the market means moving into semi-familiar territory which may risk stretching the firm's capability. Shrinkage, on the other hand, may put the organization under the risk of diluting its position with the market and may not be retrievable. The greatest risk, however, lies in diversification strategies where the firm starts to offer unfamiliar services to little known or unknown clients.

Details of risk analysis are outside the scope of this book but this section identifies three quantitative techniques that are commonly used to assess risk and make decisions under conditions of uncertainty. They are decision trees, sensitivity analysis and simulation modelling.

Decision trees. This is a technique used to evaluate future options by progressively eliminating others as additional criteria are introduced to the evaluation. It is used when a manager is faced with a number of options and he or she has to make a 'one-off' decision. This type of decision involves an element of choice on the part of the manager (e.g. whether or not to be involved in building a new type of building) and an element of chance which is beyond his or her control (e.g. the level of demand). Figure 4.4 illustrates an example concerning a property developer who has to make a strategic decision whether to fully utilize the land to construct a commercial building or to build on part of the land that can be expanded later (see method of calculation in Stevenson (1992)).

Sensitivity analysis. The assessment of risk during strategy evaluation is a subject for which sensitivity analysis is particularly appropriate. For example, if a firm wants to invest its capital in a particular venture, it often asks the question 'what happens if the capital cost turns out to be 10 per cent higher than the estimated?' Sensitivity analysis sets out to answer such a question and to measure how sensitive the outcome of the venture is to this assumption. Among the factors that may be reviewed in such an example are:

- increase in material cost of the project
- variation in running cost of the equipment
- shorter or longer plant life
- variation in labour cost.

Another example where the sensitivity analysis technique can be useful is when a firm wants to expand its business by offering a wider range of services on the assumption that the market demand will grow by, say 5 per cent p.a. Here, sensitivity analysis asks what would be the effect on the firm's profitability or growth if the market demand grew only by 1 per cent p.a. or as high as 10 per cent p.a.? The answers to these types of questions can be obtained by utilizing computer programs which can

Question for a decision tree problem

A property developer has acquired a plot of land for development. The company has the option to fully utilize the land to construct a commercial building or to build on part of the land that can be expanded later. The decision depends on future conditions of the company market. To fully utilize the land, an investment of £8 000 000 is required. The anticipated annual cashflow is £1 200 000 for high demand and £700 000 for low demand. Alternatively, the developer can build on part of the land which will cost £4 000 000 and, depending on market conditions, expansion can take place after two years if the market conditions remain good. The anticipated annual cashflows are £600 000 and £400 000 for high and low demand respectively. If a £5 000 000 expansion takes place, the anticipated annual cashflow will become £1 300 000 and £700 000 for high and low demand respectively. Assuming the project life cycle is 10 years, and there is 60% chance that the market conditions will be good and 40% chance for the conditions to be bad throughout the period, the developer has constructed a decision tree with the appropriate notations in order to decide on the optimal strategy to maximize profit.

Calculations for Nodes (see Stevenson (1992) for method of calculation):

for CN#1: $0.6(1\,200\,000 \times 10) + 0.4(700\,000 \times 10) = £10\,000\,000$

for CN#3: $0.6(1\,300\,000 \times 8) + 0.4(700\,000 \times 8) = £8\,480\,000$

for CN#4: $0.6(600\,000 \times 8) + 0.4(400\,000 \times 8) = £4\,160\,000$

for DN#2: £4 160 000 (higher value of two branches)

for CN#2: $0.6(600\,000 \times 2 + 4\,160\,000) + 0.4(400\,000 \times 10) = £4\,816\,000$

for DN#1: £2 000 000 (higher value of two branches)

Strategy: Fully utilize the land

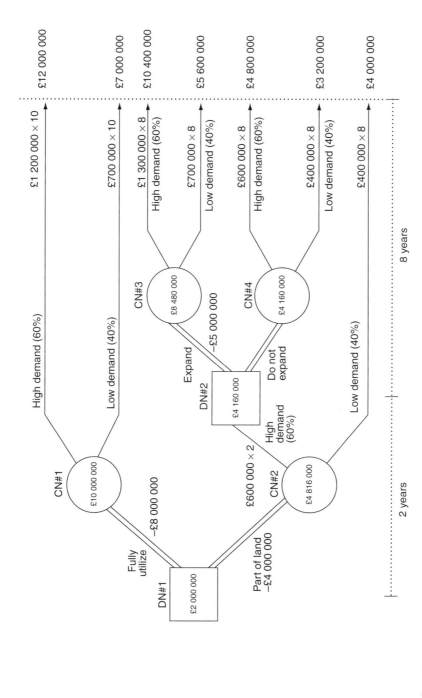

Fig. 4.4. An example of a decision tree

help strategic managers to assess the risk and decide on their strategy. It also helps managers to plan and control their resources.

Simulation modelling. Simulation modelling is another quantitative approach for solving problems under the conditions of uncertainty. It is a mathematical representation of the real-world strategy which simulates the action and reaction of the internal and external factors that affect the business strategy. A good example of a simulation modelling is a 'bidding strategy'. Here, the simulation model will need to contain basic information on the contracts such as their estimated cost, their scheduled starting and completion dates as well as information about the number of tenderers and their relative advantages in terms of location or ability, limitations on financial and working resources. This information will be fed into a mathematical model and simulated using sophisticated computer programs. The complexity of the mathematical processing of simulation modelling is not essential to understand as it is usually developed by experts in the field. However, the outcome of the model will be of great help to managers in order to make their strategic decisions. For instance, in the bidding strategy example, simulation modelling makes available a limited degree of experimentation in situations where live experimentation is virtually impossible. This is true not only in the bidding for contracts but also in many other areas of management.

Stage 4. Strategic choice

Having identified the problem and clarified the objectives of the organization, together with evaluating the alternative strategies with respect to profit, growth and risk, the next step is to choose the best course of action to the organization. In deciding between strategic options, executive management needs to ask a series of questions such as the following.

- Which option can build upon strengths, overcome weaknesses and take advantage of opportunities and minimizes threats? In other words, is there a 'fit' between the resource capability of the organization and the external environment? Or, can the resource capability be developed or 'stretched' to yield new opportunities?
- To what extent could a strategic option be put into practice?
- Can the required finance be raised?
- Would sufficient stock be made available at the right time and in the right place?
- Can staff be recruited and trained to reflect the sort of image that the company is trying to project?
- Assuming the above criteria could be met, would the strategic choice be acceptable to the stakeholders? Here, the acceptability of risk is a very important criterion.

Although such evaluation criteria are useful, there are cases where decisions are based on the leadership and management style of the organization (being autocratic in nature). Johnson and Scholes (1999) stated:

There is not a clear-cut right or wrong strategic choice because any strategy must inevitably have some dangers or disadvantages ... in the end, choice is likely to be a matter of management judgement. The selection process can not always be viewed or understood as a purely objective, logical act. It is strongly influenced by the values of mangers and other groups with interest in the organization, and ultimately may very much reflect the power structure in the organization.

Figure 4.5 is an example of a contractor whose strategic decision was purely based on its management style.

Stage 5. Action plan

After the management chooses its strategy, an action plan needs to be presented before putting the strategy into its final implementation stage. An action plan, in a strategic sense, is a theoretical framework for implementing the chosen strategy. It can be presented as a 'document' and as an 'illustration', showing many of the topics covered in the previous sections of this chapter. In particular, an action plan needs to show the allocation of resources and time when each activity takes place.

There are long-term plans and short-term plans and it is very important to distinguish between the two. The long-term plan (or strategic plan) serves as an instrument for shaping the company to meet the needs of the construction environment of the future. The short-term plan is the operating plan for converting policy into action and acts as an instrument for exercising control over the performance of the decisions.

The long-term strategic plan is prepared by the central planning department and agreed by the main board, while the short-term plan is prepared by the operating units of the company. These short-term plans have to be set within the assumptions established by the long-term plan. Such assumptions provide the unifying ideology of the expected directions of social, political and economic trends. In this way, the 'top down' approach can be blended with the 'bottom up' pattern of planning.

The short-term plan is usually converted into schedules of action, which are tasks that need to be undertaken in, say, twelve months. The financial part of the plan can be put into an overall budget. Therefore, the action plan should include the following:

- the activities involved
- allocation of financing
- allocation of human resources

Background

This company is one of the largest privately-owned construction companies in the UK. The company was founded in the early 1950s by the three members of a family. During the 1950s it operated as a small building company in the London area but in the late 1960s the company was awarded its first design and build contract. This was an important mile-stone in the development of the company and it has developed this side of the business to such an extent that it represents some 60 per cent of the £120M turnover. Much of the design work is undertaken within the organization so that clients are provided with an integrated construction service. The design service is provided by a wholly-owned subsidiary which operates on a multi-disciplinary basis using a high degree of computer-aided design and drafting.

The company has other operating divisions and these include a management contracting division, a joinery company and until recently a building services installation firm. The work-load is focused in the private sector and the company tackled work for local authorities, civil engineering projects and overseas contracts. Recently it has withdrawn from the speculative housing field. The majority of its workload is drawn from industrial, commercial and retail developments with a small section coming from a specialized market niche in laboratory construction. Remarkably the profile of clients is constant with the firm's claim that 60 per cent of current contracts are with previous clients.

The company objectives

As far as can be determined the company has two overriding objectives. One of these is internal, in that it has typical economic objectives, the other external in that it aims to have complete identification with client needs. No explicit social or community objectives could be identified.

The planning process

The strategic planning process of the firm is influenced by its size, its form of corporate leadership and its management style. The company is a large medium-sized firm and this influences the way it is managed. The form of leadership exercised is entrepreneurial as the founder of the business is responsible for all strategic decisions. This form of corporate leadership lends itself to an autocratic managerial style with all significant decisions being taken by the chairman who may (or may not) consult with the managing director and financial director.

This style of management has meant that the strategic planning process is not formalized in any way and consequently the process is intuitive and opportunistic. This process has worked for the company as the strategy of avoiding public sector contracts insulated it against large declines in public sector work. Conversely its preference for private sector contracts has given it some impetus during the 1980s. However, as private sector investment declines in the wake of rises in interest rates it remains to be seen if this will promote a preference for more formal planning methods. The evidence seems to suggest that a more formalized process is envisioned for the future. The firm has recently appointed a corporate planner who reports directly to the chairman and this development hints at a move away from the entrepreneurial style which has dominated the company over the last twenty years. The injection of formal planning will still mean that the process is conducted as a 'top down' exercise with little involvement of the operating divisions.

Fig. 4.5. An example of autocratic strategic decision making: a small national contractor with a specialized market niche in design and build construction (from Langford and Male (1991, p. 111))

- allocation of administrative resources
- the sequence and timing of each activity.

Having identified what is needed, where and when, the next step is to present the action plan. Fellows *et al.* (1998, pp. 52–54) list seven guidelines which provide a framework within which a firm can present its individual plan.

(a) *Introduction.* This section should define the scope of the plan, the period it covers, the deliberately prescribed limitations and the relationship of this plan to other previous and present plans, if any. Some idea of the broad philosophical underpinning of the plan might also be given.

(b) *Assumptions.* The assumptions that are important for an understanding of the plan should be stated. This would include statements about the extent of government intervention (e.g. registration, nationalization, mandatory fee scales, etc.), markets, clients continuing to patronize the firm, successful completion of current ventures and projects, key personnel remaining with the firm, and so on. The risk, if any, if these assumptions are not realized should be assessed and stated here or later in the plan.

(c) *Economic objectives and targets.* The broad financial expectations from pursuing the strategies stated in the plan should be given here with detailed supporting data compiled in an appendix and cross-referenced to this section. A statement of the annual economic expectations for the period covered in the plan should be given in terms of the following.

(i) *Profitability* – the expected increase in pre-tax profits on assets employed in each year of the plan. This should be given in actual figures and percentage terms, highlighting the differences between the first and last year of the plan.

(ii) *Profits* – the improvement in gross and net profits on value of work done in the period of the plan.

(iii) *Value of work done* – the increase in value of work undertaken by the firm in each year of the plan given in figures adjusted for inflation.

(iv) *Dividends* – the percentage of profits after corporation tax to be distributed to ordinary shareholders, the balance to be retained in the company.

These and other objectives could also be given in the form of ratios, as discussed earlier. Cash flow projections would be shown in this part of the plan, as would a review of the recent performance of the firm compared to the objectives of the last plan or related to similar businesses. The device of using minimum and maximum targets to give a wider spread of acceptable results as a bulwark against uncertainty could usefully be employed here.

(d) *Non-economic objectives, constraints and responsibilities.* The basic philosophy of the business mentioned in (a) would be extended in this section to indicate how the objectives and aspirations of owners, employees, clients, etc., are to be met. Constraints which have a bearing on the strategies selected, whether from sources inside or outside the business, should be stated here, as should the responsibilities the firm will assume. This section of the plan will often form the basis of a policy statement published by top management as a permanent part of company documentation and literature.

(e) *Current strengths and weaknesses.* A list of the current strengths and weaknesses of the business gleaned from the internal appraisal and possibly presented under the headings suggested in Table 4.2 would constitute this part of the plan. They should be cross-referenced to those strategies which will exploit the firm's strengths and to those strategies designed to correct or compensate for the weaknesses identified. Some weaknesses will not be resolved in the planning period and should be stated as such.

(f) *Opportunities and threats.* This section should contain only those opportunities and threats for which specific strategies have been devised and should be cross-referenced accordingly.

(g) *Strategies.* This section is the nub of the plan. There could be an introductory schedule of the strategies considered but rejected, which would be 'first reserves' if the selected strategies proved untenable. The proposed courses of action to be adopted during the plan's life, in terms of strategies and strategic modes, can be classified in any way that is appropriate to the business – by present operations, by division, by departments, by business centres, by geographical regions, by country, etc.

When the plan has been drafted and agreed by all concerned it can be published. Copies of the whole plan or parts of it should be given to those executives who will be responsible for its implementation.

Stage 6. Strategy implementation

After going through the process of selecting the appropriate business strategy, the management of the firm will then start to translate the strategy into action, as planned. In other words, making things happen. More importantly, making the right things and at the right time. Strategy implementation is a very crucial step in the strategic process and success depends on it. Management can spend a lot of time analysing and choosing the right strategy, but if those responsible for converting the choice into effective action are not present, the strategic process will remain inactive. The consequences of this are reflected in the following quotation, cited in Kast and Rosenzweig (1985):

Many … 'best-laid plans' are failing to see the light of day. Plans to innovate fizzle out after a series of task-force meetings; plans to improve quality get no further than some airy rhetoric and the hiring of a 'quality guru';… in short, many of our strategies just aren't happening. Without successful implementation, a strategy is but a fantasy.

Strategy implementation involves:

- assembling resources, as planned
- structuring work relationships
- integrating and controlling people and activities.

Here, the following questions need to be answered and should 'correspond' and 'tie' closely with the strategic plan discussed in stage 4 above.

- Who is responsible for carrying out the strategy?
- What are the key activities that need to be carried out?
- Who should do what and when?
- Is there a need for new recruitment?
- What type of management information system is needed to monitor progress?
- How will the implementation process work?

Based on the above information, the implementation of strategy requires major consideration to the following.

Effective structure and work groups (see chapters 5 and 6)
Effective leadership (see chapter 7)
Effective personnel management (see chapter 10)

Stage 7. Strategic control and feedback

Control is the phase of the management process concerned with maintaining organizational activities within allowed constraints, as measured by expectations. Strategy control is inextricably intertwined with strategic planning. For example, in order to evaluate overall performance of the firm against a five-year strategic plan, the company needs a proper feedback and control system to monitor progress. Feedback is a mechanism for identifying the need for a new or adjustable course of action to implement the strategy. Therefore, the process of plan–implement–control–feedback corresponds closely with the concept of the system approach of input–transformation–output (see chapter 2). According to Bellman (1964):

the theory of control is like many other broad theories, is more a state of mind than any specific amalgam of mathematical, scientific or technological methods.

The term can be defined to include any rationale approach by (individuals) ... to overcome the perversities of either their natural or their technological environment. The broad objective of a control theory is to make a system – any kind of system – operate in a more desirable way: to make it more reliable, more convenient or more economical.

There are six common steps in control:

(*a*) establishment of standards of performance
(*b*) measurement of performance against performance standards
(*c*) diagnosis of deviations from standards
(*d*) initiation of corrective action
(*e*) feedback from internal and external environments
(*f*) continuation of performance monitoring.

Apparent characteristics of a business strategy

From the above discussion into the process of business strategy, a number of distinguishing characteristics can be detected. Ansoff (1987) summarized these characteristics as follows.

(*a*) The process of business strategy formulation results in no immediate action. Rather, it sets the general directions in which the firm's position will grow and develop.
(*b*) Therefore, strategy must next be used to generate strategic projects through a search process. The role of strategy in a search is to focus it on areas defined by the strategy, and second to filter out the uncovered possibilities that are inconsistent with the strategy.
(*c*) Thus, strategy becomes unnecessary whenever the historical dynamics of an organization will take it where it wants to go. This is to say, when the search process is already focused on the preferred areas.
(*d*) At the time of strategy formulation it is not possible to enumerate all the project possibilities which will be uncovered. Therefore, strategy formulation must be based on highly aggregated, incomplete and uncertain information about classes of alternatives.
(*e*) When the search uncovers specific alternatives, the more precise, less aggregated information which becomes available may cast doubts on the wisdom of the original strategy choice. Thus, successful use of strategy requires strategic feedback.
(*f*) Since both strategy and objectives are used to filter projects, they appear similar. And yet they are distinct. Objectives represent the ends which the firm is seeking to attain, while the strategy is the means to these ends. The objectives are higher-level decision rules. A strategy which is valid under one set of objectives may lose its validity when the objectives of the organization are changed.

Summary

This chapter is concerned with the concept of strategy and strategic management. The rationale for undertaking a strategy is to respond to some environmental and internal forces. These forces can create opportunities but they can also be threats to the organization.

The term strategy is defined as a planned framework for achieving organizational objectives. Strategic management is concerned with taking the right strategic decision, at the right time and using the right reform to make the strategy work effectively. Strategic decisions can be diffused throughout the organization over time and therefore can have an impact on the operational decisions and the administrative decisions within the organization. In other words, effective strategic management creates a productive alliance between the nature and the demands of the environment, the organization's culture and values, and the resources that the organization has at its disposal.

Some of the reasons for undertaking a strategy are to grow, to be more productive or to provide a high job satisfaction to employees. The means of achieving growth of productivity are by: (1) diversifying the type of buildings the company constructs; (2) expanding or shrinking within the market (by type of client and/or location); (3) differentiation of building product (uniqueness), a merger or company takeover, a partnership, contracts bidding, etc.

There are two types of strategies: the planned approach and the reactor approach. The reactor approach is a 'wait and see' strategy. The planned approach follows a more sophisticated method of planning and it is more likely to be adopted by medium- and large-sized construction companies. There are seven main stages in conducting a business strategy (see Fig. 4.3). These are:

(*a*) *strategic analysis* – analysis of strengths and weaknesses of the organization

(*b*) *strategy formulation* – a scope which identifies the objectives and possible plans for achieving these objectives (i.e. alternative strategies)

(*c*) *evaluation of alternative strategies* – against growth, profit, constraints and risk involved

(*d*) *strategic choice* – which strategy is the best?

(*e*) *strategic plan* – allocation of resources with a timetable

(*f*) *strategy implementation* – making things happen

(*g*) *strategic control and feedback* – comparing the planned performance with the actual performance.

There is evidence to suggest that construction firms which adopted a systematic and sophisticated approach to planning during the volatile decade of the 1970s were more successful in riding the storm (even developing their businesses) than those construction firms whose planned effort was underdeveloped. The following case studies illustrate some of the points made in this chapter.

References

ANSOFF, H. *Corporate strategy: Present and Future*. Working paper, European Institute for Advanced Studies in Management, Brussels, 1974.

ANSOFF, I. *Corporate Strategy*. London, Penguin, 1987, revised edn.

BELLMAN, R. Control theory. *Scientific American*, September 1964, p. 186.

BARNARD, R. A strategic appraisal system for small firms. *Building Technology and Management*, September 1981, pp. 21–24.

CHANNON, D. *The strategy and structure of British enterprise*. Division of Research, Harvard Graduate School of Business Administration, 1973.

DUNCAN, R. Characteristics of organisational environment and perceived environmental uncertainty. *Administrative Science Quarterly*, 1972, pp. 313–327.

FELLOWS, R., LANGFORD, D., NEWCOMBE, R. and URRY, S. *Construction Management in Practice*. London, Longman, 1998.

GRUNDY, A., JOHNSON, G. and SCHOLES, K. *Exploring Strategic Financial Management*. Prentice-Hall, 1998.

HAGE, J. and AIKEN, M. Relationship of centralisation to other structural properties. *Administrative Science Quarterly*, 1967, pp. 72–92.

HAMEL, G. and PRAHALAD, C. *Competing for the Future*. Cambridge, MA, Harvard Business School Press, 1994.

HARVEY, E. Technology and the structure of organisation. *American Sociological Review*, 1968, pp. 247–259.

HUNT, J. *The Restless Organisation*. Wiley International, 1972.

JOHNSON, G. and SCHOLES, K. *Exploring Corporate Management*. Englewood Cliffs, NJ, Prentice-Hall, 1999, 5th edn.

KAST, F. and ROSENZWEIG, J. *Organization and Management*. New York, McGraw-Hill, 1985, 5th edn.

LANGFORD, D., HANCOCK, M., FELLOWS, R. and GALE, A. *Human Resources Management in the Construction Industry*. Harlow, Longman, 1995.

LANGFORD, D. and MALE, S. *Strategic Management in Construction*. Gower, 1991.

LANSLEY, P. Corporate planning for the small builder. *Building Technology and Management*, December 1981, pp. 7–9.

LAWRENCE, P. and LORSCH, J. *Organisation and Environment*. Harvard Business School, 1967.

LUNDY, O. and COWLING, A. *Strategic Human Resource Management*. New York, Routledge, 1996.

LUTHANS, F., HODGETT, S. and ROSENKRANTZ, S. *Real Managers*. Ballinger, Cambridge, Massachusetts, 1988, p. 27 and chapter 6.

NEWCOMBE, R. *The Evolution of the Construction Firm*. Unpublished MSc Thesis, University College, London, 1976.

NEWCOMBE, R. and HANCOCK, M. *Concepts of Management*. MSc in Construction Management by distance learning. Management in construction module. University of Bath, 1996.

PENNINGS, J. The relevance of the structural-contingency model for organisational effectiveness. *Administrative Science Quarterly*, 1975, pp. 393–410.

SHETTY, Y. and LUTHANS, F. A. Contingency Theory of Management – A Path Out of the Jungle. Reading, *Academic of Management Review*, 1979.

SIDWELL, A. *Notes on Organizational Theory*. MSc in Construction Management and Economics, University of Aston, 1980, unpublished notes.

STEVENSON, W. *Introduction to Management Science*. Irwin, 1992, 2nd edn.

TAYLOR, B. and SPARKES, J. *Corporate Strategy and Planning*. Oxford, Heinemann, 1977.

TRIST, E., HIGGINS, G., MURRAY, H. and POLLACK, A. *Organisational Choice*. Tavistock, 1963.

WILLIAMS, A. and GIARDINA, E. *Efficiency in the Public Sector: the Theory and Practice of Cost-benefit Analysis*. Edward Elgar, 1993.

Case study 1. A medium-sized regional contractor (part of a larger construction group) (from Langford and Male (1991, pp. 115–117))

Background

This company is one of eleven autonomous subsidiaries of a large construction group. The company was taken over by the group in the late 1970s after a traumatic period when the company had gone into voluntary liquidation in the wake of the recession earlier in the decade. The reasons for this failure are interesting in themselves. At the time of the liquidation the company was heavily involved in property development and the secondary bank collapse of the early 1970s took the company into liquidation. At that time the company was not diversified and had little strategic nous. Opportunism was the favoured manner of operation. The company is now in a strong position within a buoyant region of the UK and has a major presence in building, civil engineering and public works construction and has built a turnover of £70M. It has a strong tradition of direct employment and is committed to the continuation of craft training programmes.

The company objectives

Typically the firm has economic and non-economic objectives. The economic objectives are to:

1. Consistently return a satisfactory and increasing annual net profit;
2. Achieve a satisfactory return on capital employed;

3. Maintain a positive cash flow at *all* times;
4. Expand the business relative to market opportunities and staff capabilities;
5. Obtain repeat orders on a negotiated basis;
6. Stay in business.

It must be noted that these economic objectives are vague and are only of real value to the company when quantified. Such data is naturally sensitive and the company did not wish to reveal the economic targets which it had set.

The company's non-economic objectives are to:

1. Train and develop staff to enable them to fulfil their potential;
2. Maintain a high level of business integrity with a strong element of service to clients;
3. Act as a responsible member of the community;
4. Enjoy what the firm does.

The overriding objective is to expand and this expansion strategy will be discussed further.

The planning process

The process of strategy formulation in the company is driven by market analyses. Periodically a small task force is assembled to review current strategy and appraise whether new strategic directives are required. It must be noted that this is not an annual process nor does it happen at regular intervals. The background to this method is in the conduct of market research. Market research was seen as important in the late 1970s to compare the quality of market information. The task force is charged with the task of assessing opportunities and options available to the firm in the context of the expected market for construction. The task force appraises the condition of the firm and matches the external opportunities with the capacity of the firm to take advantage of these opportunities. The task force then formulates a number of strategic options and presents these to the Board of Directors. The Board then opts for a particular strategy and oversees its implementation. Two themes have run through the strategic development of the company – growth and quality assurance. The growth strategy has been implemented by an expansion of the number of depots from two offices in 1977 to eight offices in 1987 throughout the region where it operates. This growth in the number of offices has meant that projects are supervised from a local administrative centre. Thus the growth has been matched by a level of decentralization of markets. From primary interests in property development the firm has developed into general contract work and has made inroads into design and build activities for industrial and retail clients. Using the model developed by Newcombe *et al.* (1990) the company has moved from a single dominant market to a related regional market. This is illustrated in Figure 4.6.

The key to the strategy for growth was to provide a quality service to clients. Consequently the company's strategy was to encourage repeat business by providing a construction service which was quality assured.

The planning process is fairly formal with the strategy emerging from research of market opportunities and market expectations of the services that contractors will be expected to provide in the 1990s. However, this process is driven by a small number of senior executives who then have a responsibility to carry out the strategy. As such this approach may be characterized as a 'top down' approach with little involvement of the operating units. Nonetheless the commitment of the local managers to the growth and quality strategy is evident and the strategy is communicated to managers. It would appear that the senior executives enjoy the confidence of their operating managers and the culture of training and development is one of the factors which cements the commitment to strategic objectives.

	Single market	Dominant in one market	Related diversification	Unrelated diversification
Local firm	1970			
Regional firm			1989	
National firm				
International firm				

Figure 4.6. Company growth and market position

Case study 2. A progressive quantity surveying practice (from Langford and Male (1991, pp. 128–129))

Background

This practice is a large quantity surveying practice with head offices in the North of England and nineteen branch offices, some of which are based overseas. The company has developed from a traditional quantity surveying practice to one which offers specialized services to specific market sectors. The company dates from the late 1940s but it was during the 1960s and 1970s that the firm developed expertise in quantity surveying services for process and industrial engineering, and although this market has declined the expertise gained in this area enabled the practice to generate work in the building construction aspects of surveying. In common with many other surveying practices it saw diversification as necessary to enable it to develop and be synchronized with a rapidly changing external environment. Consequently the firm offers services which range from preparation of tender documents to feasibility studies and life cycle costing. More recently project management services and quantity surveying for mechanical and electrical services have been added to the workload of the practice.

Objective

The stated objective is organizational growth. The practice has sought to grow by a combination of internally generated growth and passive acquisition. This growth has resulted in the size of the organization, in terms of number of employees, being more than doubled in the period 1975–1989. Such growth was coupled with some restructuring; a small group of four partners forms the senior management team and the middle management is staffed by partners who direct the work of each branch office.

The planning process

Prior to 1984 the firm had a reactive style of strategic development. Frequently new offices were opened in response to the promise of an existing client to provide work on a development in a particular part of the country. There is other evidence of this 'reactor' approach; in an interview one of the partners revealed a strong opportunistic streak. If the partners saw a business opportunity in the market then they would 'go for it', seemingly mindful that the previously agreed strategy had not identified the opportunity as an arena for their business development. This opportunistic approach is, however, tempered by a formalized strategic planning process. The senior management formally meet once every two months to review progress on the implementation of strategy. Strategy is formulated by this group with the assistance of a development division of the practice. This division, based at the head office, has a primary role of considering organizational development. Changes in direction of strategy appear to emanate from this division and papers are presented for discussion by senior management. Therefore the strategic planning process has become much more formal.

Discussion of strategy is not accepted as part of the responsibilities of the branch offices. These units have to implement the chosen strategy and the practice recognizes that it is autocratic in its management style as policy is lowered on to these offices. However, the practice is cognisant of potential problems and a strong social life is fostered within the practice and formal communications through newsletters, etc. provide the necessary sustenance to keep the staff loyal.

Conclusions

Financial data was not available for review but the impression given was that the practice was active and progressive. The process of strategy formulation has moved from being reactive to a mixture of reactive and proactive and this fusion of entrepreneurialism and structured organizational development keeps the practice dynamic yet stable. This curious combination means that growth has occurred in an organic and a planned way; the question is whether this coalition of planning styles can sustain the relatively high morale amongst staff given the relatively centralized basis for formal strategic planning.

Chapter 5

Organizational structure

> Structure follows strategy. If the strategy establishes the objectives of the organization and determines the direction in which the organization will go, then the structure facilitates the achievement of these objectives. Structure provides the framework of an organization and its pattern of management. It is by means of structure that the purpose and work of the organization is carried out. (Chandler 1966)

In chapter 4 the view was put forward that organizations need a business strategy in order to cope with the increasing pressures of the external and internal environments. In turn, the chosen strategy requires some form of structure to make it work and achieve organizational goals effectively. This is done by means of structure where tasks are assigned, authority is exercised and power is allocated. This chapter provides an understanding of the importance of organizational structure and its effects on organizational effectiveness. The first part of the chapter discusses the subjects that are associated with organizational structure. The nature and typology of organizational structure, including the traditional (simple) structure, divisional (functional) structure and matrix (project management) structure, are then explained. Factors that affect the design or choice of structure are described and supplemented by empirical research findings. Figure 5.1 summarizes the overall principles of the chapter (also see Fig. 1.1).

Learning outcomes

To:

> ➢ understand the meaning and importance of organizational structure
> ➢ understand the topics associated with organizational structure
> ➢ identify the various types of structures

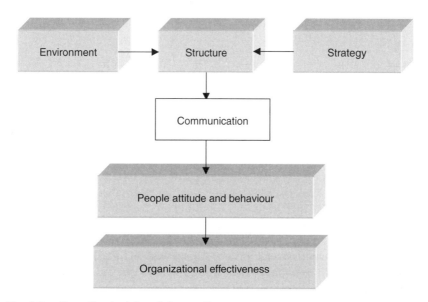

Fig. 5.1. Overall principles of chapter 5

> ➢ evaluate the main factors which are to be considered in the design of organizational structure.

The meaning of organizational structure

Every organization consists of individuals who are brought together to work as teams in order to perform specific tasks and achieve organizational and personal objectives. Those members of the organization teams are interconnected by a set of rules and procedures with some kind of structural hierarchy. Within this hierarchy, there are two essential functions that link people together, these are:

(a) the 'task' function, which refers to those activities that are responsible for the actual execution of the building process, e.g. design and construction, providing and marketing the service, and financing the organization

(b) the 'element' function, which refers to those activities that are supportive to the task function but not directly related to the specific and definable ends, e.g. personnel, management services, public relations, quality control and maintenance.

In this sense, the author has defined organizational structure as:

A mechanism for linking and co-ordinating people and groups together within the framework of their roles, authority and power. Structure can be regarded as the backbone of the organization and its effectiveness depending on how strong or weak the skeleton is.

The design principles of organizational structure can affect the organization in two ways:

(a) *technically,* where productivity and economic efficiency of the organization can be affected
(b) *socially,* where moral and job satisfaction of the employee can be affected.

Good organization does not by itself produce good performance. But a poor organizational structure makes good performance impossible, no matter how good the individual managers may be. Therefore, the design of the organizational structure should maintain the right balance of the socio-technical system. The relationship between these two systems, i.e. between structure and technological requirements of the organization and social factors and the needs of the human part, must be strong (Drucker 1989, p. 223).

Interaction between groups is usually represented by a structural diagram showing the relationship between the positions held within the organization. There are a number of possible ways of designing the structure (this will be discussed in detail later in this chapter). Figure 5.2 shows Mintzberg's five basic building blocks of organizational design, each summarized below.

(a) The *operating core* encompasses those members who perform the basic works related directly to the production process, such as the operatives and site managers on a building site.
(b) The *strategic apex* is where the general management of the organization occurs, e.g. the head office that is charged with ensuring that the organization serves its mission in an effective way and also that it serves the needs of the people involved.
(c) The *middle line* is formed of those managers with formal authority who stand between the strategic apex and the operating core, e.g. commercial and contract managers.
(d) The *technostructure* is formed by the staff analysts who design the systems whereby the work processes of others are delivered and controlled, e.g. engineers and consultants.
(e) The *support staff* provide support to the organization outside the operating workflow, e.g. secretarial and technical staff.

Within these five building blocks there is a system of co-ordination and communication for controlling the activities and the people. The following section discusses the main elements that are associated with organizational structure.

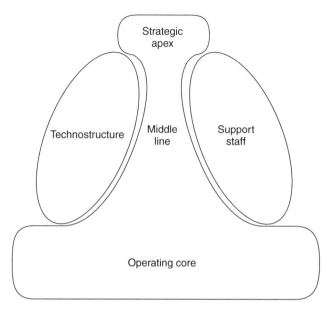

Fig. 5.2. Basic building blocks of organizational design (from Mintzberg (1998, p. 20))

Topics associated with organizational structure

The important nature of organizational structure means that it is vital to identify the interrelated elements that are closely associated with this topic (see Fig. 5.3):

- (*a*) group formation
- (*b*) communication network
- (*c*) power and authority
- (*d*) centralization and decentralization
- (*e*) mechanistic and organic systems
- (*f*) span of control.

Each of these topics is now discussed in some detail.

Group formation

Organizational structure is associated with group formation, i.e. the setting up of divisions, departments, work sections, etc. The term 'group' is commonly defined as a number of people who: (1) interact with one another; (2) are psychologically aware of one another; and (3) perceive themselves to be a group. The subject of work groups is discussed in detail in chapter 6. Briefly stated, there are common bases

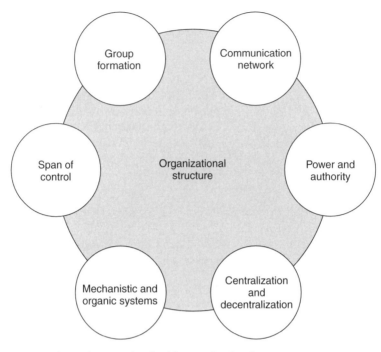

Fig. 5.3. Major topics associated with organizational structure

for the organization to form the group positions among its members, ranging from large units to small sub-units. For example, grouping by knowledge or skill, by work process and function, by time, by output, by client, by place and by project. The purpose of forming these group positions is, first, to achieve organizational objectives and second to satisfy the personal needs of those who are working within the organization. Handy (1998) summarized organizational objectives of group formation as:

- *distribution of work* – to bring together a set of skills, talents, responsibilities, and allocate to them their particular duties
- *management and control of work* – to allow work to be organized and controlled by appropriate individuals with responsibility for a certain range of work
- *problem solving and decision taking* – to bring together a set of skills, talents and responsibilities so that the solution to any problem will have all available capacities applied to it
- *information processing* – to pass on decisions or information to those who need to know
- *information and idea selection* – to gather ideas, information and suggestions

- *testing and ratifying decisions* – to test the validity of a decision taken outside the group, or to ratify such a decision
- *co-ordination and liaison* – to co-ordinate problems and tasks between functions or divisions
- *increased commitment and involvement* – to allow and encourage individuals to get involved in the plans and activities of the organization
- *negotiation or conflict resolution* – to resolve a dispute or argument between levels, divisions or functions
- *inquest or inquiry into the past.*

On the other hand, individuals use groups for one or more of the following purposes:

- A means of satisfying their social or affiliation needs, to belong to something or to share in something.
- A means of establishing a self-concept. Most people find it easier to define themselves in terms of their relationship to others, as members of a role set with a role in that set.
- A means of gaining help and support to carry out their particular objectives.
- A means of sharing and helping in a common activity or purpose which may be making a product, or carrying out a job, or having fun, or giving help, or creating something.

Group formation is therefore an essential feature of the work pattern of organizations and can influence the attitudes and behaviour of their members. People attitude and behaviour can in turn influence organizational effectiveness in terms of productivity and success. The activities of groups are not only associated with organizational structure but also with the style of leadership. This relationship is discussed in some detail in chapter 8.

Communication network

Organizational structure is associated with a communication network which is the key process of transferring information among the groups. The performance of every task within the organization depends upon the communication network that is designed to link people and clusters of people. A great deal of important information is obtained, shared, processed and acted upon by the key people working together to co-ordinate their activities. Meetings, memos, minutes, reports, etc. are all part of the communications tool. Some estimates of the extent of communication use go up to about three-quarters of an active human being's life, and even higher proportions of a typical manager's time. A comprehensive study by Luthans *et al.* (1988) directly observed 178 'real managers' in their day-to-day behaviour and found that managers devote just under a half of their daily activity to routine communication – exchanging routine information and processing paperwork. More importantly, however, is the finding that the communication activity made the biggest relative contribution to 'effective managers'. The following breakdown is a summary of the findings from that work in terms of proportions of time spent on random activities.

(*a*)	Routine communication including exchanging information and handling paperwork	44%
(*b*)	Human resource management including motivation, disciplining, managing conflict and training	26%
(*c*)	Traditional management including, planning, decision making and controlling	19%
(*d*)	Outside networking including interaction with outsiders and socializing/politicking	11%

For each type of organizational structure there is a certain type of communication network. For example, in a typical bureaucratic structure, all tasks are well understood in advance of their being performed and therefore they are effectively pre-planned. However, organizations operating in a dynamic environment with complex and changing technologies must have an information system which makes it possible to make continuous adaptations to activities. The greater the task uncertainty, the greater the amount of information that must be processed among decision makers during task execution in order to achieve a given level of performance. For example, in a straightforward project or a small organization there is a high degree of certainty concerning the task to be performed. In contrast, in a large infrastructure venture or a partnership arrangement, the tasks are highly uncertain and a great deal of information must be developed and exchanged during the execution of the project. By developing more effective communication networks, organizations strive to create more willing and effective co-ordination of diverse activities. Naisbitt 1982 (cited in Kast and Rosenzweig (1985, p. 252)) suggests that the development of communication networks as a substitute for the pyramid structure is one of the ten most prominent mega-trends affecting our lives. He says:

> *Simply stated, networks are people talking to each other, sharing ideas, information and resources. The point is often made that networking is a verb, not a noun. The important part is not the network or the finished product, but the process of getting there – the communication that creates the linkage between people and clusters of people...*
>
> *Networks exist to foster self-help to exchange information, to change society, to improve productivity and work life, and to share resources. They are structured*

to transmit information in a way that is quicker, more high touch, and more energy efficient than any other process we know.

To this end, it is worth thinking of the number of situations where:

- there has been a misunderstanding as to what information is really needed
- there has been a misunderstanding of what needs to be done and by whom
- there has been improper channel of communication when two or more groups of people are performing a particular task.

Power and authority

Organizational structure is associated with the allocation of power and authority. Power was defined by Max Weber (1947) as 'the probability that one actor within a social relationship be in a position to carry out his/her own will despite resistance'. While authority was defined as 'the right to manipulate or change others'. The allocation of power and authority is therefore an important element that needs to be considered when deciding on the type of group structure. For instance, who decides what, and with what authority, can tell a great deal about the decision making process within the organizational structure. Therefore, different types of structures can have a different power process.

There are two fundamental classification of power – legitimate power and illegitimate power. Based on these two classifications, six power bases have commonly been identified in both organizations and projects.

Legitimate power

(a) *Position power.* This is the only formal type of power which exists within the hierarchical structure of the organization and its project. Position power is usually equated with authority as being a 'legal power' where the manger (or any other person responsible for a particular task) has the right to exercise influence because of his or her position within the structure. For example, the relationship between the manger and subordinate is a position power, so is the relationship between the project manager and the site engineer. The type of relationship that exists between the person with positional power and the subordinates depends of the task and the characteristics of the group. Moreover, the strength of position power depends largely on the illegitimate bases of power. Illegitimate power relies on an individual's expertise, resources, reward capacity, information and personality. For example, the more experience the manager has, the stronger the (legitimate position) power that he/she possesses over subordinates.

The illegitimate power

(b) *Expert power.* This type of power is based on a person's distinguishing expertise and excellence among the group in a given area. For example, the functional experience of site engineers and service engineers gives them the power to make certain decisions during the building process. This is so because of their technical know how among members of the building team.

(c) *Resource power.* This is based on the perception that 'money is power'. Possession of valued resources such as finance, manpower and equipment is a useful basis for influencing subordinates. Here, the subordinates perceive the manager as a person with the ability and resources to support their position or ideas within the structure. However, the degree of resource power depends on the extent to which the subordinates need the resources.

(d) *Reward power.* This is based on the subordinates' perception that their manager can influence them because of his/her power to pay, promote and develop them.

(e) *Information power.* This is based on the view that 'information is power'. Here, the perception of the subordinates is that their leader/manager can influence them because of control over dissemination or distortion of facts and information.

(f) *Personal power.* This is the power of personality (charisma, popularity, sociability) rather than position in the organization.

From the above discussion into sources of power, it is apparent that there is a fundamental difference between legitimate power and illegitimate power. Legitimate power usually affects subordinates equally, while illegitimate power can affect different groups of people in different ways. The influence of illegitimate power depends on the extent to which the subordinate needs the resources, reward or the information. For example, one group of people could rely largely on manpower, which makes availability of resources a powerful tool to influence them. On the other hand, another group of people may be more interested in incentives and promotion, making reward a powerful tool to influence them.

Centralization and decentralization

Organizational structure is associated with centralization and decentralization of authority. In a highly centralized organization, the power of control is mainly located at the top of the hierarchical structure. In a decentralized structure, the power of control is dispersed among departments or individuals. Both centralization and decentralization

Table 5.1.   Centralization and decentralization

Features	Centralization	Decentralization
Nature of product	Need for specialization	Need for standardization
Decision making	Fast but distant from operational level	Slow but close to operational level
Economies of scale	High	Low
Admistrative support	Can be ineffective if not rationalized properly	Can be very effective if provided close to the serving activities
Co-ordination and control	Easy	More complicated
Staff training and development	Slow in providing real opportunities and therefore staff moral can be low	Fast in providing good opportunities and therefore, staff morale can be high
Application	Suitable for public services	Suitable for a large private businesses

have their own advantages and disadvantages. Table 5.1 provides the main features of both types of structures.

Mechanistic and organic systems

Organizational structure is associated with the mechanistic system and the organic system. These systems were categorized after the well known studies in the electronics industry undertaken by Burns and Stalker (1961). The mechanistic organization (closely related to democratic leadership style) was defined as a rigid structure with specialized functionally and more appropriate to stable conditions. Organic organizations (closely related to autocratic leadership style) have less formalized definitions of jobs, with more flexibility and adaptability and have a communication network involving more consultation than command. Below is a breakdown of mechanistic and organic characteristics.

The characteristics of a mechanistic management system are similar to those of bureaucracy – these are:

(a)   strong emphasis on functional specialization
(b)   concentration on individual tasks as if they were ends in themselves
(c)   co-ordination through successive hierarchical levels of superior authority

(*d*) the precise definition of rights and obligations and technical methods associated with each job

(*e*) the translation of rights and obligation and methods into the responsibilities of a functional position

(*f*) hierarchic structure of control, authority and communication

(*g*) a reinforcement of the hierarchic structure by a flow of information to the top of the hierarchy, where the final co-ordination is made

(*h*) a tendency for interaction to be vertical, i.e. between superior and subordinate

(*i*) a tendency for operations and working behaviour to be governed by the instructions and decisions issued by supervisors

(*j*) insistence on loyalty to the concern and obedience to superiors as a condition of membership

(*k*) greater importance and prestige attached to internal (local) than to general (cosmopolitan) knowledge, experience and skill.

The characteristics of an organic management system are appropriate to changing conditions that constantly give rise to fresh problems and unforeseen requirements for action which cannot be broken down or disturbed automatically arising from the functional roles defined within a hierarchic structure. It is characterized by:

(*a*) the contribution of special knowledge and experience to the common task of the concern

(*b*) the realistic nature of the individual task, which is seen as set by the total situation of the concern

(*c*) the adjustment and the continental re-definition of individual tasks through interaction with others

(*d*) the sense of responsibility not confined to a limited field of rights, obligation and methods

(*e*) commitment to the concern beyond what is laid down

(*f*) a network of control, authority and communication

(*g*) task-relevant knowledge no longer imputed to the head of the concern. It may be located anywhere in the network, this location becoming the *ad hoc* centre of authority

(*h*) a lateral rather than vertical direction of communication and communication between people of different rank resembling consultation rather than command

(*i*) communication consisting of information and advice rather than instructions and decisions

(*j*) commitment to the concern's tasks and to the technological ethos of material progress; expansion is more highly valued than loyalty or obedience

(*k*) importance and prestige are attached to affiliations and expertise external to the firm.

Burns and Stalker point out that mechanistic and organic systems represent the polar extremes of the form that such systems could take when adapted to technical and commercial change. In between these extremes is a continuum of various types of patterns which an organization can display. In other words, the range of patterns may fall anywhere on the scale's continuum. The relevant practical question is: what factors should a company consider in deciding how to design an organization? The following sections discuss this question.

Span of control

Organizational structure is associated with span of control (SOC). The term SOC means: 'how many individuals should report to each manager and who should report to whom?' Based on this principle, there are two organizational structures:

(a)   the narrow span of control with a tall structure and
(b)   the wide span of control with a flat structure.

In a tall structure, the chain of authority is rather long with relatively small groups, while in a flat structure, the levels of authority are fewer with relatively large work groups at each. The selection of the shape will depend on the level of control that the managers need over their subordinates as well as the degree of co-ordination required between the groups in order to perform the tasks.

Graicunas (1937) developed a mathematical formula for the SOC. The limitation of the number of subordinates who can effectively be supervised is based on the total of direct and cross-relationships:

$$R = n(2^n/2 + n - 1)$$

where n is the number of subordinates and R is the number of inter-relationships.

Urwick (1947) suggests that the SOC should not exceed five, or at the most six direct subordinates whose work interlocks. At the lower levels of the organization, where there is less interlocking, or where responsibility is concerned more with the performance of specific tasks, the SOC may be larger.

Practical studies into organizational structure suggest that the design of SOC depends mainly upon the:

(a)   nature of the organization
(b)   the task to be performed
(c)   the technology used
(d)   the ability and quality of the managers
(e)   the effectiveness of co-ordination and the nature of the communication and control system.

For example, the Woodward (1965) study found that:

> *The figures relating to the span of control of the chief executive, the number of levels in the line of command, labour costs, and the various labour ratios showed a similar trend. The fact that organizational characteristics, technology and success were linked together in this way suggested that not only was the system of production an important variable in the determination of organizational structure, but also that one particular form of organization was most appropriate to each system of production. In unit production, for example, not only did short and relatively broad based pyramids predominate, but they also appeared to ensure success. Process production, on the other hand, would seem to require the taller and more narrowly based pyramid.*

According to Carzo and Yanouzas (1969, p. 189), 'the greater number of levels in the tall structure can interrupt the vertical flow of information more frequently'. However, the flat structure requires more discussion and consultation. In effect, 'the greater time required for decisions to pass through several levels of a tall structure can be offset by the time required to resolve differences and co-ordinate the efforts of many subordinates in a flat structure'. Carzo and Yanouzas also found evidence of greater status differences in the tall structure, which impeded information flow and so required the managers to be more careful in their data collection. However, when the experiment was measured against profit and return on investment, the tall structures performed better. They wrote (p. 190):

> *The superior performance of the groups under the tall structure may be explained by the fact that their decisions were subjected to more analysis than the decisions of the groups under the flat structure. The intermediate supervisory levels provided the means for repeated evaluation of decisions. In addition, the narrow span of supervision in the tall structure permitted a much more orderly decision and communication process. Freed from the burdens that arise from having many subordinates, decision makers appeared to be able to develop a better understanding of the problem.*

If the SOC is too wide it becomes difficult to supervise subordinates effectively and this places more stress on the manager. With larger groupings, informal leaders and sub-groups or cliques are more likely to develop, and these may operate contrary to the policy of management. There may be a lack of time to carry out all activities properly. Planning and development, training, inspection and control may suffer in particular, leading to poor job performance. A wide SOC may limit opportunities for promotion. Too wide a SOC may also result in a slowness to adapt to change or to the introduction of new methods or procedures.

If the SOC is too narrow this may present a problem of co-ordination and consistency in decision making, and hinder effective communications across the organizational structure. The morale and initiative of subordinates may suffer as a result of too close a level of supervision. Narrow spans of control increase administrative costs and can prevent the best use being made of the limited resource of managerial talent. They can lead to additional levels of authority in the organization, creating an unnecessarily long scalar chain.

Types of organizational structure

In order for the organization to achieve its goals and objectives, the tasks allocated to individuals need to be co-ordinated in a cohesive manner through the organizational structure. Organizational structure is a continuous development and should be constantly under review alongside the aim and objectives of the company. The following should be included in such a review.

- The pattern of authority relationship between the people (managers and operatives) and/or departments/divisions.
- The chain of command. Organizations and sites will have longer and/or more complex communication links which lengthen the chain of command. This will affect the ability to control contracts financially and organizationally. Here, there will be the problem of how much to delegate.
- Area offices/head offices/sites – how should functions and services be distributed? Which services are to be done centrally and what advantage is there in having an expensive head office which creates an expensive overhead charged on the organization? Economies of scale can be achieved by grouping activities.

There are three types of organizational structure:

(*a*) the traditional simple structure (also known as craft structure)
(*b*) the functional structure (also known as line manager structure)
(*c*) the matrix structure (also known as task structure).

The simple structure

A simple or a craft structure organization has an informal line relationship among its members. It is the type of organization that is common to most businesses at their development stage. It consists of an owner who starts the business and who undertakes most of the management responsibilities, perhaps with a partner. It is characterized by:

- centralized power
- a wide SOC

- direct supervision
- informal communication
- single decision making
- flexibility of workflow
- having a reactive strategy (wait and see)
- fast reaction to a dynamic environment.

The simple structure is fine if the chain of command involves only line management, so each manager controls, say, ten subordinates. However, in modern organizations there are advisory staff functions (such as marketing, personnel, R&D) and consequently the pyramid gets bigger and more unwieldy. These trends of modern organizations, which are caused by:

- centralization of control data
- centralization of planning data
- techniques covering the company as a whole
- project managers following a job from start to finish
- increasing size and complexity of companies
- increasing number of specialists

can be countered by an alternative pattern of organizational structures, such as the functional or the matrix structure.

The functional structure

When the simple/craft organizations grow, informal communication becomes increasingly inadequate for co-ordination. Therefore, new levels of management must be developed and direct supervision must be increasingly relied upon for co-ordination. This signals the arrival of the functional structure.

A functional structure is based on a grouping of all the specialists in autonomous departments. Thus, each specialist department provides a common service throughout the organization. Figure 5.4 shows a typical organization chart for the functional structure, together with its advantages and disadvantages. In this structure, line managers and the staff (who provide the service) exercise a formal authority over their subordinates only and not across the structure. In other words, the service specialists have no direct authority over those who make use of the service. For example, the personnel manager has no authority over staff in other departments – this is the responsibility of the line manager. However, in construction, some individuals can hold a line management position and at the same time provide a professional service. For instance, the quantity surveyor can have a line management relationship with the chief surveyor and can also have a staff relationship with the site manager.

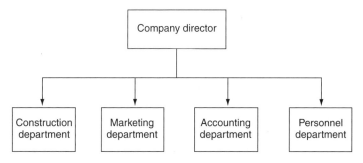

(A) Functional structure by department

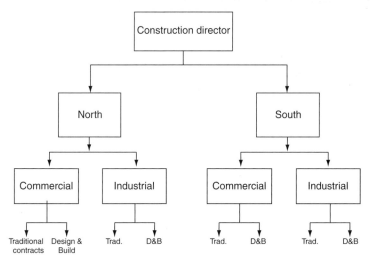

(B) Functional structure by region and contract type

Advantages of functional structure	Disadvantages of functional structure
(i) Total control of executive managers	(i) Difficult to co-ordinate between departments
(ii) Clear roles and responsibilities of departments	(ii) Difficult to adapt
(iii) Specialist divisions	(iii) Difficult to diversity

Fig. 5.4.   Functional structure of an organization

The functional structure is characterized by:

- decentralization of functional power (full departmental autonomy)
- a narrow span of control
- direct and indirect supervision
- formal communication
- integrated decision making
- interdependency of the workflow, processes, sales and socializing
- having a planned strategy
- being a slow reactor to a dynamic environment.

The main advantage of this structure is that it allows for high production control at a senior level and a clear definition of roles and authority. However, there are disadvantages, particularly as the organization becomes larger and more diverse. Langford *et al.* (1995, pp. 66–67) wrote:

> *. . . in the wide expansion of diversification, construction firms find it necessary to rethink the line and staff structure. Companies expanding their operations often in a geographical sense, tend to divide their functions according to area and to decentralise a number of the administrative functions. This leads to a degree of autonomy and accountability (especially for profit and costs) within the local division whilst Head Office retains strategic control. A similar pattern can be observed when a firm diversifies. Here, they are likely to divide the organization according to product e.g. housing, commercial, industrial, civil engineering, etc. In both cases the object is to provide a structure capable of the flexibility and quick repose necessary for effective operation.*

The matrix structure

With the continuous growth of organizations and as a result of projects becoming more large and technologically complex, it has become necessary for organizations to add a horizontal dimension to the traditional functional structure in order to improve co-ordination and functional integration among individuals and groups. The matrix structure can facilitate this integration whereby the normal vertical hierarchy is overlaid by some form of lateral authority, influence or communication (Knight 1976).

For example if, as part of the organizational strategy, a construction company expands its operations on a multi-geographical scale and also introduces new construction divisions, it needs a better system of communication among the divisions and a complete rationalization of resources in order to achieve integration and efficiency. The matrix mechanism will provide a balance of formal power, which distinguishes its characteristics from functional, and line and staff structure. Figure 5.5 shows a typical organization chart for the matrix structure.

Mintzberg (1998) notes in his discussion of matrix structure that:

> *. . . it is one thing to have four product managers, each with a manufacturing, marketing, engineering and personnel manager reporting to him, or to have four integrating managers each seeking to co-ordinate the work of four functional managers with the line authority, or even to combine the latter into market-based task forces, and quite another thing to force the product and functional managers to face each other with equal formal power.*

The matrix structure can be applied at two levels.

(*a*)   At organizational level where line managers and the supporting staff form a relational grid. This means that people with specialist

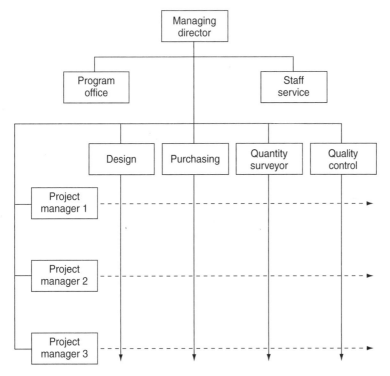

—— line authority exercised over departmental staff through direct chain of command
- - - project authority exercised over selected staff assigned from departments as appropriate.

Fig. 5.5. The matrix structure (adapted from Delbecq and Filley (1974))

knowledge have to be integrated with the management structure in an informal matrix structure. In this structure, the individual authority relationship defined previously as 'functional' now becomes part of the actual structure under the heading of staff relationships (Mullins 1999).

(b) At project or operational level where project managers and organization staff form a team relational grid. This grid provides liaison between departments where considered necessary for the elements of a particular project. This is known as a formal project management matrix structure. In this structure, a two-way flow of authority and responsibility can be established between members of the project team and organization staff. Within the functional department authority and responsibility flow vertically down the line, but the authority and responsibility of the project manager flow horizontally across the organizational structure.

Therefore the matrix structure is characterized by:

- shared expert and functional power
- a narrow span of control
- direct supervision and operational control
- two-way formal communication
- integrated group decision making
- interdependency of the workflow, processes, sales and socializing
- having a reactor strategy
- having a fast response to a dynamic environment.

These characteristics of the matrix structure will generate the following advantages.

(a) It allows efficient use of resources where specialized individuals can be shared and transferred from one task to another or among the projects.

(b) It provides a high integration and flexibility among individuals at organization and project level, leading to greater task integration and a wide range of functional activities. For example, at project level, the relationship between the project manager, architect, quantity surveyor, engineer, site manager and even the main contractor and sub-contractor is very close and the team is continuously in contact with each other thought the operation or the building process. This relationship will create a 'team' work spirit.

(c) It facilitates a high quality and fast decision making approach since each group have the expertise and power required to make a decision collectively – this will reduce the risk of one individual dictating his/her interest.

(d) The matrix structure can balance the conflicting objectives of the client (such as time and cost) with that of the business (such as economic operation and technical development).

(e) It is a highly motivating structure because each position member of the matrix feels that he/she is part of achieving the goal and objectives of the organization or the project.

The concept of the matrix structure does, however, present a number of difficulties, as follows.

(a) There can be an element of role ambiguity as to who is responsible for what – this may lead to conflict. Moreover, role ambiguity can lead to role overload with an individual being given too much work to do by independent superiors.

(b) The matrix structure may decrease the quality of reporting where a limited number of staff report directly to the project manager. Moreover, staff may prefer to report to their own functional group. This can result in reducing the extent of the project manager's authority over staff from other departments and of losing the support of other functional managers.

Having identified the main difficulties of the matrix structure it has to be stressed that the advantages listed above outweigh the inherent disadvantages. In particular, Ronald (1990, p. 344) writes:

Matrix organizations tend to have a high level of performance in dealing with complex, creative work products. Also, because the amount of interaction among members in the matrix structures, and the high levels of responsibilities they possess, matrix organizations usually have greater worker job satisfaction.

Factors influencing the choice of organizational structure

There are four basic factors that can influence the structural design of an organization (see Fig. 5.6):

(*a*) Organizational characteristics
 (i) Age
 (ii) Size
 (iii) Subordinates

(*b*) Organizational management
 (i) Managers' personality and values
 (ii) Goals and objectives
 (iii) Strategy

(*c*) Operation
 (i) Task
 (ii) Technology

(*d*) Environment
 (i) External
 (ii) Internal

Organizational characteristics

Age and size

The size of an organization, especially in terms of the number of people employed and units produced, influences the kinds of co-ordination, direction and control reporting system, and hence the organizational structure. When an organization is small, interaction is confined to a relatively small group – communication is simpler, less information is required for decision making and there is less need for formal organizational aspects.

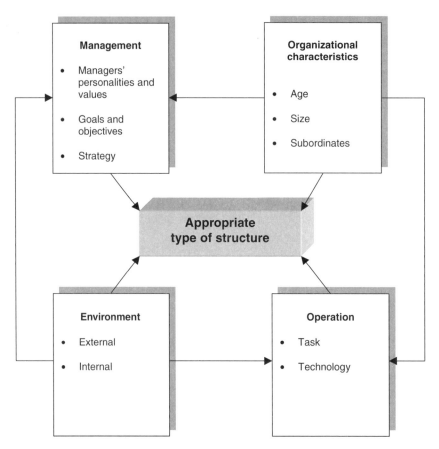

Fig. 5.6. Factors influencing the type of organizational structure

Research by the Aston Group into the design of organizational structure found that the size and degree of dependency on other organizations are what actually influence the structure. Pugh and Hickson (1989) wrote:

The larger the organization, the more likely its employees are to work in very specialized functions, following standard procedures and formalized documentation; that is, it will score highly on structuring of activities and have many of the appearances of bureaucracy. The more it is dependent on only few supplier or customer units, or even just one..., the less autonomy it will have in its own decision making, and even those decisions that are left to it are likely to be centralized within itself rather than decentralized.

As organizations grow, they pass through a number of calm, evolutionary and revolutionary periods. Figure 5.7 shows a model developed by Greiner (1972) which describes a sequence of crises as the organization

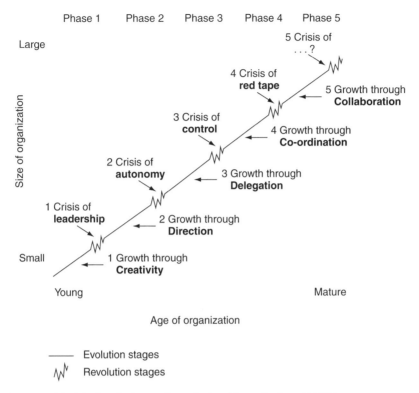

Phase 1   Phase 2   Phase 3   Phase 4   Phase 5

Fig. 5.7. Model of evolution and revolution (from Greiner (1972))

lurches from too much central control and uniformity to too much diversity and too little co-ordination.

The subordinates

Some research evidence seems to suggest that a major contribution to organizational effectiveness will derive from adapting the structure to accommodate more adequately the psychological needs of organizational members. Writers on people and organizations, such as Argyris (1965) and Herzberg *et al.* (1959), have drawn attention to the conflict that is likely to prevail between a traditional definition of formal organizational structure and the needs of psychologically mature individuals. Herzberg developed a two-factor theory of employee motivation, which suggests specific structural adaptation to provide 'job enrichment' through which to enhance motivation and performance. In order words, before designing an organizational structure, it is necessary to consider a number of forces affecting the subordinates' behaviour and performance. The subordinates' desire for independence, skill and motivation for assuming responsibility, need for a sense of achievement, etc. will greatly influence the organizational structure.

It can be argued that, compared to unskilled workers, skilled workers and professional personnel are more involved in their jobs and are more anxious for opportunities to have a high degree of autonomy in their jobs and to participate in making decisions relating to them. Studies consistently show that scientists as well professional employees want autonomy and job freedom. They prefer not to be commanded in the same way as other employees in an organization.

Moreover, some workers have positive attitudes towards work (sometimes called 'motivation seekers') while there are others who seem relatively unaffected by the same conditions (called 'maintenance seekers'). Perhaps the significant difference is that maintenance seekers reach a state of relative fulfilment at the primary needs level, whereas motivation seekers continue to be motivated by the need for a higher level of social security. This implies that certain forces in the subordinates will have substantial influence in designing an organizational structure.

The above is a brief analysis of selected elements and how they might influence a company's actions in designing the structure of an organization. This analysis scarcely exhausts all the elements in these forces. Looking at the selected few, however, one can begin to understand which types of design might lead to organizational effectiveness. The strength of each of them will, of course, vary from instance to instance, but a management system which is sensitive to them can better assess the problems it faces and determine which mode of organizational pattern is most appropriate.

Most organizations are formed through evolutionary processes rather than by conscious design. At certain stages design or redesign takes place, but this is merely a codification or modification of the results of the evolution. An adequate framework for developing organizational theory should make it possible to increase the role of a conscious design process in the development of an organization. Hopefully, the suggested model would provide such a framework.

Characteristics of managers

The designing of an organization at any instance will be influenced greatly by the many forces operating within the managers' own personalities. They will, of course, perceive their organizational problems in a unique way on the basis of their background, knowledge and experience. Their initial decisions will be in terms of what market the organization will enter, the level of competition, the location, the characteristics of the organization, who will be the boss and who will directly influence the organization's structure. All these have to be made in the context of the relationship between the environment and the managerial philosophy of the entrepreneurs involved (Shetty and Luthans (1980)).

Chandler (1966) clearly identified a strong relationship between the strategy adopted by the company and its organizational structure. His work supported the hypothesis that 'in order to achieve a high level of performance the design of the structure needs to match the perceived strategy'. Therefore, corporate goals and the selected structural design of the organization are impersonal procedures which are affected by the characteristics of the managers.

An important element influencing structural design is the managerial view on the level of freedom and autonomy that every individual should have in their department or place of work. McGregor (1960) argued that the style of management adopted is a function of the manager's attitudes towards human nature and behaviour at work. He put forward two assumptions, known as theory X and theory Y, which are based on popular assumptions about work and people, respectively. The organizational structure emerging from the managerial value system implied by the view that man is inherently lazy and pursues goals contrary to the interests of the company will not be the same as that which emerges from the opposite image of human nature. Thus, the implicitly held management value system manifests itself in contrasting organizational designs.

Therefore, the underlying value system of the managers can have an impact on the ways in which work is organized, such as the distribution of decision-making authority, levels of SOC and shape of the organization. A theory X value system might predominantly lead to an organization closer to mechanistic structure, which will emphasize high specialization, close control, centralization of decision making, etc. A theory Y value system might predominantly lead to job specialization, wide spans of control, a flatter organizational structure and decentralized decision making, etc.

Operation

Task

The operations performed by an organization can have an impact on an analysis of the organization and its design. Different types of products (e.g. civil engineering and housing products) require different organizational structures to suit efficient execution of the tasks and its technology. The task and technology are very much influenced by the external environment (see the discussion on the effect of the environment below). The construction industry environment is regarded as highly uncertain and the construction operations are non-repetitive, requiring an organic structure. However, within the main tasks are supporting activities, such as the purchasing department, which are more predictable and require a mechanistic structure or bureaucracy. Burns and Stalker (1966) wrote:

> *The whole concern [a yam processing company] can be seen as a three-sided pyramid of power, technical expertise and knowledge circumstances. At every step down from the top there was less authority, less technical expertise and less information. Each person's task was clearly laid down and defined by his superior. He knew just what he could do in normal circumstances without consulting anyone else; just what point of deviation from the norm he should regard as the limit of his confidence; and just what he should do when this limit was reached i.e. report to his superior. The whole system was designed to perceive normality and stability.*

Technology

A number of empirical research studies have been conducted to investigate the impact of technology on organizational structure. Among the most significant is the work of Joan Woodward at the South East Essex Technical College (1953–1957) and this is now covered in some detail.

The Joan Woodward study (1965). This research studied the organizational structure of 100 firms. It revealed some interesting insights into the relationship between technology, organizational structure and business success. Sidwell (1980) summarized Woodward's research as follows.

The method was to analyse and classify the structures and characteristics of the firms and to try and relate this to success.

Variety of structures in the firms studied. Woodward found that the number of distinct levels from board to operations varied from two to twelve. The span of control of the chief executive varied from two to nineteen and that of the first line supervisor from seven to ninety. Other factors varied and they did not appear to be related to size and type of industry or success or failure. According to classical theory the most successful firms should have been those with the best structured and optimum organizational structure, but Woodward's findings were more than that.

In her research, a scale of technical complexity of processes was constructed measured by the extent to which production process is controllable and its results predictable. Below are the production groupings identified by the research.

Group 1 – Small batch and unit production
1. Production of simple units to customers' orders (5 firms)
2. Production of technically complex units (10 firms)
3. Fabrication of large equipment in stages (12 firms)
4. Production of small batches (7 firms)
5. Production of components in large batches subsequently assembled diversely (3 firms)

Group 2 – Large batch and mass production
6. Production of large batches, assembly line type (25 firms)
7. Mass production (6 firms)
8. Process production combined with the preparation of a product for sale by large-batch or mass-production methods (9 firms)

Group 3 – Process production
9. Process production of chemicals in batches (13 firms)
10. Continuous flow production of liquid gases and solid shapes (12 firms)

Eight firms were unclassified because production was too mixed or changing.

Table 5.2 shows the organizational structures of the 100 firms. However, within these groupings the firms were not consistent as to the way in which the structure was applied or in the character of the sub-properties. As regards the application of structure, Woodward found that the following two groupings proposed by Burns and Stalker (1966) applied.

(a) *Mechanistic.* Classical type used for stable situations; very structured. This structure is characterized by the rigid breakdown of components into functional specialisms, a precise definition of duties, responsibilities and authority.

(b) *Organic.* Unstructured type; for situations of change this is an adaptable structure with little formal job definition and communication processes. It is also informal in the forms of consultation used.

Table 5.2. Organizational structure of the firms in Woodward's study

Type		Number of firms
(a)	Predominantly line organization	35
(b)	Functional organization	2
(c)	Line/staff organization	39
(d)	Unclassifiable	4
Total		100

Results of Joan Woodward's study

(a) Firms using similar technical methods had similar organizational structures, i.e. there is not one overall set of organizational types but the type of structure varies with the type of industry.

(b) Organization sub-properties varied on a scale of technical complexity, but in various ways.

    (i)   The number of levels of authority increased up the scale from 1 to X. Similarly labour costs decreased as technological complexity increased from 1 to X, as did the ratio of indirect labour to hourly paid workers; the proportion of graduates employed also increased.

    (ii) The span of control of first line supervisors reached a peak in mass-production process types and then decreased.

    (iii) The ratio of managers and supervisory staff to total personnel decreased from unit production to process production.

(c) There was no significant relationship between the size of the firm and the system of production (i.e. unit, mass, process).

(d) No relationship was noted between conformity with classical rules and success. However, a subsequent study showed that when firms were grouped in relation to their system of production, those having an organizational structure closest to the median (optimal) for that group were most successful.

(e) Finally, an important element of technology, which is also related to the organization pattern, is the nature of the workflow. Here two interesting findings emerged.

    (i)   The amount of discretion given to subordinates seems to vary according to the type of specialization where the activities of one individual or department are closely dependent on other individuals or departments and these are characterized by more lateral relationships in order to obtain effective co-ordination between specialized groups. At the same time, under this type of specialization the subordinates have a 'vested interest' in their own typical point of view or approach to problems and are unable to see the impact of their actions on others. Only personnel at the top would note the interests of the total organization and thus be able to see the overall picture and integrate the efforts of the different parts in order to achieve the overall organizational goals.

    (ii) Under parallel specification – where workflow is organized so as to minimize the amount of co-ordination – employees see themselves as responsible for the total process, something with an observable output, and are able to see the total efforts rather than a part. Under this system natural teamwork develops as each person sees that their contribution is needed to complete the total work. For these reasons, under parallel specification, a more organic type of organization may be appropriate, but independent specialization may call for a less organic type of structure and less and less delegation of authority to the lower level.

Evaluation of Woodward's results. The most significant aspect of Woodward's research, which contradicts the classical theory of basic organization types applicable to all organizations, is the conclusion that it is the technology process which determines what the optimum organizational structure should be, that different technologies impose different kinds of demands on individuals and organizations and that these demands can be met through an appropriate structure and that the successful firms are those that have the correct structure for their technology.

The degree of control and the type of organizational structure will depend on two aspects:

(a) the type of people involved – for example, people have different reactions to authority according to their upbringing, their education and training, personality, motives for working and the type of industry (different industries will attract certain types of people).

(b) the number of decisions and processes involved, i.e. Woodward's complexity of technology.

The relationship between technological elements and construction operations. The above research and discussion on the influence of technology on the design of organizational structure were more focused towards manufacturing industries. So how significant is the effect of technological elements on the design of organizational structure in construction operations? The short answer to this question is that the bespoke nature of construction projects means that some research into mass and process production may not be fully applicable or feasible on construction sites. No doubt, over the past two decades or so there have been significant advances in construction methods, fixing techniques and materials used to execute the tasks, but these advanced industrialized technological movements can be regarded as small when compared to the progress in levels of automation and robotics used in manufacturing. Therefore, it might be fair to say that, in construction, the effect of the task on the design of organizational structure has a greater impact than the effect of technology (Newcombe and Hancock (1996)).

The environment

In chapter 3 the view was put forward that the overall element of the environment can have a significant effect on organizations, including their aims and strategy. Studies by Lawrence and Lorsch (1967), Burns and Stalker (1966), Trist *et al.* (1963) and Galbraith (1973) all supported the proposition that the environment can have direct and indirect effects on organizational structure and that the most effective pattern of organization is one that can adjust to the changing environment. This is all down to brainpower, according to Galbraith (1973), who studied the effect of greater decentralization by saying that 'one brain can no longer cope with the amounts of information that a complex environment creates'. It has been argued that the pattern of these environmental pressures will, over time, generate different levels of uncertainty requiring different structural accommodation.

Lawrence and Lorsch study (1967)

Previous sections in this chapter have reviewed the work of Burns and Stalker (1966) on the 'mechanistic' and 'organic' patterns of organization. According to their study, in science-based industries such as electronics where innovation is a constant demand, the organic type of organization is made appropriate. Lacking a frozen structure, an organic organization grows around the point of innovating success. Studies of communication reinforce the point that the optimal conditions for innovation stem from a lack of hierarchy. An organization not primarily concerned with technological innovation but preoccupied with production problems requires a mechanistic type of structure, where co-ordination is facilitated.

Lawrence and Lorsch undertook a study of six firms in the plastics industry, followed by a further study of two firms in the container industry and two firms in the consumer food industry. They attempted to extend the work of Burns and Stalker and examined not only the overall structure, but also the way in which specific departments were organized to meet different aspects of the firm's external environment.

According to Mullins (1999), Lawrence and Lorsch sought to answer the following questions.

(a) What are the differences in the environmental demands facing various organizations, and how do these demands relate to the internal functioning of effective organizations?

(b) Do organizations operating in a stable environment make greater use of the formal hierarchy to achieve integration and, if so, why? Is it because less integration is required, or because decisions can be made more effectively at higher levels of the organization or by fewer people?

(c) Is the same degree of differentiation in orientation and departmental structure found in organizations in different industrial environments?

(d) If greater integration is required among functional departments in different industries, does this influence problems of integrating different parts of the organization and the methods of achieving integration?

The word 'functional' was used to indicate major aspects or departments of the organization such as research, production and marketing. The first stage of the study was an investigation of six firms in the plastics industry which were operating in relatively comparable, dynamic environments. The internal structures of the firms were analysed in terms of 'differentiation' and 'integration'.

Differentiation describes 'the difference in cognitive and emotional orientation among managers in different functional departments' with respect to:

- the goal orientation of managers, for example the extent to which attention was focused on particular goals of the department
- the time orientation of managers and relation to aspects of the environment with which they are concerned, for example longer term horizons, or short-term horizons and problems requiring immediate solutions
- the interpersonal relations of managers to other members, for example a managerial style based on concern for the task, or on concern for people relationships
- the formality of structure, for example the extent of mechanistic or organic design.

Integration describes 'the quality of the state of collaboration that exists among departments that are required to achieve unity of effort by the demands of the environment'. It is the degree of co-ordination and co-operation between different departments with interdependent tasks. Lawrence and Lorsch's view of integration was not the minimizing of differences between departments and the provision of a common outlook, it was the recognition that different departments could have their own distinctive form of structure according to the nature of their task, and the use of mediating devices to co-ordinate the different outlooks of departments. Given the possibility that different demands of the environment are characterized by different levels of uncertainty, then it follows that individual departments may develop different structures. The study of the firms in the plastics industry supported this hypothesis and Lawrence and Lorsch found a clear differentiation between the major departments of research, production and sales.

- Research was more concerned with the long-run view and was confronted with pressures for new ideas and product innovation. The department operated in a dynamic, scientific environment and had the least bureaucratic structure.
- Production was more concerned with the here and now, short-term problems such as quality control and meeting delivery dates. The

department operated in a fairly stable, technical environment and had the most bureaucratic structure.

- Sales were in the middle between research and production. The department was concerned with chasing production and had a moderately stable market environment.

The two most successful firms were those with the highest degree of integration; they were also among the most highly differentiated. This view of differentiation and integration was confirmed in the subsequent study of firms in the container and consumer food industries. In this part of the study a comparison was made of both high- and low-performance firms operating in different environments. The aim was to discover what forms of organizational structure are required for different environments. It was concluded that the extent of differentiation and integration in effective organizations will vary according to the demands of the particular environment.

- The more diverse and dynamic the environment, the more the *effective* organization will be differentiated and highly integrated.
- In more stable environments, less differentiation will be required but a high degree of integration is still required. Differences in the environment will require different methods of achieving integration.

The mechanisms used to achieve integration depend on the amount of integration required and the difficulty in achieving it.

- In mechanistic structures, integration may be attempted through the use of policies, rules and procedures.
- In organic structures, integration may be attempted through team-work and mutual co-operation.
- As the requirements for the amount of integration increase, additional means may be adopted, such as formal lateral relations, committees and project teams.
- When there is a high degree of differentiation, the use of assigned 'integrators' or possibly a separate unit with a number of integrators were suggested. Because they are not dominated by any particular perspective these integrators can help resolve problems of co-ordination and work programming between different departments.

It is important, however, to achieve the right balance of integration. Too great a level of integration may involve costs which are likely to exceed possible benefits. Too little a level of integration is likely to result in departments 'doing their own thing', lower quality decisions and failure to make the best use of resources.

Lawrence and Lorsch do not see the classical and human relations approaches as being out of date but as part of a continuum of patterns of organization and management related to the environment in which they operate. The work of Lawrence and Lorsch is an extension of this continuum and their case for 'a contingency theory of organizations' has provided a further insight into the relationship between organizational structure and the demands of the environment.

Mintzberg's (1999) hypotheses on the effect of the environment on organizational structure

Dynamic, complex, hostile and diverse environments were defined in chapter 3 (pp. 31–33).

(a) *The more dynamic the environment, the more organic the structure.* In a stable environment, an organization can predict its future conditions and so, all other things being equal, can easily insulate its operating core and standardize its activities and establish rules, formalize work, plan actions (or perhaps standardize its skills instead, i.e. form a mechanistic structure). Conversely, a dynamic environment will drive the structure to the organic state. Support for this hypothesis comes from the work of Duncan (1972), Ansoff (1974), Harvey (1968) and Hunt (1972)

(b) *The more complex the environment, the more decentralized the structure.* Here, the three elements of task, technology and size of the company are crucial in determining the type of environment that the firm is facing. Support for this hypothesis comes from the work of Duncan (1972), Lawrence and Lorsch (1967), Galbraith (1973), Hage and Aiken (1967) and Pennings (1975).

   In construction, this means that companies that build large and technologically complex projects require a much greater division of work, with many more specialists needed to cope with the complexity. For example, the characteristics of the clients and their projects are technically sophisticated and the market is more diverse. This, therefore, demands a great deal of decentralization of decision making to the various specialists in order for the firm to handle the complexity of the environment.

(c) *The more diversified the organization's market, the greater the propensity to split it into market-based units.* In other words, diversification breeds divisionalization. Support for this hypothesis comes from largely from the works of Chandler (1962) and Channon (1973). Chandler coined the phrase 'structure follows strategy'. In a study of large American corporations he noted the following.

   While the strategy of diversification permitted the continuing and expanded use of a firm's resources, it did not assure their efficient employment. Structural reorganization became necessary ... It became increasingly difficult to co-ordinate through the existing structure the different functional activities to the needs of several quite different markets.

Channels of communication and authority as well as the information flowing through these channels grew more and more inadequate. The wants of different customers varied, and demand and taste fluctuated differently in different markets ... In time, then, each major product line came to be administered through a separate, integrated autonomous division. Its manager became responsible for the major operating decisions involved in the co-ordination of functional activities to changing demand and taste.

(d) *Extreme hostility in its environment drives any organization to centralize its structure temporarily.* This situation occurs when an organization faces extreme hostility, e.g. the sudden loss of its key client or source of supply, attack by the government, or whenever its survival is threatened. Since it must respond quickly and in an integrated fashion, it turns to its leader for direction. Therefore the firm moves, temporarily, from centralization to decentralization in order to tackle the crisis very quickly. At a certain stage, however, the organization would be facing two forces – one is complexity, which requires decentralization, and the other is hostility, which requires centralization. However, should the crisis be solved, the organization will return to full decentralization. Naturally, this situation of double environmental forces requires a very strong leadership to get balance between strategy and structure right.

(e) *Disparities in the environment encourage the organization to decentralize selectively to differentiated work constellations.* No organization has ever existed in an environment uniformly dynamic, complex, diverse, or hostile across its entire range. In other words, certain departments (e.g. marketing) may need to centralize their decision making and so organize in an organic form. Other departments within the same organization may be in a much more stable environment (e.g. the material purchasing division) and so organize in a mechanistic form.

Configurations of the organization

Throughout chapters 4 and 5, the reader was introduced to a number of structural and strategic terminologies, such as specialization, standardization, centralization, decentralization, co-ordination, divisionalization and environmental sophistication. These terminologies describe forces that configure the organization from one type of structure to another. Figure 5.8 summarizes the key features of Mintzberg's five configurations (1999) in terms of a set of forces that pulls organizations in five different structural directions (also see Fig. 5.2).

(a) First is the pull exercised by the strategic apex to centralize, to co-ordinate by direct supervision, and so to structure the organization as a Simple Structure.

(b) Second is the pull exercised by the technostructure, to co-ordinate by standardization (notably of work processes of the tightest kind) in order to increase its influence, and so to structure the organization as a Machine Bureaucracy.

(c) Third is the pull exercised by the operators to professionalize, to co-ordinate by the standardization of skills in order to maximize autonomy, and so to structure the organization as a Professional Bureaucracy.

(d) Fourth is the pull exercised by the middle managers to Balkanize, to be given the autonomy to manage their own units, with

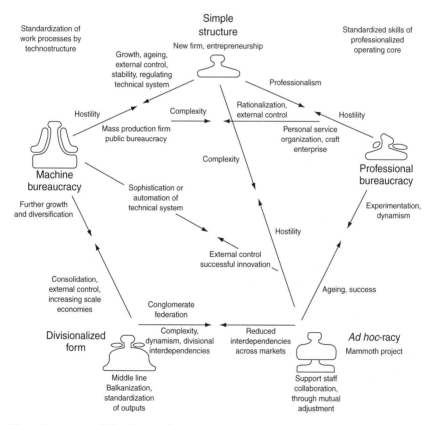

Fig. 5.8.   Basic building blocks of organizational design (from Mintzberg (1998, p. 471))

co-ordination restricted to the standardization of outputs, and so to structure the organization as a Divisionalized Form.

(e) Fifth is the pull exercised by the support staff (and by the operators as well in the Operating *Ad hoc*-racy), for collaboration (and innovation) in decision making, to co-ordinate by mutual adjustment, and so to structure the organization as an *Ad hoc*-racy.

Each of these five structures is influenced by the factors described earlier in this chapter, which exert their pull on the organization, Once again these factors are:

(a) organization characteristics
(b) management characteristics
(c) the operation
(d) environment.

The relationship between organizational structure and performance

Unfortunately, the amount of construction management research is relatively low when compared with other areas of management research. However, the works of Channon (1978) and Lansley *et al.* (1974) into the relationship between structure and performance are most interesting.

The Channon study (1978)

The study by Channon (1978) of the strategic, structural and financial histories of the largest 100 service industry companies for the period 1950–1974 is particularly relevant here as it includes seven construction corporations – Richard Costain, Taylor Woodrow, John Laing, George Wimpy, Trafalgar House Investments, Wood Hall Trust, and London & Northern Securities. Figure 5.9 is an extract from Fellows (1991) which summarizes the study.

If business strategy is the process of formulating and implementing a strategic plan and strategic management is the dynamic element which steers and motivates business action, then the organizational structure of the firm is the framework within which both strategy and strategic management are both meaningless outside the context of a business organization; it follows, therefore, that strategy and structure must be interrelated (Fellows *et al.* 1991).

The Ashridge Management Research (Lansley et al. 1974)

This research examined the relationship between organizational structure and management style and their influence on organizational effectiveness

In Channon's study:

Strategy was defined as the extent of diversification and international activity together with the acquisition policy adopted.

Structure was classified in terms of the formal organisation structure (i.e. functional, holding company, multidivisional, critical function) and the corporate leadership mode (i.e. entrepreneurial, family, and professional management).

Financial performance was measured using conventional accounting ratios for growth and profitability.

The findings of the research confirmed Chandler's thesis, that structure follows strategy, as the companies had diversified from offering a single product or service, to offering a range of related or unrelated services or products, so the pressure for organisational change proved irresistible if efficiency was to be maintained, with functional forms giving way to the more appropriate holding company and multidivisional structures. Significant relationships were also found to exist between the strategic and structural variables and financial performance.

The strategy of related diversification, extending the original business by the addition of related business activities, gave superior financial performance to either limited, or unrelated, diversification. As might be expected, an aggressive acquisition policy proved to be a very effective vehicle for achieving rapid business growth, but resulted in inferior profitability performance. Increased international activity did not, in general, lead to better financial performance, but in the case of the construction companies did give greater stability and continuity of workload by offsetting the effects of fluctuating demand at home.

The influence of formal organisation structure on financial performance was less definite, with higher growth being associated with multidivisional structures; and greater profitability with functional and critical function structures. There were, however, significant increases in all aspects of financial performance when companies switched from the holding company to the multidivisional form. The most interesting structural implication was the impact of the corporate leadership style on financial performance. Entrepreneurial-led businesses considerably out-performed both family-led and professionally managed businesses on all the performance measures. In turn, family firms achieved better financial results than those firms run by professional managers. This would seem to emphasise the importance of an equity stake in the business; the shareholdings of professional managers are generally low. It is interesting that many of the construction corporations were dominated by entrepreneurs, or their descendants.

There was a marked contrast between the strategies of the long-established construction companies – Costain, Taylor Woodrow, Laing and Wimpy – and those of the newer conglomerates. The older companies had grown rapidly between 1918 and 1939 as house builders, and during World War II had become involved in civil engineering projects for the war effort. The post-war domestic rebuilding programme provided the opportunity to further develop major contracting expertise and the possibility of pursuing a strategy of related diversification through backward integration into the manufacture of construction materials and forward integration into property development, particularly during the property boom of the 1960s and early 1970s. In contrast the newer companies had been created since 1945 by individual entrepreneurs and were much more diversified than the major contractors, with interests in property, investment, contracting, engineering, house building, shipping, hotels, newspapers, and so on. These firms had reached the top 100 service industries group very quickly through a strategy of aggressive acquisition as opposed to the slower and largely internal expansion of the older construction companies.

Fig. 5.9. Channon's study (from Fellows et al. (1991, pp. 23–25))

measured in both 'human' and 'financial' terms. Account has also been taken of related contextual factors such as 'task', 'size' and 'environment' of a company. Using information collected from a sample of fifty small and medium size printing and building firms the authors elaborated a conceptual model involving the following independent attributes.

(*a*) Attributes related to organizational structure:
    (i) *Integration* – assessed by the extent to which the activities of the members of the management system are closely co-ordinated in relation to overall objectives.
    (ii) *Control* – assessed by the extent to which the activities of members of the management structure are laid down by higher authority and subject to close review on the one hand, or are more the result of the exercise of discetion and processes of discussion and consultation on the other hand.
    (iii) *Environment* – the extent to which the activities of the management system are concerned with the regulation of the internal affairs of the organization or with managing the organization's relationships with the environment.

(*b*) Attributes related to management style:
    (i) *People orientation* – assessed by combining two scores. One reflects the extent to which senior management was perceived as consultative rather than autocratic in style; the other concerns the extent to which senior management was seen to emphasize the importance of building high employee moral.
    (ii) *Task orientation* – assessed on the basis of scored responses to two questions. One of these is to do with the extent to which senior management was perceived as being willing to act on suggestions aimed at improving efficiency. The other reflects the extent to which senior management is perceived as giving propriety to improving the efficiency of the firm. Here, some adjustments were made for the building industry to reflect different patterns of association between the data.

The validity of this model has been operationally tested and examined against the background of evidence reported by other research works on the contextual determinants of organizational structure and management style. Subsequently, different patterns of association between 'organization' and 'style' and company performance were found for the two industries (printing and building) and an important outcome of

Table 5.3. *Lansley's research sample*

	Number of printing firms	Number of building firms
High integration with low control (organic structure)	3	5
High integration with high control (bureaucratic structure)	6	6
Low integration with low control (anarchic structure)	7	7
Low integration with high control (mechanistic structure)	8	6

the research was the production of further evidence in favour of the contingency theory of organization.

Four organizational structures were identified; these are shown in Table 5.3. The structural variables were derived from a variety of sources, as follows.

(a) Respondents' perceptions of the organizational structure compared with the 'official' or top management view of the structure.

(b) A measure of the extent to which the management structure of the enterprise is 'steep' or 'flat' in configuration.

(c) The extent to which respondents agree with each other about their organizational relationships, both vertical and horizontal.

(d) The average number of communications contacts reported by each respondent.

(e) The extent to which respondents agree with each other about the pattern of communications in the firm.

(f) The extent to which communication takes place outside the chain of command.

(g) Respondents' perceptions of the effectiveness of the company's formal communication channels.

Measuring performance

The criteria for measuring performance were grouped as follows.

(a) Performance in human terms
  (i) *Satisfaction* – with job and company.
  (ii) *Information* – the extent to which people perceived the communication system in the firm as effective.

(iii) *Change* – respondents' perceptions of the effectiveness with which their firms managed change.

(b) Performance in commercial terms

(i) *Profitability* – a combined measure based on return on capital employed and profit on turnover.

(ii) *Growth in sales turnover.*

Results

Given the different characteristics of the two industries studied, the printing firms performed well using bureaucratic structures and a task-oriented management style. This is due to the fact that printing firms have relatively short production cycles and the tasks are executed sequentially with a high degree of mechanization.

Production cycles in building firms are is usually longer, the tasks are executed simultaneously and sequentially with some degree of mechanization. There is a high tendency for firms with organic or anarchic structures (i.e. those with low control) to achieve better all-round performance than bureaucratic or mechanistic firms. The investigating team confirmed the view that the building industry is very much more heterogeneous in nature and that different types of building firms faced quite different tasks and hence required different forms of structures. The following groupings and related structural requirements were hypothesized, n being the sample number.

(a) General contractors ($n = 6$). For these firms each new contract brings fresh and unfamiliar problems creating a need for considerable flexibility with few opportunities for routinization of operations. At the same the need for co-ordination and teamwork is considerable. Hence the organizational requirement is for an organic structure.

(b) Specialist contractors ($n = 8$). Contracts tend to follow a set pattern and operations can be largely routinized. At the same time the requirement for teamwork remains high and the appropriate form of structure is bureaucratic.

(c) Small works firms ($n = 6$). Here also much of the work can be routinized. At the same time it is carried out by small units which can work independently of each other. The requirement is therefore for high control and integration, i.e. a mechanistic structure.

(d) Firms that put most of the actual construction work out to subcontract ($n = 4$). These firms have much in common with architectural partnerships. They do not require either high control or high integration. Their activities are entrepreneurial, creative and mediated through personal relationships rather than

Table 5.4. *Lansley's findings*

	High overall performance	High commercial performance	High human performance	Low overall performance
Appropriate structure ($n = 11$)	4	3	4	0
Inappropriate structure ($n = 13$)	1	3	1	8

formal channels of organization. The appropriate form of structure for this group of firms is, therefore, anarchic.

The companies in the building sample can now be classified according to whether or not they have an organizational structure appropriate to their type of task. When this is done the relationship with performance is as shown in Table 5.4. It can be seen that once differences in the nature of the task have been taken into account there is a strong relationship between appropriateness of structure and performance.

In conclusion, this study added further weight to the argument that there is no one best way of organizing a business. Effective organization is contingent upon the purpose that the organization is seeking to fulfil and upon the nature of the tasks to be managed. Moreover, the research also added to the evidence in favour of the view that the amount of uncertainty in the task is a key factor in determining the appropriateness of a particular organizational design. The extent to which managers receive specific (as distinct from general) guidance from such findings is, however, affected by two related problems. One is the difficulty of approximating the amount of uncertainty present in any given situation. The other is that uncertainty stems from many sources – the market, government legislation, the economic climate, the nature of the work and materials used, the technology employed and so on. The general proposition that the higher the uncertainty in the overall task the less appropriate is an organizational structure that is designed to achieve a high level of *control* over its members only goes so far. It does not help the individual manager. An amount of uncertainty present in the task facing his organization does not specify the form or organizational structure which will lead to the achievement of a given level of control. In this very important sense, therefore, organization design must remain largely a matter of managerial judgement. Judgement will be better exercised in the framework of the kind of generalized knowledge and helpful insights produced by research of the kind carried out by Lansley *et al.*

Summary

This chapter has emphasized the importance of organizational structure. The types of structures and the factors that influence selection of the appropriate structure have been discussed.

Structure follows strategy and is defined as a mechanism for linking and co-ordinating people and groups together within the framework of their roles, authority and power. Structure can be regarded as the backbone of the organization.

There are simple, functional and matrix types of structures. Each has its own application and selection of the appropriate structure for an organization depends on the task, the size of the firm, the subordinates, the managers and the environment. There is evidence to suggest that structure can influence effectiveness, in particular, the attitude and behaviour of the people working within the structure. This in turn influences productivity and efficiency. We now turn to the study of groups within the organization.

References

ARGYRIS, C. *Organization and Innovation.* Irwin-Dorsey, 1965.

BURNS, T. and STALKER, G. *The Management of Innovation.* London, Tavistock Institute, 1966.

CARZO, R. and YANOUZAS, J. Effects of flat and tall organisation structure. *Administrative Science Quarterly,* 1969, pp. 178–191.

CHANDLER, A. *Strategy and Structure.* New York, Anchor Books, 1966.

DELBECQ, A. and FILLEY, A. Program and project management in a matrix organization: A case study. (Monograph No. 9, Graduate School of Business, Bureau of Business Research and Service, University of Wisconsin, Madison, 1974).

DRUCKER, P. *The Practice of Management.* Oxford, Heinemann Professional, 1989, p. 223.

FELLOWS, R., LANGFORD, D., NEWCOMBE, R. and URRY, S. *Construction Management in Practice.* London, Longman Scientific & Technical, 1991.

GALBRAITH, J. *Designing Complex Organizations.* Reading, MA, Addison-Wesley, 1973.

GOWLER, D., LEGGE, K. and CLEGG, C. (Editors) *Case Studies in Organisational Behaviour and Human Resources Management.* London, Paul Chapman (part of Sage Publishing), 1998.

GRAICUNAS, V. Relationship in organisation. *Papers on the Science of Administration.* University of Columbia, 1937.

GREINER, L. *Evolution and Revolution as Organisations Grow.* 1972.

HANDY, C. *Understanding Organizations.* London, Penguin, 1998, 5th edn.

HERZBERG, F., MAUSNER, B. and SYNDERMAN, B. *The Motivation to Work.* New York, Wiley, 1959.

KNIGHT, K. Matrix organisation: A review. *The Journal of Management Studies*, 1976, pp. 111–130.

LANSLEY, P., SADLER, P. and WEBB, T. Organisation structure, management style and company performance. *Omega, The International Journal of Management Science*, **2**(4), 1974, pp. 467–485.

McGREGOR, L. *The Human Side of Enterprise*. London, Penguin, 1960.

MINTZBERG, H. *The Structuring of Organizations*. Englewood Cliffs, NJ, Prentice-Hall, 1998.

MULLINS, L. *Management and Organizational Behaviour*. Boston, MA, Pitman, 1999, 5th edn.

NAISBITT, J. *Ten New Directions Transforming Our Lives*. New York, Warner, 1982, pp. 192–193.

PUGH, P. and HICKSON, D. *Writers on Organisation*. London, Penguin, 1989.

URICK, L. *The Elements of Administration*. Boston, MA, Pitman, 1947, p. 38.

WEBER, M. *The Theory of Social and Economic Organization*. New York, Free Press, 1947.

WOODWARD, J. *Industrial Organization*. Oxford, Oxford University Press, 1965.

Case study. The growing pains of Harvey (Engineers) Ltd (from Gowler *et al.* (1998, pp. 225–36))

Organizational setting

Harvey (Engineers) Ltd is the vision of one man, Mr Harvey. Starting as a 'one man band' in 1970, he has been centrally involved in the development of the company to this very day. With the support of his wife, the company reached a record annual turnover of four and a half million pounds in 1990, which approached six and a half million pounds in real terms by the middle of that year. The company currently employs over a hundred personnel. Over the years the company evolved a very simple multi tasking functional structure, headed by Mr Harvey, and reflected in the emerging Senior Management team (see Fig. A). This prevailed until around 1987. The 'Lawson Boom' in the construction industry in 1988 onwards, and the surge of business that resulted, threw this slow evolutionary process of emergent organizational design into turmoil. To cope with a rapid expansion of business, new staff were recruited quickly, raising questions about their appropriate place in the existing organization structure, its continued suitability, and issues of career progression and management development.

Until this time only those employees with long service were considered for positions of responsibility as they had 'grown up with the company' and had therefore gained the trust of Mr Harvey. All had been employed in shopfloor or menial worker positions. The increased demand, however, required the injection of new personnel into newly developed roles as it was realized that, by dividing responsibilities and task areas, a more efficient and effective service to the customer could be achieved. It is the consequences of this change in personnel practice this case study aims to address, as well as the issues that arose when the market pendulum began its regressive swing.

Background

The company was founded in the south of England in 1970. Having occupied a number of jobs in his life, Mr Harvey saw an opportunity to develop a business in farm building construction. Thus 'Harvey (Engineers)' was born. At this time the numbers employed were few, relying mainly on family members to help out, as and when necessary. But the numbers employed by the company grew steadily and, in 1975, two of the current senior management personnel, Mr Dawson and Mr Lishman, were taken on as manual staff. In 1979, through the advice of an external accountant, the company acquired limited status, with the appointment of Mr and Mrs Harvey as the joint stock holders of the enterprise. It was at this time that a further ten employees were introduced to accommodate a market boom in the industry. Although, traditionally, the focus of the company was on steel fabrication, gradually its portfolio began to change with the complementary addition of civil engineering. This was stimulated by the recession that arose in the agricultural building industry in the early 1980s which instigated a shift of focus to a new and yet similar market: that of the industrial building.

Although the shift in market sector was successful a further development evolved from this action; the company switched its main operational focus. The majority of current trade is now acquired through the company's talents in civil engineering rather than through its traditional expertise in steel fabrication work. However, the company in a sense has the best of both worlds, for it can offer both services to the customer; the construction of a building by skilled civil engineers, and the steel fabrication supports for the building under construction. This eliminates the need to subcontract for one or other of these facilities, giving Harvey (Engineers) Ltd a perceived source of competitive advantage in the construction industry.

In order to get a clear picture of the company's operating practices, it is vital that we assess the role of the founder within the organization, as management practices he has established over time undoubtedly affect the performance of present Senior Management personnel in their daily routines and in their communications with the newly acquired Middle Management employees.

There is no doubt over the extent of Mr Harvey's commitment to the company. He still shows a keen interest in the business and all of its activities, and often comments on the 'millions of duties' he must still perform: 'He's a workaholic. He never stops … the other night he was here at ten o'clock at night to pick up a truck … and that was him here at ten o'clock at night!' (Pre-Contracts Manager, Phil Vokes).

Although his level of involvement in the company is high, a desire to pursue other external interests was expressed by Mr Harvey. Before he is prepared to relinquish his current position, however, he has stated the need for reassurance that, in his absence, the organization will continue to operate effectively. The alternative, to sell the company as a going concern, is not an option Mr Harvey is prepared to consider because of strong family involvement and a son who hopes to take owner-ship at some stage: 'The alternative was to sell out and retire type of thing, but I don't see any point in it. Adam's one of the reasons for that. He's head over heels in the company … what he decides to do is what the company will decide to do basically' (Mr Harvey).

Such a statement, suggesting the possible withdrawal of Mr Harvey from the company, is strongly contradicted by other accounts. For example, the results of a previous DTI report on the company, completed in 1986, stimulated the following response when Mr Harvey questioned one of the conclusions made: 'basically [it] said that I should retire and get out … said that I should stand down as Managing Director and put in a Managing Director and me go as Chairman. I didn't think it was a good idea … to get an outside man in would absolutely upset everything'.

This view is also substantiated by some of the now senior-management personnel:

> *I don't think John [Mr Harvey] will ever retire, personally. I did ask this question at one meeting, 'What was the retirement attitude of the board of the company', and I was told in no uncertain terms by Mrs Harvey, 'You don't have to retire here. Nobody has to retire unless they want to', and she turned to John and she says, 'and you're certainly not retiring!' … John keeps telling me, 'You better get somebody to back up for you.' I just say, 'I'll see you out, you old bugger, don't you worry!'*
>
> (Quantity Surveyor, Ken Pearson)

The devastating effect of losing the centre-piece of the organization and other key members without a considered succession strategy, is clearly an issue that is avoided.

Although at the helm of the company's development, Mr Harvey has utilized the skills of other employees. Indeed he differentiates his company from others because of the 'type' of people holding senior management positions: 'None of us are really paperwork minded because we've all come up from the shopfloor and this is probably the difference between us and a lot of other companies because they work with professional men.'

The General Manager, Pete Dawson, has the following account of how he came to work for Mr Harvey:

> *How long have I been here? Thirteen or fourteen years I think. I came in to operate the saw in the workshop. I worked for Billing Steads before that. I was made redundant, he went way down, so I was looking for a job. At the time I would take anything, so I got on the saw working for John. It was a temporary job, type thing, see how it went. From there I took charge of his workshop and started organizing things.*

The Civil Engineering Manager, Ian Lishman, tells a similar story. Being slightly younger than the General Manager he explains how his career has progressed within the company from the position of steel erector to the senior management post he now occupies. Ian Lishman comments on the change he has experienced in this management role in the last six or seven years: 'For a beginning it was, what can I say, 50 per cent of your time office work and organizing and 50 per cent actually physically labour and work. As it got bigger the gap went, then it was all office work really.' It is these two employees who have supported Mr Harvey for the longest period of time, since 1975.

In 1984 Ken Pearson was employed in the capacity of a buyer, having moved on from the loss of his own 'multi-million pound organization', according to his own attribution. Since his appointment, Ken has gained increasing influence within the company and has become a prominent member of the senior management team in the capacity of quantity surveyor. It is these three employees who represent the functional core of the senior management. The fourth member, Jackie Griffiths, having been with the company since 1980 in a clerical capacity, has been appointed Office Manager. With the external appointment of Phil Vokes, in 1990, to Pre-Contracts Manager, the existing Senior Management structure was complete (see Fig. A).

These personnel needed increasing support as the demand for industrial and other buildings grew in the mid-to-late 1980s. A functional structure began to evolve in accordance with the new demands, twelve months prior to the events outlined, in 1989 (see Fig. B). All of the appointments to 'middle management', excluding the site agents, came from

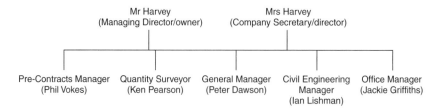

Fig. A.   Senior management team

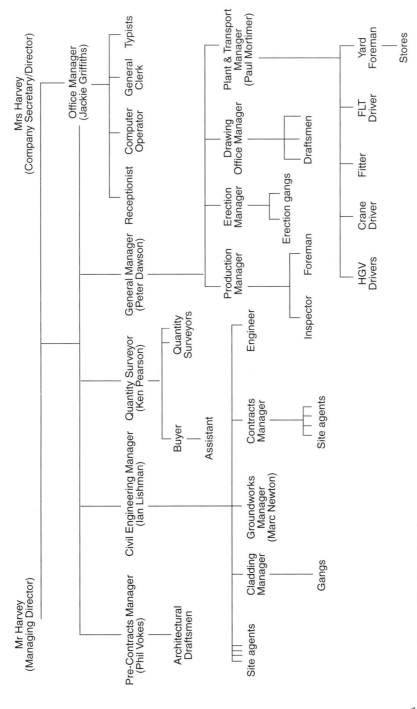

Fig. B. Harvey (Engineers) Ltd

external appointments. Mr Harvey justifies the appointments as an 'injection of professionals', as these individuals all had relevant higher/further educational or previous broad experience.

The new functional structure, however, gave rise to numerous difficulties, which were expressed by those who participated in the formalized version of what once was an *ad hoc* structure.

Problem experienced

With the increase in organizational size, the need to develop 'systems' for various procedures was recognized and acted upon. The effectiveness of these 'systems', designed by Mr Harvey, was questioned, especially by the middle management. A basic lack of trust became apparent as the senior management's roles became increasingly overloaded as their ability and willingness to delegate to more professional (and, hence, potentially threatening) middle management remained minimal.

Problems relating to communications were expressed, especially by the new Plant and Transport Manager, Paul Mortimer. He is responsible for setting up new sites and getting all the necessary equipment and materials to the location ready for work to commence on a given date. In order to do this there is certain information he obviously requires: 'Oh, like everybody thought somebody had told me, and somebody thought Pete [General Manager] would have told me, and Pete thought Ian [Civil Engineering Manager] would have told me, and Ian thought somebody else had told me, and in the end nobody had bloody well told me.' (Plant and Transport Manager, Paul Mortimer)

This problem was not exclusive to middle management, as the following comment from the General Manager, Pete Dawson, illustrates: 'the main problem we have is getting information . . . Like we're guessing most of the time.'

The postal system provides an ideal example of this point. All mail is delivered to, and opened by, Mr Harvey, regardless of the notification of addressee. This is a technique he utilizes in order to keep himself informed of actions within the company. He also receives a copy of every outgoing letter before it is sent. Should he not agree with the contents the letter is stopped. Because of his increasing outside interests, and therefore spasmodic attendance, post may go unopened for relatively long periods of time and replies are sent without his knowledge:

> *it's a slow turn-round time as well. Sometimes John [Mr Harvey] sits on stuff for three or four days, waiting for important quotes and all the rest of it. He sees it as addressed to whoever, has a quick look at it and doesn't see the relevance. He doesn't know the relevance of how important it is.*
>
> (Plant & Transport Manager, Paul Mortimer)

This slow response is detrimental to the company's performance and has created significant morale problems throughout the organization. Such formalized but ill-considered systems instigated for the benefit of the founder can therefore be seen to have caused immeasurable damage to the whole organization.

In spite of some attempts at formalization, significant gaps, reflecting the traditional culture, still remain. For example, no official job descriptions or outlines have been given to any of the individuals employed by the company, as Mr Harvey believed this would inhibit the flexibility of the company should people decide to work to rule. This has caused numerous concerns to be voiced by employees but none have been directed towards Mr Harvey himself: 'It's debatable really what the hell I am, quite honestly' (General Manager, Pete Dawson). 'The first month I was here I could have gone away. I could have been in tears. I was very depressed because I didn't know what they were expecting from me' (Groundworks Manager, Marc Newton).

This lack of clarity on given job roles has led to considerable confusion. Individuals either overlap in completion of tasks (hence jobs are done twice) or, as in the case of informing the Plant & Transport Manager of a new site, tasks are not completed at all. The boundary between senior and middle management responsibility has also been left undefined: 'lack of organization again. We're tripping ourselves up badly' (General Manager, Pete Dawson).

This 'lack of organization' was recognized and yet no time was allocated for its resolution because of the prevalence of the belief that 'the pressure of work' made it impossible to find time to resolve the problem. The source of pressure was perceived to emanate from the boom in the industry and was therefore seen to be beyond the organization's control. This feeling of environmental determinism was reflected in the explanation Mr Harvey expressed for his company's massive expansion of sales from just over £1 million in 1988 to sales exceeding £4.5 million in 1990!: 'I can't say that anything caused the expansion other than just natural growth.' As a result of this fatalistic belief in environmental determinism the company operates in a vicious circle of confused, reactive 'seat of the pants' management.

Although the complaints highlighted above are expressed throughout the organization, the newly appointed middle-management tier are experiencing specific problems relating to their personal roles. For example, all letters going out from a functional area have to be signed by the senior management representative. Middle management believe the reasoning behind this 'system' again is lack of trust: 'I write letters and yet I can't sign them. For thirty-odd years I've been writing to everybody from the Prime Minister downwards, but suddenly I'm not allowed to do that any more ... to my mind I should be if I'm accepted into the company and found trustworthy' (Contracts Manager, Dean Halden).

Middle management meetings were originally held to allow such issues to be raised. These were cancelled. The reason given for this, once again, was the 'pressure of work'. Meetings were recently reinstated whereby senior management and middle management join to discuss operational issues alone:

> *In the middle management meetings that we had it's been brought up time and time again. 'Look,' you know, 'I'm whatever manager. I'm getting paid this money to do..., why can't I get on and do it?' You know. Whether it's a lack of trust or whatever ... but if it's a lack of trust, then the guy shouldn't be in the job, you know.*
>
> (Plant & Transport Manager, Paul Mortimer)

A good example of the atmosphere between these parties is an incident whereby a member of middle management mentioned they were discontented with the practice of senior management taking the minutes at such meetings. This comment was later followed by Mr Harvey, at a senior management meeting, commenting on how rarely he actually received a copy of this information!

Senior management hold conflicting opinions on the believed inadequacies of the middle-management tier: 'you're employing men but you're not taking the load off. It's still drifting back to the same people' (Civil Engineering Manager, Ian Lishman), which they convey to Mr Harvey: 'In other words, we've now increased the salaries of these people, and increased people as well, but we're getting no more management out of them. All we're getting is followers' (Mr Harvey).

Nevertheless, some senior management were prepared to take responsibility for the occurrence of this situation: 'Yeh, but we're paying him the wage to do it; but, we've bugger all to blame but ourselves because were not feeding him the information either to work on ... we're not actually telling him to do it either' (Civil Engineering Manager, Ian Lishman).

No recognition of middle management's grievance of wanting more responsibility was expressed, nor any suggestions made as to how these issues could be resolved. Some senior managers were more perceptive of the situation than others, but the majority still tended to follow the belief that they were 'carrying' middle management personnel.

Middle management have their own explanation of the problems they now face, which rests on the fundamental assumption they are 'different' from those people who have been employed by the company in the past:

> *I mean a lot of these, don't forget, are local, they've grown up with the firm. They don't know anything outside it. All they know is Harvey (Engineers) Ltd. It's a small firm, it's built up. You know they're just not aware, maybe they are aware I don't know, maybe they're just not interested but the likes of meself, and the others, you know, we've been in our own*

respective fields.... You can't say they're slow to change, they just don't want to change.

(Plant and Transport Manager, Paul Mortimer)

Many of middle management have tried taking their grievances directly to Mr Harvey but have been cautioned by him for evading the correct procedure; they must go through the chain of command.

One of the loudest voices of unrest came from the Plant & Transport Manager, Paul Mortimer, who was blatant in his criticism of the company's management policies and yet is still respected throughout the organization due to a macho manner in tune with the culture of both company and industry. He questions the ability of some senior managers to adapt to their newly found 'managerial' role:

if he's not capable of doing the job, he shouldn't be doing it. That is a clear black-and-white definition ... they're too well established now. I could wipe out this management team quite easily. Put in people with far less experience and they'd do a damn sight better job.

Certain members of the senior management team have also expressed concern with regard to their new administrative and supervisory roles as they feel they are ill-equipped to oversee the specialized areas for which they are now responsible. The General Manager, Pete Dawson, is one such individual who is actually responsible for overseeing Paul Mortimer, the Plant & Transport Manager: 'I suppose I'm General Manager really, but to my mind I shouldn't be. I should be concentrating on the fabrication side, because that's the one that I know best. I'm feeling my way in the others and I would say jobs aren't getting done properly.'

Just as such debates were starting to come to a head throughout the summer of 1990, there was a substantial turnaround in the building industry. A market that was once booming suddenly began to regress as customers began to check their spending and investment in properties. The action taken by the company in response to this unanticipated slump was to silence all voices of discontent. Perceived environmental constraints now led to a 'seat of the pants' course of action.

In the space of three weeks, the middle management band of time organization was halved (see Fig. C). The explanation senior management offered for this action was that of 'trimming the dead wood', a conclusion that reflected their view that the elaborated structure was, in any case, ineffective and expensive.

The company therefore reverted back to the simple structure and *ad hoc* practices prevalent before the insertion of middle management, with senior roles remaining unaltered. The danger exists that although the organization has regressed to its earlier form, the environment is very different from that in which such a structure was last successful, and the key members are another five years older.

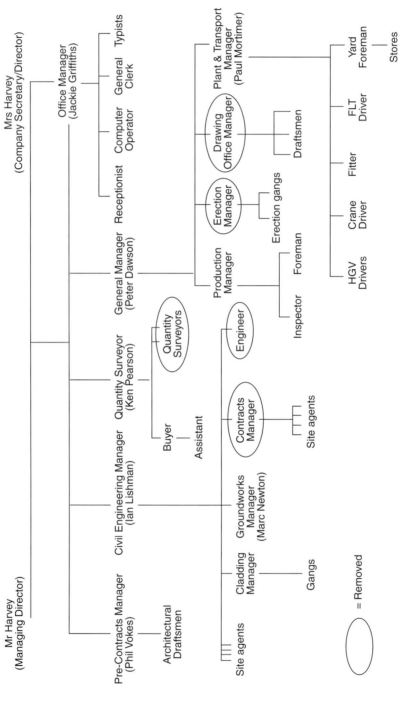

Fig. C. The current situation

Chapter 6

Work groups

The design of organizational structure is associated with grouping people into units and sub-units to achieve individual and organization objectives. A cohesive work group provides greater integration, which leads to better co-ordination and managerial control.

Chapter 5 discussed the organizational structure and the mechanisms of interrelating people together within the framework of their roles, power and authority. The formation of work groups within the structure is another important feature of the organization and can be regarded as the building blocks of the organization as a whole. Group formation and cohesiveness can influence the satisfaction of its members and their morale. This in turn will affect people attitude and behaviour towards work which will then have an impact on the high level of productivity and organizational effectiveness. This chapter highlights the importance of forming a cohesive group and the relationship between work groups and organizational effectiveness. Figure 6.1 summarizes the overall principles of chapter 6 (also see Fig. 1.1).

Learning objectives

To:

> ➢ understand the meaning and purpose of work groups
> ➢ identify the various types of groups
> ➢ identify the main factors that influence group cohesiveness
> ➢ realize group conflict.

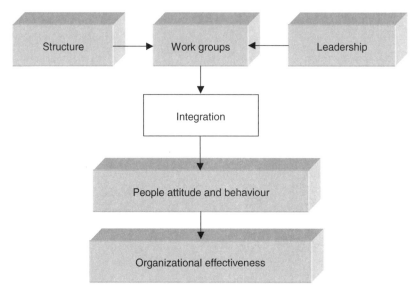

Fig. 6.1.   Overall principles of chapter 6

The meaning of groups

Having decided on an organizational strategy and designed a structure to fit the strategy, it is then important to form (or reform) the working groups within the divisions, departments and units. Group formation is a dynamic process and can take place at any stage during the development of the organization. What is really important is for the management to ensure compatibility and coherence among members of the group as well as among the various groups within the hierarchical structure of the organization.

Group cohesiveness provides high integration to the work process, which leads to better co-ordination and managerial control. Group norm will be developed over a period of time and will affect people attitude and behaviour. Research studies (discussed later in this chapter) have shown that the more cohesive the group, the higher the level of productivity and member satisfaction. The term 'work group' is commonly defined as a collection of individuals:

(*a*)   who have significantly interdependent relations with each other
(*b*)   who are psychologically aware of one another
(*c*)   who perceive themselves to be a group by reliably distinguishing members from non-members
(*d*)   whose group identity is recognized by non-members

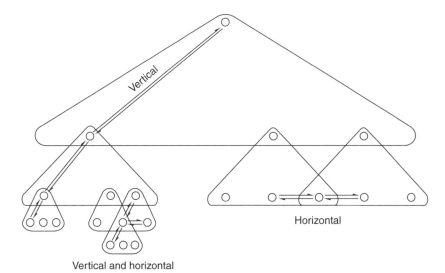

Vertical and horizontal

Fig. 6.2. Overlapping group structure and the linking-pin (from Likert (1967, p. 167))

(e) who have differentiated roles in the group as a function of expectations of themselves, other group members and non-group members

(f) who, as group members acting alone or in concert, have significantly
interdependent relations with other groups (see Berelson and Steiner
(1964) and Schien (1988)).

This definition implies that there is a high level of interaction among
individuals within the organization. The proper formation of work
groups and the high level of integration of their members has an important
significance for the management. Likert (1967) asserted that there ought to
be an overlapping mechanism between group members, vertically and
horizontally, with a 'linking-pin' process between them by which the
superior of one group is a subordinate of the next group. Figure 6.2 is an
example of the overlapping structure showing the linking-pins which
can improve communication, co-ordination and managerial control.

Interactions among the group members can take two forms: formal and
informal. They are both interrelated and play an important part in the
organization.

Formal groups

Formal groups are created as a process mechanism within the formal
structure of the organization. They are characterized by 'task-centred
behaviour' where the tasks are divided and co-ordinated among group

members with formal roles and duties. They are generally occupied at any one time by one person (for example, the manager) or sometimes two (the manager who has expertise and the leader who has the power to get the task done). In other words, formal groups are official and legitimate and supported by positional power or authority. Task forces, project teams, committees, departments, divisions, all fall into the formal group category.

Informal groups

Informal groups are created as a result of personnel interaction and friendship among colleagues with no official constraints. They are characterized by 'socio-emotional behaviour', where work is executed and information is passed among group members on an informal basis. The informal group was evident in Mayo's Hawthorne experiments (Mayo 1933) (discussed in chapter 2). Roethlisberger and Dickson (1939) state that:

> *Many of the actually existing patterns of human interaction have no represen-*
> *tation in the formal organization at all.... This fact is frequently forgotten*
> *when talking about industrial situations in general.*

Although, the interactions are informal and invisible, they can still have a significant effect on the behaviour of the organization. A lack of direction and clear information flow within the formal structure can give rise to uncertainty and suspicion. It can also have economic and behavioural consequences on organizations. For instance, there can be a conflict of interest between the formal groupings (the task function) and the informal groupings (the social function). This potential conflict was an area of concern to classical theorists which threatened to stamp out informal groups altogether. The theorists felt that informal group patterns were invisible and therefore insidious. Informal groups could not be seen on the organizational chart and were therefore perceived to be somehow threatening and beyond control.

The purpose of groups

Organizations and individuals at work can derive certain benefits from forming and becoming a member of a group. Handy (1998) provided the following purposes of groups:

(a) *Organizational purposes* (*the formal task functions*). Organizations use groups, or teams and committees for the following reasons.
   (i)   For the distribution of work. To bring together a set of skills, talents, responsibilities, and allocate to them their particular duties.

(ii) For the management and control of work. To allow work to be organized and controlled by appropriate individuals with responsibility for a certain range of work.

(iii) For problem solving and decision taking. To bring together a set of skills, talents and responsibilities so that the solution to any problem will have all available capabilities applied to it.

(iv) For information processing. To pass on decisions and information to those who need to know.

(v) For information and idea selection. To gather ideas, information or suggestions.

(vi) For testing and ratifying decisions. To test the validity of a decision taken outside the group, or to ratify such a decision

(vii) For co-ordination and liaison. To co-ordinate problems and tasks between functions or divisions.

(viii) For increased commitment and involvement. To allow and encourage individuals to get involved in the plans and activities of the organization.

(ix) For negotiation or conflict resolution. To resolve a dispute or argument between levels, divisions or functions.

(x) For inquest or inquiry into the past.

(b) *Individuals' purposes* (*the social functions*). Individuals use groups for one or more of the following purposes.

(i) A means of satisfying their social or affiliation needs, to belong to something or to share in something.

(ii) A means of establishing a self-concept. Most people find it easier to define themselves in terms of their relationship to others, as members of a role set with a role in that set.

(iii) A means of gaining help and support to carry out their particular objectives.

(iv) A means of sharing and helping in a common activity or purpose which may be making a product, or carrying out a job, or having fun or giving help, or creating something.

Bases for grouping

There are several common bases for the organization to group positions into units and units into larger ones; these are as follows.

- *Grouping by knowledge or skill*. Positions can be grouped according to the specialized knowledge and skills that members bring to the job. Contractors, for example, group bricklayers in one department, joinery men in another and apprentices in a third.

- *Grouping by work process and function*. Units can be based on the processes or activities used by the worker. For example, work can be grouped by marketing, finance, engineering, quality control, and so on.

- *Grouping by time.* Groups can be formed according to when the work is done. In construction this refers to shift work.
- *Grouping by output.* Here, the units are formed on the basis of the products made or services rendered. A large construction company may have separate divisions for each of its product lines – for example, one for housing, another for commercial, a third for industrial, and so on.
- *Grouping by client.* Groups can also be formed to deal with different types of clients. A contractor, for example, may have different departments for private and public contracts.
- *Grouping by place.* Groups can be formed according to the geographical regions in which the organization operates. For example, a UK operation could include groups allocated to the North, South, East, West and the international operations might include Asia, Africa and the Middle East.
- *Grouping by project.* Each project in itself can become an organization and therefore groups can be formed according to individual projects.

The criteria for selecting groups are:

- homogeneous backgrounds
- common objectives
- common interests
- compatible personalities
- shared resources
- own territory.

Interdependence and communication networks

In every organization there are various types of communication networks (or patterns) that exist among the groups. The level of interaction among members of a group is influenced by the structuring of channels of communication. On the subject of interdependence and communication, Leavitt (1951) conducted an experiment with interesting lessons in the management of teams. He set up a number of six-member teams each with different ways of communicating within the team; this was controlled by having partitions between the members and specific rules for the passing of written messages between them. He then set two problems. In the first, he gave each member of the team a differently coloured marble and asked them to discover, as a team, the range of colours they possessed. In this experiment the team that was structured

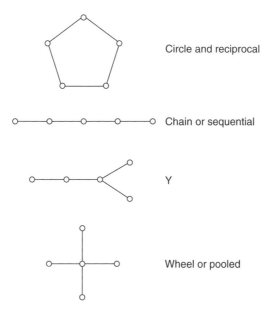

Fig. 6.3.   Basic communication networks (from Berelson and Steiner (1964, p. 356))

hierarchically with one man at the top through which all communication had to pass was the most successful.

In the second experiment, he gave the team six pink marbles each of a slightly different shade. This presented a far more difficult problem, with no simple black or white decisions, but which required a great deal more discussion and comparative analysis. In this case the team which was structured most suitably for group discussion was not successful.

Leavitt's study and the subsequent research by Berelson and Steiner (1964) and Thompson (1967) have resulted in the design of a series of communication networks. Figure 6.3 shows the four common forms of interdependence:

- circle and reciprocal
- sequential or chain
- Y chain network
- pooled or wheel.

Circle interdependence is a decentralized network and solutions can be reached quicker than the sequential pattern. It is appropriate for tasks that change frequently. Reciprocal interdependence is an extension of the circle shape. It is also a decentralized network and appears to work best where a high level of interaction is needed among all members of the group. It is appropriate for complex open-ended problems. The ability of the person who is leading the web determines the outcome of the pattern. The reciprocal is usually inflexible if the nature of the task changes.

Sequential interdependence and the Y network are centralized networks with information flows along a predetermined channel. They are appropriate for simple problem solving tasks, requiring little inter-action among members of the group.

Pooled or wheel interdependence is a centralized network and solutions to problems can be reached very quickly. It is appropriate for simple closed-ended problems. The person at the centre of the wheel is the leader of the group who acts as the focus of activities and information flows as well as the co-ordinator of group tasks.

Factors affecting group cohesiveness and effectiveness

Much organizational effectiveness depends on the cohesiveness of the group members. Group cohesiveness will influence the level of integration among members of the group. Integration in turn affects co-ordination and managerial control, which leads into group norm and then effectiveness (see Figure 6.4). The influencing factors and outcomes of group cohesive-ness are listed below and each is then discussed in turn.

(*a*) The influencing factors:
     (i)   management and leadership
     (ii)   the operation (task and technology)
     (iii)   organizational structure and size of group
     (iv)   characteristics of the group members
     (v)   group development and maturity.
(*b*) The outcome:
     (i)   integration
     (ii)   co-ordination and communication
     (iii)   managerial control
     (iv)   group norm
     (v)   group attitude and behaviour
     (vi)   group effectiveness and success.

The influencing factors

Management and leadership

The style of leadership can affect the cohesiveness of the group directly and indirectly. For example, a democratic style allows group members opportunities for participation which can increase cohesiveness and aid the integration of group and organizational goals. Similarly, an autocratic style may have the same effect by causing threats to the group which will

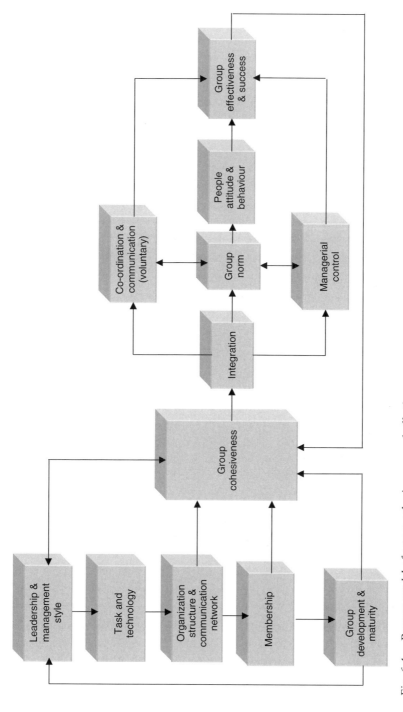

Fig. 6.4.   Process model of group cohesiveness and effectiveness

enhance cohesiveness. Therefore the appropriate style of leadership depends on the characteristics of the group (see chapter 8).

In Likert's (1961) research, 200 companies were studied in an attempt to determine the performance characteristics of different types of organizations. His research identified four types of management systems, namely:

System 1   Exploitative authoritative
System 2   Benevolent authoritative
System 3   Consultative
System 4   Participative group.

One of the main conclusions drawn from Likert's research was that, the nearer the behavioural characteristics of the leaders to system 4 (i.e. leadership with a high degree of teamwork), the more likely this will lead to long-term improvements in labour turnover and high productivity, low scrap, low costs and high earnings. As Davis (1977) put it:

Leadership is part of management. Managers are required to plan and organize, for example, but all we ask of leaders is that they influence others to follow.... Leadership is the ability to persuade others to seek defined objectives enthusiastically. It is the human factor that binds a group together and motivates it toward goals.... It is the ultimate act that brings to success all the potential that is in an organization and its people.

Moreover, harmony and cohesiveness within the group are more likely to be achieved if personnel policies and procedures are well developed and perceived to be equitable with fair treatment for all members.

The operation: task

The nature of the task can determine how people should be brought together and when it is necessary for them to communicate and interact regularly with each other in the performance of their tasks. There are certain criteria which need to be considered when assigning tasks to the people. Hunt (1992) summarized them as follows.

- Choose a task capable of involving all members.
- Give the group a concrete, not abstract, task.
- Clarify a definite beginning and end for the task, and make clear how the effectiveness of the decision will be assessed.
- Choose people who can 'get along' – balance is essential for performance.
- Give the group sufficient autonomy to carry out the task.
- Reward the group as a whole (rewarding individuals breaks the cohesion in the group).

- Structure the task for the group to include at least:
  - a precise statement of the objective(s)
  - a precise statement on the method of presenting the group decision(s)
  - time and cost limits.
- Choose a task requiring a variety of skills and experience, not those of an expert (often an expert alone is much more competent than a group).
- Choose a task which needs close co-ordination, through which people will learn from each other.
- Restrict the size of the group to five or six (although the research data are conflicting on group size).
- Select problems where the administrative cost and time or the social benefits support a group solution – that is, justify the choice of a group.
- The more able the members, the better the decision.
- The more aware the members are of group processes, the better the decision.
- Co-operative groups are better problem solvers than competitive groups.
- Creative groups, where members choose one another, make better decisions.
- Better decisions result when the task and maintenance leadership roles are filled in a way that leads to co-ordination, thus overcoming the slowness, tangential discussion, loss of focus and other inefficiencies of groups.

The operation: technology

The technology involved in executing work can also affect work groups. The term technology can be subdivided into 'process technology' and 'information technology'.

Process technology refers to the means by which the tasks are put together. In particular, changes in emphasis that occur when building technology tends towards system or component building. The change in emphasis that it brought about in the design process is not one which can be shown by structural or process models. These changes are product-oriented and Hunt gives examples of the consequences of a tendency towards a system or component buildings as:

- the client loses an individually tailored building
- the designer becomes more closely linked with the manufacturer
- the contractor becomes an assembler
- quality control becomes vital.

This is one example of how a change in procedure or technology can have an influence on the behaviour of the building team whatever the configuration. It is probably true, however, that some configurations may be better able to cope with certain changes or procedural constraints than others. This may depend on the flexibility and capabilities of the individuals and the group.

Information technology, on the other hand, demands new patterns of work organization and can have an impact on the structure of groups. The movement away from large-scale centralized organizations to smaller working units can help create an environment in which workers may relate more easily to each other. For example, a contractor may need to introduce a new technology to replace the traditional method of executing the job, so providing opportunities for communication and group decision making. The more easily members can communicate freely with each other the more likelihood there is to be group cohesiveness. Therefore, improvements in telecommunications will lead to a more cohesive group.

It has to be said though, that people communication can be the cause of a cohesive group as well as being the outcome. In order words, communication can lead to cohesiveness and cohesiveness can result in better communication.

Organizational structure and size of group

The nature of the operation (e.g. organizational tasks or project tasks) determines the design of the organization/project structure. The structure gives a set of positions and roles, and the designer of the structure needs to determine how these positions should be grouped into sections, units, departments, divisions, etc. and how large these units should be. Both of these questions are related to the design of the superstructure of the organization and have been discussed in some detail in chapter 5. Briefly, simple tasks require little communication among members of the group and a centralized structure with one person in the middle can supervise individuals and produce good results. As the tasks become larger and more complicated, more people will be needed, thus increasing the size of the groups. As the size of the group increases, there will problems of communications and co-ordination among members of the group which require a higher level of managerial control. It is generally accepted that cohesiveness becomes more difficult to achieve when the group size exceeds ten to twelve members. Consequently, the manager divides the people into sub-groups. It has been noted that the optimum size of the work group should not exceed seven members. Large work groups tend to have more absenteeism and lower morale. Large in this context, however, seems to be twenty members or over. Thus, proper design of the structure can stimulate cohesive groups.

Characteristics of group members

Distribution of roles. The term 'role' relates to the activities of an individual in a particular position. The relationship of individual roles to group cohesiveness is apparent. For example, a role sets certain job parameters within the group such as rights, duties, obligations and privileges of individuals. The more clear and balanced these parameters are, the more cohesive the group. A typical successful team should contain people with the following roles:

- chairman/co-ordinator; focuses team on goals, manages interaction
- shaper; strongly task-oriented, full of energy, prevents inertia, extroverted
- plant; innovative, original thinker, creative
- resource investigator; extrovert, gathers information, networks, negotiates
- monitor–evaluator; evaluates conflicting ideas analytically, considers options carefully
- team worker; builds harmony, team spirit, maintenance-oriented
- completer (finisher); picks up loose ends, check details, ensures completion
- implementer (company worker); does routine methodical jobs, directs others, work hard
- technical specialist; expert knowledge, experienced, professional (Belbin, 1993).

Creative teams require a balance of all these roles and comprise members who have characteristics complementary to one another. Good examples of the nine types listed above would prove adequate for any challenge, although not all types are necessarily needed.

Homogeneity and compatibility. The more homogeneous and compatible members of the group in terms of background, interests, beliefs, attitudes and values, the more cohesive the group. Moreover, employees who vary widely in terms of age, skill, social status, etc. are unlikely to achieve cohesiveness and this may be a cause of disruption and conflict.

Group stability. Cohesiveness can be achieved when members of a group are together for a reasonable length of time, and changes occur only slowly. If members are frequently changing, members will not have the opportunity to get to know each other and so develop cohesively. Research by Katz (1982) showed that stable groups tend to be high producing groups. A study of fifty R&D project teams in the research laboratory of a large US corporation illustrates how subtle, unrecognized changes can affect performance. Kast and Rosenzweig (1985, p. 341) cited Katz's research and reported that:

> *the average tenure of team members (scientists and engineers) was calculated, and project performance (innovativeness) was rated independently by the seven top managers of the research laboratory. A curvilinear relationship was found; that is, project performance was lowest when group longevity (average tenure of team members) was less than two years or more than five years. Project performance was highest for groups with average tenures of two to five years. These results showed the effects of getting started and learning to work together, as well as the effects of being together too long. The explanation that seems most plausible stems from data on communication patterns. Intraproject, organizational, and external professional communication all decreased after about three years. This suggests a degree of complacency and lack of zeal in seeking new ideas and exchanging information. The average age of project team members was not a factor; the key was average tenure – how long a particular group had been together. These findings suggest some design criteria for management: (1) accelerate group development in the initial stages of a project with team building efforts, (2) rotate individuals among projects reasonably often, and (3) facilitate (require?) internal and external communication at all stages of a project.*

Physical setting. Social interaction is necessary to stimulate cohesiveness. Members of a group need to be physically close to one another and need to communicate freely with each other.

Group development and maturity

The degree of cohesiveness is also affected by the manner in which groups progress through the various stages of development and maturity. Tuckman and Jensen (1977) identified four main successive stages of group development and relationships: forming, storming, norming and performing. In certain operations, these stages will eventually lead to a final stage of adjourning. Each is now discussed in a little more detail.

(i) *Stage 1 – forming.* This initial stage is marked by uncertainty and even confusion. At this stage, group members start to develop mutual acceptance and membership, establish the purpose of the group, hierarchical structure, task, roles and responsibilities, or even the leader for the group. There is likely to be considerable anxiety as members attempt to create an impression, to test each other, and to establish their personal identity within the group.

(ii) *Stage 2 – storming.* This stage of development is characterized by conflict and confrontation. At this stage people get to know each other better and will put forward their views more openly and force-fully. Disagreements will be expressed among members about tasks, roles and duties. This may lead to conflict and hostility.

(iii) *Stage 3 – norming*. In this stage, the members begin to settle and con-flict and hostility start to be controlled by establishing guidelines and standards, and developing their own norms of acceptable behaviour. The group will have the 'we' and 'our' feeling with high cohesion and group identity.

(iv) *Stage 4 – performing*. This is the stage where the actual functioning of the group starts. Group members will show cohesiveness and teamwork spirit. At this stage, members co-operate with each other instead of competing. Members would be motivated to achieve a high level of productivity.

(v) *Stage 5 – adjourning*. This represents the end of the group but, in some tasks, it might never be reached. However, for construction project teams, or task forces with a specific objective, once the objective is achieved, the group will disband or have a new composition, and the stages will start all over again.

The more successful the group, the more cohesive it is likely to be, and cohesive groups are more likely to be successful. For example, the satisfactory completion of a task through co-operative action can increase harmony in the group (see the outcome of group cohesiveness below).

The outcome

Integration

Figure 6.4 shows that the design of the organization structure influences group cohesiveness. A cohesive group can lead into an integrated team of people, working closely together to complete a specific task. Lawrence and Lorsch (1967) define integration as 'the quality of the state of collaboration among units that have to work together'. They found that successful companies used task forces, teams and project offices to achieve co-ordination. There was a tendency to formulize co-ordinative activities that had developed informally and voluntarily.

Co-ordination and communication

Co-ordination and communication can be classified as administrative and voluntary. In an administrative sense, a cohesive group can make it easier for the management to co-ordinate members of the group together. In a voluntary sense, a cohesive group means that co-ordination depends on the willingness of individuals to find means to integrate their activities with other group members.

Similarly, the content of messages, the manner in which they are communicated and received and thus the extent to which the process is successful can be determined not only by the group's formal or administrative structure, but also by preconceptions that members have about each other.

Managerial control

Another outcome of a cohesive group is high managerial control. The term control can be interpreted in a number of ways. Within the context shown in Fig. 6.4, managerial control is concerned with the regulation of people behaviour towards achieving organizational effectiveness. It involves the planning and organization of work functions, and guiding and regulating staff activities. Control provides a check on the execution of work and on the success or failure of the operations of the organization.

The operations of groups can influence the functioning of control systems. Informal group 'norms' (discussed below) and peer pressure can be one of the most powerful forms of control. Going back to the Hawthorne study, Mayo (1933) observed that the experimental group did not follow company policy on the reporting of production figures. Workers had developed their own patois or slang, reinforcing its solidarity by establishing standards of attitude and behaviour. Although actual production varied, the workers officially reported a relatively standard amount of output each day, and in order to remain a member of the informal group the supervision acquiesced to this. Membership of a cohesive and effective work group can be a source of motivation and job satisfaction. Socialization can help create a feeling of commitment to the group and reduce the need for formal managerial control. With the development of autonomous work groups, members have greater freedom and wider discretion over the planning, execution and control of their own work. In order to maintain co-operation and commitment of staff the manager must continually review (at both individual and group level) the operation of the control system and the progress made in achieving objectives. This includes full participation of staff in discussions on the operation of control systems that affect them, on the difficulties and problems experienced, and on decisions concerning remedial action and future plans (Mullins 1999).

Group norm

Group norm is one of the commonly observed outcomes of group behaviour. Norms are developed when the group members start to co-operate with one another in a cohesive manner. Group members accept each other's ideas and compromise their opinions, which leads to establishing norm. As group cohesion increases, the amount of interaction between group members increases and the amount of agreement in group opinion also increases. In a model developed by Homans (1982) the dynamics through which group norms emerge and influence the activities of group members were illustrated. Homans suggested that all group behaviour consists of three basic elements, namely activities, interactions and sentiments. The following is a summary of the findings.

(a) Activities refer to things that people do ... all activities refer in the end to movement of the muscle of men.

(b) Interactions refer to communications of any sort between individuals. These communications need not be verbal, they can be physical such as two people using a saw.

(c) Sentiments are internal states of the human body and include motives, drives, emotions, feelings and attitudes. Sentiments thus range from fear and hunger to affection. Unlike activities and interactions, sentiments cannot be seen or observed.

Homans went further and noted that group behaviour can be described in terms of an external system and an internal system, each of which contains its own activities, interactions and sentiments. Homans believes that viewing group behaviour in terms of an external and an internal system can help managers better visualize the dynamics or behaviour of a group.

- The external system is composed of the required activities, interactions and sentiments which the group must carry out to survive.
- Internal activities, interactions and sentiments emerge from the work group itself. Groups often establish norms (which are types of sentiment) that say 'no group should produce more than X number of units per day'. This norm is communicated to new and existing members through various kinds of interactions: verbal admonitions, frowns, etc. As a result, the emergent activity of the group – in this example its production level – is often much lower than management planned for the group.

Another characteristic of group norm is its strength. Strength of a group is defined as the extent to which members of the group agree with each other and support one another. The stronger the group the more cohesive it is, and the better the group members will be able to withstand pressures emanating from outside. Pressure exerted on an individual by other members within the organization is likely to be less effective if the person is in a more highly cohesive group than in a less cohesive one. Problems or complaints can be easier dealt with if an individual is in a more cohesive group.

The greater the group cohesiveness and, therefore, the more attractive the group is to an individual, the greater is its influence on the individual's evoked set of choices and their consequences (Litterer 1967). Moreover, the more attractive a group is to an individual the more congruent his/her evoked set is likely to be with the norms and opinions of the group. For those courses incongruent with group standards, the individual is aware that the group can make the consequences of choosing them far from desirable. First, it is more disturbing for a person to be dropped from or ostracized by a group that is highly attractive than from one that has relatively little attraction for him. Second, the more cohesive group has clearer opinions about what it expects, making a violation of its expectations easier to detect. Last, because opinions are more uniformly held in a highly cohesive group, the break will be more likely to be with all group members.

Group attitude and behaviour

When the group reaches the 'performing' stage (see group development above), it will behave in certain characteristic ways, very much as if it had a life of its own, independent of the lives of the individuals included in it. Graham and Bennett (1995, p. 89) listed the following characteristics of group behaviour.

(a) The group will produce a settled system of personal relationships and customs.

(b) These customs sometimes include restrictions on output.

(c) Individuals will often behave more in the way the group expects than as they would if left to themselves.

(d) The group exerts great pressure on all its members to conform to its own standards of behaviour.

(e) Newcomers to the group are often made to feel unwelcome. Groups vary in this respect just as individuals vary in their ability to become easily accepted by a group.

(f) The group tends to resist change imposed on it, and will react to it slowly because of the threat to its existence, its security, its customs and its pattern of relationships.

(g) Unofficial leaders emerge in the group, changing according to the needs of the situation at the time. When the group is in open conflict with the management, for example, it may choose as its leader a person whom its members would normally describe as an agitator. When conditions settle down, a new leader might emerge who would be a more diplomatic person.

(h) A group often seems to follow the same motivation process as an individual – searching for and eventually perceiving satisfying goals. A group can be frustrated and show the negative reactions of aggression, regression, resignation and fixation.

(*i*) The character of a group will not change because one person leaves it or joins it, unless that person is extremely influential.

(*j*) An external threat or the competition of another group will increase the cohesiveness of a group.

Group effectiveness and success

The visible outcome of a cohesive group is its efficiency and productivity. The term efficiency is defined as 'doing things in the right way'. In a work situation, productivity is normally measured by the ratio of output to input over a period of time. In a more simple term, productivity can be measured by cost and time of production. Naturally, the efficiency of the group and its productivity level depends on many dependent and independent factors. Among these factors is group cohesiveness.

There is increasing evidence which points to the power of group influences upon the functioning of organizations. In those situations where the management has recognized the power of group motivational forces and has used the kind of leadership required to develop and focus these motivational forces on achieving the organization's objectives, the performance of the organization tends to be appreciably above the average achieved by other methods of leadership and management. Membership of groups which have common goals to which they are strongly committed, high peer group loyalty, favourable attitudes between superiors and subordinates, and a high level of skill in inter-action can clearly achieve far more than the same people acting as a mere assemblage (Likert 1961).

In the building trades industry, work groups are continually being assembled, assigned to work for a while on a project (such as a house or an office building), and are broken up when the project is complete. Upon completion, the individual workers need to be regrouped differ-ently for a later project. Usually these groupings are made by the foremen who select men personally known to them, often on the basis of what they perceive to be the worker's competence in his craft. A study was conducted by Raymond H. Van Zeist (1952, pp. 175–185) cited in Litterer (1967, p. 87), where the productivity of two types of construction groups was measured against time and cost of production. In this study, one project was selected where some construction crews were chosen in the usual fashion, while others were assembled on the basis of personal choices made by the workers themselves. Each man was asked to indicate a person with whom he would most prefer to work, and work groups were formed to follow these choices as closely as possible.

The results showed rather clearly that those groups assembled on the basis of the personal choices of the members had significantly higher

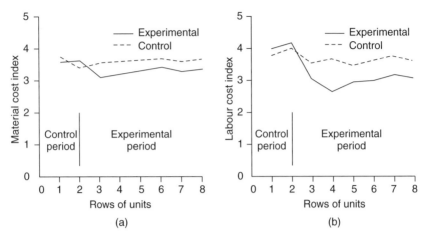

Fig. 6.5. (a) Fluctuations between experimental and control groups on materials costs for an entire three-month period. (b) Fluctuations between experimental and control groups on labour costs for an entire three-month period (from Litterer (1967, p. 87))

job satisfaction, lower turnover rates, lower indices of labour cost, and lower indices of materials cost (see Fig. 6.5). Litterer argued that, although in this research, the results showed that the effect of self-selection in promoting cohesiveness was high with apparently resultant high productivity, it would be erroneous to presume that cohesiveness built on such grounds would always yield high productivity.

In other research carried out by Back (1952), where groups were formed on the basis of the personal attractiveness of the members, the group tended to stretch discussions out as long as possible in order to continue the pleasant conversations. As a result, they seriously reduced the speed with which they completed their assigned tasks. In yet another research into work groups by Fiedler (1954), where productivity was high, the group members did not have any great personal attraction for one another.

These three works have provided an interesting paradox. In the first research, high personal attractiveness and high productivity go together. In the second, high personal attractiveness goes with low productivity, and in the third, a relatively low personal attractiveness accompanies high productivity. This paradox was explained by Litterer (1967) in the following.

First, all three research groups were highly cohesive but not for the same reason. In two cases cohesiveness rested on personal attractiveness, in the other on team success and the purpose of the group. Second, productivity was measured by some system external to the group. In some cases, productivity in group terms was the same or congruent with those of the investigator, whereas in the second case they were to a considerable degree mutually exclusive. In the second case the group would have to turn its attention and conversation to solving technical problems, which would keep members from enjoying one another's company, the basis of their cohesiveness. Hence, productivity based on the assigned task would have been unproductive from the standpoint of the group.

Litterer went further to note that there is usually less variability in productivity within a highly cohesive group than within a group that has low cohesiveness. That is, all members of a highly cohesive group tend to produce at a similar level; in a group with low cohesiveness some members may be producing at a high level and others at a low level. A highly cohesive group is able to exercise control over the productivity of members, as evidenced in the uniformity of the production of the individual group members. If group control over individual production was fixed at a high rate, management or the experimental investigator would admit that high productivity was being achieved. On the other hand, if the control of the group fixed production at a low rate, management would not obtain the desired productivity. The important point here is that high group cohesiveness promotes high group control over the variation in productivity performance among group members. The *level* of group production, often specified by a norm, is dependent on other factors.

Although the relationship between the level of group production (or better, the group standard) and productivity in management terms has not been well studied, we are able to identify some relevant factors. Let us begin by recalling that both the group and management (or the investigator) have their own objectives with regard to productivity, or, to put it more rigorously, there are two systems each with its own standards. If the two sets are congruent, there is little problem. However, if management wants a high volume of production to get lower costs but the work group wants a low volume of production to keep its jobs longer, the two production standards differ. When the production standards of management and the group vary considerably and group cohesiveness is high, it is doubtful that any individual performance of a group member will match the standards set by management. On the other hand, even if the standards differ considerably, but cohesiveness is low, it is likely, or at least possible, that some group member's performance will approach the management's standard. Often, of course, group and management standards do not differ in only a single dimension (for example, quantity produced) but in several aspects of output. It would be perfectly possible to have a work group that defined productivity in terms of quality first and quantity second, where management's order of preference was the reverse. Group effort in producing a high-quality output may reduce the quantity produced, giving management both a quality and quantity it does not want.

Team building

The principle of creating a cohesive group or units within the organization can also be applied to building a project team. As mentioned before, each project in itself can become an organization and therefore a building team is formed according to client and project characteristics. The building team usually comprises groups of people from the client organization, consultants and specialized firms who are brought together to design and construct the building project.

The fragmented nature of the construction industry, where design is separated from construction, places great dependence on the competence of the building team in setting up the building process and bringing the work to a successful completion. Many earlier reports and research conducted in the 1960s and 1970s (such as the Emmerson (1974) and the Banwell (1964) reports) stated that there is a lack of liaison between the architect and other professionals and contractors, and between them and clients. It has continuously been argued that in no other important industry is the responsibility for design so far removed from the responsibility for production. These reports emphasized the need to reform the organizational approach to building projects. Building project management was seen to be a passive procedural activity but the movement towards a more dynamic integrated approach was later suggested by Higgins and Jessop (1965).

Higgins and Jessop clearly identified that the problem of communication within building teams was created to a large extent by the attitudes and perceptions about the values of contributors to the building industry. The most important drawback to the traditional approach, as noted by Higgins and Jessop, is the lack of effective communication and co-ordination between members of the building team. In other words, it is the nature of the relationships between the communicators which creates the difficulties for communications structures. Five problems of communication were outlined, namely:

(*a*) communication with prospective clients
(*b*) communication between clients and advisers
(*c*) communication within the design team
(*d*) communication related to the contract
(*e*) communication within the construction team.

Higgins and Jessop then went further and noted that:

> *if building is thought of without the people involved, it can be seen as a chain of interdependent operations called the Technical System, i.e. briefing, design, estimating, billing, supplying, etc. To undertake these operations, a wide variety of resources, e.g. material and skill, remain under the control of*

people and organizations which are called the resource controllers (i.e. The Social System).

The central problem arises from the fact that the basic relationship which exists among 'resource controllers' has the character of interdependent autonomy. There is a lack of match between the technical interdependence of the resources and the organizational independence of those who control them. Any attempt to re-order the division of responsibilities among resource controllers that might arise from a purely technical study would run up against deep-seated difficulties of conflicting values and vested professional, technical and commercial interests.

In subsequent research by the Tavistock Institute (1966), a thesis exploring the foregoing problem of communication among building teams was presented and provided a model of the structure and functions of the building industry. Two important characteristics that are incorporated into any model of the building process were identified – interdependence and uncertainty. The construction industry as a socio-technical system and its performance was seen as being dependent on the communication between and the interdependence of the participants. The building team was described as a sub-system within the overall system of environment.

Based on the competitive tendering procedure, it was reported that within the building process there are five closely related sub-systems:

(*a*)   a system of operations
(*b*)   a system of resource controllers
(*c*)   a system of formal controls
(*d*)   a system of informal controls
(*e*)   a system of social and personal relations.

Traditional competitive tendering was criticized by professionals as being unable, in a situation of certainty about all factors affecting time and cost, to provide the basis for a valid and protective contract. There were two main types of attacks on the problem of the unsatisfactory nature of the organization, functioning and communications in the building industry Firstly, exhortations to return to the formal system in its pure form, i.e. directive functions, which was deplored. Second, a call for some new form of system to incorporate the more adaptive characteristics of the informal system.

Thus, the socio-technical analysis and the three dimensions described by the Tavistock Institute (1965, 1966) of complexity, uncertainty and interdependency had a great impact on the introduction of alternative forms of team building in an attempt to achieve a wide co-ordination of control of the building process (such as package deals in the late 1960s and management contracting by the early 1970s).

Before continuing further, the element of integration and its relation to team building should also be considered. Principally, the changing technologies, procedures, materials and complexity of the building process are such that the sequential approach of independent professionals to the formation of design and construction solution is unable to provide an efficient solution to the client's requirements. As mentioned earlier, the problems in communication within the building industry were documented over 30 years ago by the Tavistock Institute and integration was seen as a necessary solution to the interdependence and uncertainty involved.

The notion of integration of the building team has been reported in a number of studies, such as the Banwell (1964) report, Sidwell (1982), Naoum (1989), the Latham (1994) report and the Egan report (1998). Evidently, high integration among members of the building team can help to improve the performance of the project. It is also important that each team and sub-team should be composed of people with various characteristics. The most important role in team building is the leader of the team.

This serves to emphasize the view put forward earlier in this chapter that group relationships are of prime importance for the successfully run project. Furthermore, for group relationships to work effectively, interpersonal relationships and behaviour must likewise operate in an effective manner. Perhaps the most commonly observed aspect of group behaviour is the establishment of a positive attitude toward objectives which can lead to norms. For example, the move away from conventional procurement procedures has meant that the role of the architect has had to change from being the leader of the building team to being part of the team. Designers have therefore had to change their attitude towards new procurement methods and accept input from the contractor. This change of attitude can improve communication and increase harmony among members of the team, leading to a high level of performance.

A study on construction times for industrial building by NEDO (1983) concluded that:

> *It is not the form of contract which primarily determines whether targets are met but the attitude of the parties to which the form of contract may contribute. The standard form of contract offers penalties for delays but not incentives for speed. Industry and customers should look for ways of sharing the benefits from improved performance.*

Turner (1986) referred to the benefit of high integration of a harmonious team. He stated:

> *by breaking down the 'us and them' syndrome, the professionals and the management contractors are able to pool together their once fragmented*

expertise for the benefit of the project. Thus the participants in the construction industry can work together as a team rather than being excessively concerned with their own individual roles, vice versa other participants.

Group conflict

Conflict is another important subject that is usually associated with work groups. Conflict is commonly defined as fight, struggle, quarrel or bitter argument. It may take place between individuals, groups, organizations and countries. For example, a conflict between employers and workers can arise because of differences in opinions and roles. A conflict between two neighbouring countries can escalate because of territorial claims. This definition implies that conflict tends to be associated with negative features and situations which result in inefficiency. However, conflict within groups and organizations is not necessarily a bad thing. Some conflict can also result in positive outcomes. For example, competition and a healthy argument can improve standards, provided they are properly managed. Figure 6.6 shows how conflict can affect organizational performance both positively and negatively. At the far left, performance is low because of little conflict with no new ideas or few challenges. At the far right, performance is also low because of high conflict with lack of co-ordination, managerial control and, perhaps, chaos. A functional range is shown in the middle – enough conflict, but not too much. Within this range an appropriate amount of conflict, facilitates idea generation and creativity. Thus, the task for managers

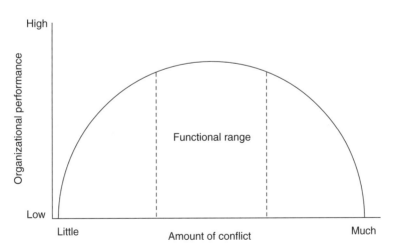

Fig. 6.6. Conflict and organizational performance (from Kast and Rosenzweig (1985, p. 344))

is not necessarily to eliminate conflict but to encourage and maintain a functional amount by proper control of people (Kast and Rosenzweig 1985).

As we have seen, conflict can have negative as well as positive effects on individuals, groups and organizations. Among the negative effects of conflict are:

- lack of teamwork
- escalated competition
- frustrated arguments
- poor communication
- frustration
- friction
- hostility and jealousy
- personal defeat
- aggression
- low morale.

Among the positive effects of conflict are:

- people working harder to fight defeat
- controlled competition
- healthy arguments
- innovation and creativity.

Causes of conflict

(a) *Differences in personality.* This is also known as personality clash. This type of conflict arises when two people disagree about a particular issue because of their different disciplines and beliefs. Disagreements of this type often become highly emotional and take on moral overtones. Such conflicts are not based on technical merits but purely on social or cultural backgrounds.

(b) *Differences in interests and objectives.* There is likely to be conflict when two people or groups are dependent on each other but with differing interests or objectives. The higher the degree of interdependence of the groups, the more crucial becomes the relationship of their interest and objectives.

(c) *Clarity of role.* A role is the pattern of behaviour that an individual within the organization is expected to display in occupying a particular position. Sometimes the actual behaviour of the individual differs from that expected and this can result in conflict. This difference can be due to role incompatibility or ambiguity.

There are three types of role conflict: between the person and the role, intrarole and interrole. The person–role conflict is between the person's personality and the expectations of the role. As an example, imagine a project manager and a union member appointed to head up a new section engineering team. The new team leader may not really believe in keeping close control over the workers and it goes against this individual's personality to be hard-nosed, but this is what is expected of a project manager. Intrarole conflict is created by contradictory expectations about how a given role should be played. Interrole conflict results from the different requirements of two or more roles that must be played at the same time.

(*d*) *Structural.* The role conflict described in (*c*) above can be used as a basis for analysing conflicts that arise as a result of structuring or re-forming the organization. Earlier in this chapter it was pointed out that the organization is made up of overlapping and interlocking role sets. Figure 6.7 gives an example of the interacting role set concept of organization. The figure shows only three possible role sets from a large design and build organization. The construction manager, general area manager and designer are called the focal

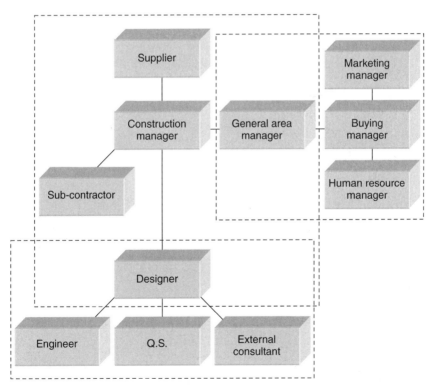

Fig. 6.7. Overlapping role sets (modified from Luthans (1998, p. 314))

persons of the sets shown. The sub-contractor, supplier and con-sultant roles are vital in their respective sets but would not be included within traditional organizational boundaries. They are external to the traditional organization. The designer is a member of the construction manager role set but is also a focal person for another role set. The general area manager is shown as a member of two role sets. The overlaps can result in role conflicts and ambi-guities. Such dynamics become important in intergroup conflict analysis and provide the theoretical foundation for the need for today's interfunctional teams (Luthans 1998)

(e) *Contractual*. Tasks and responsibilities that are demanded will be different from what is agreed. If the contract is unclear, it may be differently perceived by each party, leading to conflict.

(f) *Resources*. Due to economic pressures, most organizations today have very limited resources. Groups within the organization have to compete for their funds, space, manpower, etc. The more limited the resources are, the greater the potential for conflict.

(g) *Territory*. This is the space that forms the boundary between divisions and groups. Within this boundary, the group has special rights which can be claimed as theirs and not somebody else's. Violation of the group's territory will result into conflict. Such violation can involve information or physical space.

(h) *Jealousy*. Intergroup hostility and jealousy comes out as a result of:
   (i) when an individual is promoted to a higher position while others with similar credibility remain in the same position
   (ii) when someone receives non-contractual benefit from the management (such as a car or a bonus) while others do not
   (iii) when information is given to one group of people but not to others.

Summary and conclusion

A work group is another important aspect of people and organizational management. It is closely associated with the design of organizational structure. A work group is commonly defined as a collection of individuals who are dependent on each other, who are psychologically aware of one another, who perceive themselves as a group, who have exclusive identity with differentiated roles, who, as group members, have significantly interdependent relations with other groups.

Similar to organizational structure, a work group can be formal or informal. A formal group (also known as task-centred behaviour) has formal roles and duties and follows rules and procedures set by the organization. Informal groups (also known as socio-emotional behaviour) are based on friendship and social interaction. Although informal groups have no legal constraints, they can still have a significant effect on organizational effectiveness.

The purpose of forming a group is to fulfil organizational objectives such as distribution of work, information processing and decision making as well as individual objectives such as personal satisfaction and establishing self-concept. To achieve these objectives, there are several common bases for the organization to group positions into units and units into larger ones; these are grouping by knowledge or skill, by work process and function, by time, by output, by client, by place and by project.

Research studies have shown that the more cohesive the group, the higher the productivity and job satisfaction. Group cohesiveness leads to high integration which results in high co-ordination and managerial control. This in turn develops a group norm with a high level of effectiveness. Among the factors that can influence group cohesiveness are:

- management and leadership style
- task and technology
- structure and communication network
- group membership
- group development and maturity
- group success.

The dynamic nature of work groups can result in conflict. conflict can take place as a result of:

- differences in personality
- differences in interests and objectives
- clarity of role
- poor structure
- ambiguous contract
- lack or sharing resources
- territory
- jealousy.

Conflict, if managed properly, can also have a positive effect on individuals, groups and organizations. Among the positive outcomes of conflict are (1) working harder, (2) healthy competition and argument, (3) generation of innovation and creativity.

References

BACK, K. Influence Through Social Communication. *Journal of Abnormal and Social Psychology*, **46**, 1952, pp. 9–23.

BANWELL, H. *The Placing and Management of Building Contracts.* London, HMSO, 1964.

BELBIN, R. *Team Roles at Work.* Butterworth-Heinemann, 1993.

BERELSON, B. and STEINER, G. *Human Behaviour.* New York, Harcourt, Brace & World, 1964, p. 326.

DAVIS, K. *Human Behaviour at Work.* New York, McGraw-Hill, 1977, 5th edn, p. 107.

EGAN, J. *Rethinking Construction.* The Construction Industry Task Force. Department of Environment, Transport and the Regions, London, 1998.

EMERSON, I. *Survey of Problems before the Construction Industry.* London, HMSO, 1974.

FIEDLER, F. Assumed Similarity Measures as Predictors of Team Effectiveness. *Journal of Abnormal and Social Psychology,* **49**, 1954, pp. 381–388.

GRAHAM, H. and BENNETT, R. *Human Resources Management.* Boston, MA, Pitman, 1995, 8th edn.

HANDY, C. *Understanding Organizations.* London, Penguin, 1998, 5th edn.

HIGGINS, G. and JESSOP, N. *Communication in the Building Industry.* London, Tavistock Institute, 1965.

HIGGINS, G. and JESSOP, N. *Interdependence and Uncertainty.* London, Tavistock Institute, 1966.

HOMANS, G. *The Human Group.* New York, Harcourt, Brace & Co., 1982.

HUNT, J. *Managing People at Work.* McGraw-Hill, 1992, 3rd edn.

KAST, F. and ROSENZWEIG, J. *Organization and Management.* New York, McGraw-Hill, 1985, 5th edn.

KATZ, R. The effects of group longevity on project communication and performance. *Administrative Science Quarterly,* March 1982, pp. 81–104.

LATHAM, M. *Constructing the Team.* London, HMSO, 1994.

LEAVITT, H. Some effects of certain communication patterns on group performance. *Journal of Abnormal and Social Psychology,* **46**, 1951, pp. 38–50.

LIKERT, R. *New Patterns of Management.* New York, McGraw-Hill, 1961.

LIKERT, R. *The Human Organisation.* New York, McGraw-Hill, 1967, p. 156.

LITTERER, J. *The Analysis of Organizations.* New York, Wiley, 1967.

LUTHANS, F. *Organizational Behaviour.* New York, McGraw-Hill, 1998, 8th edn.

MAYO, E. *The Human Problems of an Industrial Civilisation.* London, Macmillan, 1933.

NAOUM, S. *An Investigation into the Performance of Management Contracts and the Traditional Method of Building Procurement.* PhD thesis. Department of Building, Brunel University, Middlesex, 1989.

NEDO report. Faster Building for Industry. *Building Economic.* London, NEDO, 1983.

ROETHLISBERGER, J. and DICKSON, W. *Management and the Worker.* Cambridge, MA, Harvard University Press, 1939, p. 552.

SCHEIN, E. *Organizational Psychology.* Englewood Cliffs, New Jersey, Prentice-Hall, 1988, 3rd edn.

SIDWELL, A. *A Critical Study of Project Team Organizational Forms within the Building Process.* PhD thesis, Department of Construction and Environmental Health, The University of Aston, 1982.

THOMPSON, J. *Organization in Action*, McGraw-Hill, 1967.

TUCKMAN, B. and JENSEN, M. Stages of small group development. *Group and Organizational Studies*, December 1977, pp. 419–427.

TURNER, D. *Design and Build Contract Practice.* London, Longman, 1986, p. 13.

VAN ZELST, R. Sociomettrically Selected Workteams Increase Productivity. *Personnel Psychology*, **5**, 1952, pp. 175–185.

Case study. Chelston plc

The Engineering Design Department

Chelston plc is a large mining and exploration group, with its own Engineering Design Department. The Department is organized (see chart) into 6 sections, of fairly equal size, which are based on engineering specialisms – mechanical, civil, etc. Each section has a manager, controlling approximately 5 senior engineers, 12 engineers and the section's draughting personnel.

The Department works as an internal 'engineering consultancy' to the rest of the group. The projects with which the Department becomes involved range from multi-million pound ventures lasting from 3–4 years for new Chelston developments to relatively short projects for alterations or repairs to existing operations sites. The Department has existed for many years, following a Board decision to have as much engineering design work as possible carried out 'in house', for reasons of control, flexibility and cost. It was deliberately created as an 'internal consultancy', with many staff coming from consultancy practices. The image of a 'professional practice' has remained over the years, the Department responding to requests from operating divisions as an external consultant would to a client. Its professional reputation is considerable in the various specialisms, with regular contributions to professional journals and to conferences.

Project management

While a few projects require the skills of only one specialism, the larger majority involve a range of specialisms. The range varies between projects and over the life of a given project.

Projects are managed by Project Managers, who are not part of the specialist engineering sections. They, like the Specialist Section Managers, report to the Assistant General Manager. Each Project Manager (there are currently 7 in Post) has a staff of 2 or 3 Planning Engineers, and 2 Planning Assistants.

Specialist Engineers are assigned to projects by their Section Managers but they remain part of, and work physically in, their section areas, which are on different floors of the building. An engineer may spend all of his time on one project or have it divided between 2 or 3 projects.

The flow of work into organizations has usually been at a level which fully occupies the existing staff. Fairly regularly external consultants are used when the flow of projects creates a load which exceeds staff capacity.

The success of the Department lies in the specialist skills of its engineering sections and in the ability of Project managers to integrate these skills into effective project teams. While this works fairly well, there are problems.

Project Managers do not have as much control as they think necessary over the specialist engineer members of their project teams. The establishment of a team for a project is based on discussions between a Project Manager and Specialist Section Managers who have the detailed knowledge of the disposition and workload of their staff across projects. In some projects, the nature of the scheme allows specialists to work relatively independently of each other. In many projects, however, close teamwork is needed between specialisms to facilitate the development of an optimum design which solves the design problem and is also economical. This integrated teamwork is sometimes 'short of the mark'. In addition, members of teams are sometimes changed at short notice because of a Section Manager's need to achieve a balance of staff across projects.

Staffing

While there is a flow of staff into and out of the organization this is kept to a minimum by the General Manager's salary policy which is intended to reduce the problems associated with high turnover among well-qualified professional staff. The Department uses the services of a salary survey organization and regularly adjusts its salaries above the survey norms.

Projects Managers have mainly been recruited from outside and are in the age range 35–45 while most Section Managers have been promoted internally and are aged 45–55.

The General Managers, who established the Department, will retire in 3 years' time. The Assistant General Manager, who is 45, was recruited a year ago from a consultancy practice which Chelston had regularly used. He was appointed in order to take some of the managerial workload from the GM, to allow the GM to concentrate more on liaison work with the rest of the organization. Chelston's mining and exploration business has had to respond more rapidly to external competitive developments in recent years and it has become increasingly important that the Engineering Design Department keeps in touch with developments in their early stages.

Organization changes

The organization structure of the Department has long been the subject of discussion. There are generally two views:

- make the existing structure work more effectively
- change to a full project team structure.

Specialist Section Managers support the first view arguing that a project team structure would dilute the specialist competence for which the Department is renowned. The arguments on both sides are well known and regularly rehearsed, with each side confident in its own analysis.

Six months after arriving, the Assistant General Manager conducted a review of the Department's operation by talking individually to all Specialist Section and Project Managers, and by visiting contacts in comparable organizations. The review was stimulated by staffing and co-ordination problems which were becoming critical in one of the Department's major projects.

His initial conclusion was that considerable advantages in efficiency and co-ordination could be gained by re-organizing on a full project team basis. His outline plan was to:

(i) Reduce, by about 60%, the size of the Specialist Engineering Sections. They would continue to provide a focus on developments in the various specialist areas and to carry out projects which were largely restricted to one specialism. The Section Mangers would have an involvement in the annual performance review of relevant engineers working in project teams.

(ii) Create 5 interdisciplinary project groups from the engineers released from the specialist sections. These project groups, each led by a Project Manager with appropriate administrative and planning support, would handle the flow of larger, interdisciplinary projects which accounted for approximately 70% of the Department's work. Projects managers would also he able to call on the services of engineers remaining in the specialist sections if work loads became too heavy.

Current situation

This is as far as the Assistant General Manger's thinking has gone. He realizes that there are a number of issues which still require resolution.

The General Manager gave general approval to the plan, saying that the structural debate needed to be resolved in one way or the other. However, because of the scale of the change involved, he asked the Assistant General Manager to 'mull it over' for a couple of weeks before a final discussion at which a decision would he made.

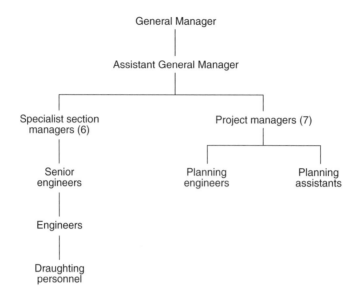

Chapter 7

Organization culture

The basic philosophy, spirit and desire of an organization have far more to do with its relative achievements than do technological or economic resources, organizational structure, innovation, and timing. All these things weigh heavily on success. But they are, I think, transcended by how strongly the people in the organization believe in its basic precepts and how faithfully they carry them out. (Tom Watson, Chair of IBM, 1963)

This chapter provides an understanding of the concept of culture and how culture can affect people's values and behaviour towards achieving organizational goals. The first part of the chapter defines the term culture and determines its main characteristics. It also examines various types of organization cultures and explains their link with organizational structure, which was discussed in chapter 5. Factors that influence the choice of culture are discussed and the relationship between the issue of culture, strategy and performance is addressed. The chapter links organizational goals with the human resources dimension of the organization, in terms of transmission of required values and behaviour. Figure 7.1 summarizes the overall principles of chapter 7 (see also Fig. 1.1).

Learning objectives

To:

> ➢ understand the concept and importance of organizational culture
> ➢ identify the various types of culture
> ➢ evaluate the main factors that influence the type of culture
> ➢ understand the relationship between culture, strategy and company performance.

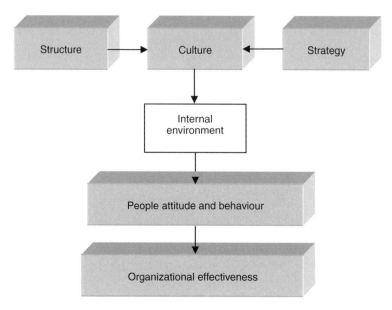

Fig. 7.1. Overall principles of chapter 7

The concept of culture

The concept of culture was first known to represent, in a very broad and holistic sense, the qualities of any specific human group that are passed from one generation to the next. This includes religion, way of life, values and beliefs of people. This is known 'social culture'. People born in a particular culture are expected to believe and behave differently to others. Similar to the social culture, each organization has its own culture dominated by its values and behaviour. This is known 'organizational culture'. Organizational culture has commonly been defined as (see Kotter *et al.* (1992), Scholz (1987) and Williams *et al.* (1993)):

> *the way things are done and operated within the internal environment of the workplace. It has a number of features including: common beliefs; pattern of behaviour, norms; values and rules that are exercised among members of the organization. These features are strategically driven and they are usually established through the company founders or the new managers/leaders. The closer the values and beliefs among members of the organization, the stronger the culture.*

The following factors are examples of cultural matters related to organizations:

- the characteristics of the people employed by the organization

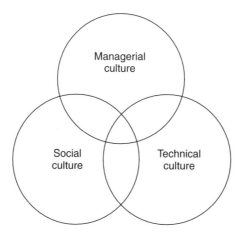

Fig. 7.2. The three dimensions of organizational culture

- the level of qualifications required for professional employees
- the level of past experience required
- the recruitment process
- rewards and promotion of employees
- training of employees
- the system used for career development
- social activities available
- decision making level
- the type of power that is exercised within the organization
- how much risk the company takes
- line managers, involvement (or not) in strategic decisions
- subordinates' awareness of company objectives
- subordinates' awareness of company problems
- the system of communication and co-ordination used
- information documentation system used.

Overall, if the above issues are put into a conceptual model, Fig. 7.2 provides a basis for one showing that there are three major dimensions of organizational culture:

(a) *Social culture.* This refers to the way individuals behave and the means in which people are motivated at work. It also includes social activities that take place within the organization. For example, 'out of work' activities such as sports and social clubs.

(b) *Technical culture.* This means that the organization has a culture related to the techniques used for executing the tasks, equipment, processes and any other facility which transfers inputs into outputs. Naturally, the techniques used depend on the characteristics of the task which in turn affect the organizational structure and culture.

(c) *Managerial culture.* This includes the style of management and organizational structure. It refers to ways in which the tasks are divided (differentiated) and the manner in which the activities are co-ordinated (integration). Differentiation and integration will create a pattern of power and authority within the organization which in turn can be developed into a particular culture.

In order for organizations to survive the external pressures of the environment, they need to continuously change their culture to fit the environment in which they operate. Changing culture is usually associated with changing strategy. A change in strategy requires a change in organizational objectives, work methods, structure, systems, training and eventually, people's values and behaviour. The term value in a cultural context refers to matters that are difficult to visualize and hard to change even when the group members change. For example, a manager's care about customers and an executive's policy regarding long-term debt. On the other hand, the term people behaviour refers to matters that are more visible and easier to change – matters in which new employees are encouraged to follow their fellow workers. For example, being hard working and friendly or being tough and decisive.

In addition to social and organizational culture, there is also an 'industry culture' where certain patterns of attitude and beliefs dominate the behaviour of its people. The fragmented nature of the construction industry, where design is separated from construction and a large proportion of the work is sub-contracted, means that there is 'cultural diversity' among the different specialized firms engaged on any given project. This point was expressed by Michael Latham (1993), who stated that construction suffers from a culture of confrontation. He reported:

I have found a general mood of change. It is widely acknowledged that the industry has deeply ingrained adversarial attitudes. Many believe that they have intensified in recent years. There is also general agreement that the route to seeking advice and action from lawyers is embarked upon too readily. While a relatively small number of these legal disputes actually reach formal court hearings, the culture of conflict seemed to be embedded and the tendency towards litigiousness is growing. These disputes and conflicts have taken their toll on morale and team spirit. Defensive attitudes are commonplace. A new profession of 'claims consultants' has arisen whose duty is to advise some participants in the construction process how they should seek to make money out of the alleged mistakes or shortcomings of their participants. While clearly the existing culture of claims provides its own justification for such services, it is difficult to imagine a starker illustration of adversarial arrangements within the construction process itself.

The Harrison/Handy culture types

In 1972 Harrison identified four types of organizational culture related to the way the organization is structured, these are: power, role, task, and person. Later in 1978, Handy reworked Harrison's ideas distinguishing the four cultures using simple pictograms (Handy 1998). One of these cultures might dominate the entire organization, or different cultures may exist in various parts of the firm; what might suit some organizations or departments at some time is not necessarily appropriate forever. Figure 7.3 illustrates Handy's four types of culture.

Power culture

The power culture stems from a single central source, as in a small business that has begun to expand or in a large organization that has begun to be divisionalized. Its structure is best pictured as a web. Here, there are few rules and procedures with little or no bureaucracy. These cultures put a lot of faith in the individual at the centre of the web (i.e. the

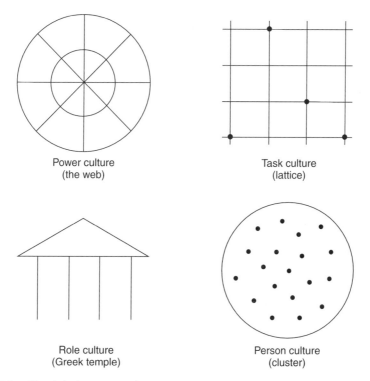

Power culture
(the web)

Task culture
(lattice)

Role culture
(Greek temple)

Person culture
(cluster)

Fig. 7.3. Handy's four types of organizational culture (from Handy (1998))

spider) but little in committees. All important decisions are taken by a handful of powerful people and precedents are followed. Therefore, in these organizations, individuals with powerful positions will prosper and be satisfied to the extent that they are power-oriented, politically minded, risk-taking and rate security as a minor element in their psychological contract. Resource power is the major base in this culture with some elements of personal power in the centre. Employees working within a power culture may suffer from low morale.

The fundamental feature of the power culture is the ability to move quickly to the changing conditions of the external environment; such an organization can react well to threat or danger. However, company size is a problem with this type of culture. As the organization grows in size, the web can break because it seeks to link too many activities. Nevertheless, organizations can remain in the web structure by spawning other organizations, producing other spiders. Handy referred to the GEC company in the UK as an example of a multi-web organization. The company continued to grow but was careful to give maximum independence to the individual heads of the linked organizations.

The role culture

The role culture is highly bureaucratic. It operates through formal roles and procedures and there are clearly defined rules for settling disputes. The role culture can be pictured as a Greek temple where it rests its strength in its pillars, its functions and specialists. These pillars are strong in their own right (such as finance, purchasing and construction) and they are co-ordinated at the top by a narrow band of senior managers.

In the role culture, the job description is often more important than the individual who fills it and position power is the main source of power (see chapter 5). It will succeed as long as it can operate in a stable or predictable environment. If the market, the product needs or the competitive environment changes, the role culture is likely to forge straight ahead confident in its ability to shape the future in its own image. Collapse, replacement of the pediment by new management, or takeover, is then usually necessary.

Role cultures offer security and predictability to the individual. They offer a predictable rate of climb up a pillar. On the other hand, such a culture is frustrating to those who are power-oriented, who want control over their work, who are eagerly ambitious or are more interested in results than method.

The task culture

The task culture is job- or project-oriented. It seeks to bring together the appropriate resources and people at the right level of the organization, and to let them get on with it. Its accompanying structure can be pictured as a net. There is no single dominant leader; all group members concentrate on completing the collective task. A task culture will encourage flexibility in approach and is ideal for a changing environment. However, the task culture finds it hard to produce economies of scale or great depth of expertise. According to Handy (1998), you cannot organize a large factory as a flexible group. Although the technical person in the group may be clever and talented she will, by virtue of having to work on various problems in various groups, be less specialized than her counterpart in a role culture. The task culture therefore thrives where speed of reaction, integration, sensitivity and creativity are more important than depth of specialization.

Expert power is the major base for this culture, more so than position or personal power. This will utilize the unifying power of the group to improve efficiency and to identify the individual with the objective of the organization. Therefore, under normal situations, job satisfaction is high for individuals and there is much group cohesion.

However, top management control in the task culture can be difficult. When resources and people are scarce, top management has to rationalize the resources in order to control methods as well as results. Alternatively, team leaders begin to compete, using political influence, for available resources. In either case, morale in the work groups declines and the job becomes less satisfying in itself. This new state of affairs necessitates rules and procedures or an exchange of methods of influence, and the use of position or resource power by the managers to get the work done. In short, the task culture tends to change to a role or power culture when resources are limited or the total organization is unsuccessful. Therefore, it is a difficult culture to control and inherently unstable by itself.

The person culture

The person culture is one in which the individual is the central focus and any structure exists only to serve and assist the individuals within it. If a group of individuals decides that it is in their own interests to band together in order to do their own thing, share an office, a space, some equipment or even clerical and secretarial assistance, then the resulting organization would have a person culture. Its accompanying structure can be pictured as a cluster. Examples are architects' partnerships and some small consultancy firms.

Individuals with this orientation are not easy to manage. There is little influence that can be brought to bear on them. Being specialists, alternative employment is often easy to obtain, or the individuals have protected themselves by tenure so that resource power has no potency. Position power not backed up by resource power achieves nothing. They are unlikely to acknowledge expert power. Coercive power is not usually available; only personal power is left and such individuals are not easily impressed by personality.

Characteristics of culture

Beside culture being historically based, heterogeneous and partly un-conscious, there are two other key characteristics of organization culture.

(a) *Culture is dynamic in nature*. It can be stable over a period of time, but never static. Figure 7.4 shows how a particular culture can change over time. Environmental crises are usually the driving force for re-evaluating some values or set of practices. As a result, the strategy of the company will change, leading to market diversification and/or geographical expansion. In order to implement the new strategy, organization structure and the system will be newly designed or modified, resulting in people taking new positions with fresh ways of doing things. If the new company policy is proved to be successful, then it will be adopted for a long period of time and become 'cultural'. If not, then the organization needs to revisit its strategy and re-form the accompanying structure (also see Fig. 4.3 in chapter 4).

(b) *Culture is a socio-technical system with input and output process*. Williams *et al.* (1993) illustrated organizational culture within the context of the external environment, where organizations operating in different markets, technologies and legal restraints have different skill and resource needs. Variations place different demands and constraints that result in different socio-technical systems. Variations in organizational learning cause differences in culture. Strategies, procedures and behaviour adopted by the management create the work environment for other members, but the management is a product of the culture itself (see Fig. 7.5).

The best fit

The values and behaviour that become embedded in a particular organization have the tendency to generate one of the above types of culture (power, role, task or person). In certain cases, more than one culture can be noticed in a particular organization. None of these cultures is suitable to all organizations.

Modern theories of organization are increasingly persuaded of the wisdom of the appropriateness of the match of people to systems, task and environment, of the interrelations between the four, of what has

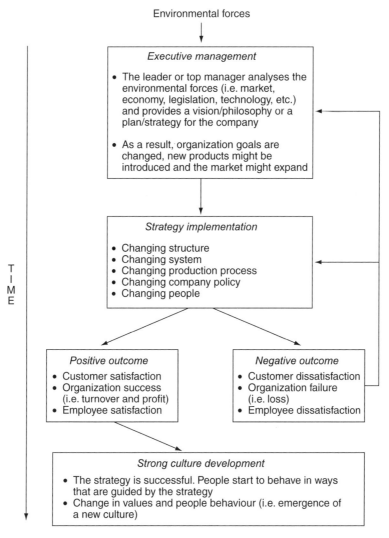

Fig. 7.4. Cultural development

come to be called the system approach to management theory. According to Handy (1998), this is a word sufficiently vague to cover all manner of specific approaches but it tends to connote interrelationships, feedback mechanisms and appropriateness of fit. The culture/structure approach to describing organizations is not really a subset of systems theory but it shares with it a concern for linkages and appropriateness. The literature contains a number of illustrations of the influence of culture on structure, particularly on the use of power, authority and bureaucracy.

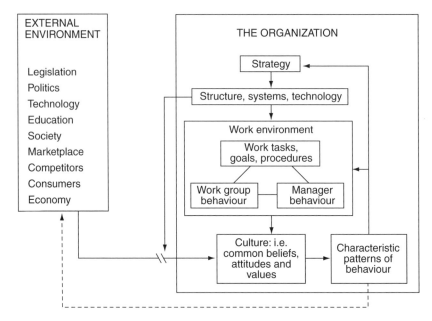

Fig. 7.5.   Culture as a socio-technical system (from Williams et al. (1993, p. 53))

Scholz (1987), in his model of strategic fit, focused on corporate culture as an important aspect of corporate strategy, in particular he argued that corporate culture is capable of solving the 'problem of strategic fit'. He considered both strategy and culture as elements of a dualistic model which provides answers to the question of how to create strategic fit. Within Scholz's model there is a typological approach to determine the specific type of culture. The three dimensions used are Ansoff (1987) on 'evolution induced culture', Deal and Kennedy (1982) on 'external induced culture' and Johns (1983) on 'internal induced culture'.

Theoretical framework of factors that contribute to a change of organizational culture

In order to develop a culture, the manager will be concerned with creating an environment which will influence the type of culture. Figure 7.6 summarizes the factors that determine organization culture under four broad headings:

- Organizational characteristics:
  - size and age
  - founders' values

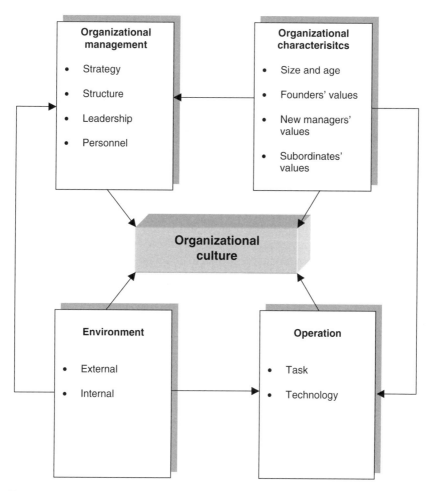

Fig. 7.6.   Factors influencing the type of culture

- ○ new managers' values
- ○ subordinates' values.
- • Management:
  - ○ strategy and structure
  - ○ leadership
  - ○ personnel management.
- • Operation:
  - ○ task
  - ○ technology.
- • Environment:
  - ○ external
  - ○ internal.

Organizational characteristics

Size

In chapter 5 the relationship between size and choice of organizational structure was discussed and the view was put forward that the size of an organization, especially in terms of the number of people employed and units produced, influences the kinds of co-ordination, direction and control reporting system and, hence the organizational structure. Where an organization is small, interaction is confined to a relatively small group and communication is simpler, less information is required for decision-making and there is less need for formal organization aspects. This phenomenon tends to form a power culture.

As organizations increase in size, problems arise with communication and co-ordination. This will push the organization toward a functional structure which shifts the power from the centre, resulting into a role culture with positional power. Further organizational growth means diversity in projects and/or areas. This will push the organization toward a matrix structure which shifts the power to the experts, resulting in a task culture.

Founders' values

Almost all organizations start with an owner who has an idea to establish a new business, perhaps with a partner. At the beginning, the founder forms a set of rules with certain values and beliefs and the founder expects that the core groups will respect and share these values and beliefs. At that stage the size of the organization is small and the owner can impose his/her beliefs on the workforce without too much difficulty.

New managers' values

As organizations grow in size, new managers will emerge or be employed. This new management system often heralds its arrival by a change of culture. The new managers have their own views concerning the method of operating, including the level of freedom and autonomy that every individual should have in their department or place of work. As a result, a new philosophy will emerge within the organization. For example 'systems instead of politics' which is equivalent to 'role replaces power'; 'efficiency not bureaucracy' which is equivalent to 'task instead of role' (Handy 1998).

McGregor (1960) argued that the style of management adopted is a function of the managers' attitudes towards human nature and behaviour at work. He put forward two assumptions, known as theory X and theory Y, which are based on popular assumptions about work and people (this is covered in chapter 5, p. 98).

Subordinates' values

As people join the organization, they bring with them their own values and beliefs which may or may not be compatible with the organization's own values. A mismatch between people and organization will result in a weak culture and consequently organization failure. There will be, however, a learning curve for new employees as they learn how things should be done within the organization. They will be told about the organization's philosophy and method of operating. Nevertheless, these new employees are bound to have strong values and beliefs concerning certain issues which are different from those of the organization and their values are very difficult to change. So long as the position of these employees stays static within the organization structure, these differences in values would not be effective. However, at a certain stage, the organization will grow and individuals will be promoted and, perhaps, become the new managers. At that stage a new culture begins to emerge.

Management

Strategy and structure

As noted earlier in chapters 5 and 6, the strategic change of most organizations is accompanied by a change in structure. Changes in an organization's structure and system will continuously or unconsciously change the culture gradually. A person's self-concept and values are in part a product of their culture, reference groups and their education and training. The formal task role can vary through a change in organization design and through a change of a person's position within the organization. Therefore, a change in the personnel of the organization, such as promotions or the appointment of a new director, or for that matter, new subordinates, will change the formal task role and, eventually, change the culture.

There is also evidence to suggest that a changing structure is likely to be a pre-condition of fostering a new culture. For example, in a study by Williams *et al.* (1993), the relationship between structure and culture was examined using four of their case studies. The following was reported.

> *In the first case, the organisation realized that it would not be possible to develop an entrepreneurial culture in the direct force while this was part of the essential bureaucratic structure of the organisation as a whole. Here, it was necessary to take the Direct Labour Organisation out of the traditional Authority structure and set it up as an independent operation in its own right. It even became necessary for the DLO to override some of the formal control mechanisms operating elsewhere in the Authority. The success of the DLO's restructuring and culture change is undoubted.*

In the second case, the company's cultural messages reflected changes in production methods and organisational structure. The company moved towards a greater 'task oriented', with less demarcation and high level of flexibility. At shopfloor level, this was achieved through a grading structure based on the range and flexibility of job skills. At more senior levels, it was achieved through a reduction in the number of management layers and the development of management teams not committed to specific functions. The 'loosening' of the traditional structure was accompanied by promotion and greater awareness of overall company values.

In the third case, the company underwent a process of decentralisation, developing management control from Head Office. Head Office became an abling rather than a controlling function. These structural changes reflected the company's overall intention of moving from paternalism towards a culture of greater initiative and interdependence.

Finally, in the fourth case, the new organisation was consciously designed as a very 'flat' hierarchy, with few management layers. The intention was that the customer should be as close as possible to senior management. This in turn reinforced the company's general culture of accountability and customer awareness.

Leadership

The issue of leadership is discussed in more detail in chapter 8. It is sufficient here to say that people have beliefs about their leaders, and their leaders' strengths and weaknesses can influence their work culture. Furthermore, they will have values and beliefs about what constitutes good leadership.

Leadership is an essential part of the process of management and it is also an integral part of the social structure and culture of the organization. If the manager is to be successful in dealing with people and influencing their behaviour and actions, this requires a leadership style which helps to foster a supportive organizational culture – a type of leadership that goes beyond profitability. For example, to what extent is emphasis placed on long-term survival or growth and development? How much attention is given to avoiding risk and uncertainties? Or how much concern is shown for broader social responsibilities? The organization must give attention to all key areas of its operation. The combination of objectives and resultant strategies will influence culture, and may itself be influenced be culture (Mullins 1999).

According to Brown (1998), effective leadership and workable organization design and development programmes must be based on sensitivity to, and understanding of, culture. Excellent leaders are not merely aware of their organization's basic assumptions, they also know how to take action to mould and refine them (see mini case in Fig. 7.7).

Personnel management

Personnel management can act as an agent for changing the culture. It can influence the culture through varied initiatives. Some of the initiatives are aimed at changing attitudes and values directly and others to changing the behaviour and values of the people. Examples of personnel initiatives are:

- recruitment
- staff training and development
- payment and reward systems
- staff appraisal
- health and safety
- employee relations.

The issue of personnel management is discussed in detail in chapter 10.

Operation

Task and technology

When the organization changes its strategy, this does not mean a change in structure only, but also in the nature of the work and hence on the people employed. As mentioned in chapter 5 (pp. 99–102), the Woodward (1965) study demonstrated that technology was an important factor in organizational change. Previous studies do not all point towards one or other of the cultures, but Handy (1998) reported the following.

(a) Routine, programmable operations are more suitable to a role culture than any of the others.

(b) High-cost, expensive technologies, where the cost of breakdown is high, tend to encourage close monitoring and supervision and require depth of expertise. Both are more appropriate in a role culture.

(c) Technologies where there are clear economies of scale by mass production of heavy capital investment tend to encourage large size and thence role cultures.

(d) Non-continuous discrete operations, the one-off job. unit production these technologies are suited to power or task cultures.

(e) Rapidly changing technologies require a task or power culture to be dealt with effectively.

(f) Tasks with a high degree of interdependence call for systematized co-ordination and suggest a role culture. In markets where co-ordination and uniformity are more important than adaptability a role culture will therefore be appropriate.

People and organizational management

In 1952, Francis Bouygues founded the famous French construction company. Noted for his determined, dynamic and plain-speaking style Bouygues was a product of the prestigious Hautes Ecoles (the French equivalent of Oxbridge, Yale and Harvard). It is, however, his proud and charismatic character rather than his educational background which is usually said to be responsible for his creation of one of the largest construction firms in the world, and which has earned him the nickname *le roi du Béton* (King Concrete).

Having borrowed the start-up capital from his father, by 1956 he was able to start creating the first of many subsidiaries, which currently include companies involved in real estate, offshore oil platforms and television. One reason for this phenomenal expansion was that during the 1950s France's industrial growth rate was 50 per cent (compared with 15 per cent in the UK) and hotels, schools, roads and hospitals – the Bouygues Group's principal concerns – were all high on the priority list. The result was not only that the organization built some of the best-known Parisian landmarks but that it grew into an 80 000 employee, worldwide conglomerate.

Accounting for Bouygues' rapid advancement, commentators have suggested that his personality, drive and characteristically French exploitation of the 'old boy network' all played a role. For example, the French Government's choice of Bouygues as the controlling stockholder when it privatized the televison station TFI in 1987 was rumoured to be an entirely political decision. Within the organization, Bouygues was described by his senior colleagues as 'despotic', 'a megalomaniac', a 'boss without scruples' and 'ruthless'. Indeed, he has been likened to a combination of Lee Iacocca, Donald Trump and Robert Maxwell. What this meant in practice was that he was firmly in control, and given to using rousing rhetoric and symbolism in order to create and sustain a vigorous corporate culture.

The development and management of culture was evidently a priority for Bouygues. In fact, all new recruits are soon subject to intensive enculturation processes, including a training programme that involves a presentation of the group's history, peppered with anecdotes from company folklore. Other channels for communicating cultural beliefs and values include a charter that expounds twelve principles (such as teamwork, quality and success), which are familiarly known by employees as the Twelve Commandments. These messages are taken up and reiterated by the numerous in-house magazines and bulletins, the largest of which, *Minorange*, is distributed to the home of every employee.

Bouygues has also sought to influence the culture of his organization in more subtle ways. Thus, managers are expected to dress stylishly (what the French call b.c.b.g. (*bon chic bon genre*)), while the $200 000 000 head office was built in the style of a modern chateau and called 'Challenger'. The company not only has its own logo but its own colour, minorange, a reddish hue, and a privileged group of elite builders created by Francis himself in 1963, called *Les Compagnons du Minorange*. This grouping has been encouraged to develop its own values, such as craftsmanship and fraternal relations, distinctive clothing, its own magazine, and a special budget for ceremonies, professional awards and initiation rituals.

It should be recalled that construction work is a predominantly male province and that the typical Bouygues manager is French, male, around 35 years old, has a baccalaureate and has been with the firm for five or more years. Interpersonal address was rather formal ('vous' being preferred to the more familiar 'tu'), and it was said that Bouygues preferred his female staff not to wear trousers. This does not mean that the organization is backward-looking in many important respects; training is better funded than in many firms, worker participation was encouraged through quality circles and unions (despite their relative weakness in France) are recognized.

With the culture of the organization firmly in place, in 1989 Francis, then 67, decided to step down in favour of his youngest son, Martin. While certain differences in style (Martin is a far quieter man, and more democratic in a collegiate sense, than his father) and strategy (Bouygues is now even more highly diversified than before) are noticeable, the question is, to what *degree* is the organization able to retain its original identify, and to what extent is this desirable?

Questions

1. What means of shaping culture did Bouygues employ?
2. Do you think that the culture of the Bouygues Group must inevitably change now that its founder and dominant leader has retired?
3. What steps can be taken to minimise the impact of the departure of a dominant leader on a culture that he or she has created?

Fig. 7.7. Mini case-study – leadership and organizational culture in the Bouygues group (cited in Brown (1998, p. 49)). Source: adapted from K. Meudell and T. Callen, 'King Concrete – an Analysis of the Bouygues Group', in Derek Adam-Smith and A. Peacock (eds) (1994)

Technological considerations do not always push in the same way. High-cost, rapidly changing technologies will leave the culture ambivalent between role and task. So will a need for swift reaction but high co-ordination. In general, however, the tendency towards increasing auto-mation and high investment in technologies of work is pushing cultures towards a role orientation.

It has to be stressed, however, that this technological move is rather limited in the construction industry when compared with the advances in manufacturing. As reported in chapter 5, the bespoke nature of construction projects means that some of research into mass and process production may not be fully applicable.

Environment

Companies try to promote a culture that can deal with a changing world, for example, when a contractor makes a certain minimum percentage of contracts come from relatively new types of clients and projects. This type of firm has a culture norm of being willing to take some level of risk to adapt to the environment and enter a new market. Other firms do not confirm this perspective, mainly because its current culture fits the environment and the environment is not changing. Thus, such firms might argue: Risk taking for what? Adaptation to what? Innovation for what? As long as a corporate culture promotes change and is not overtly political, it will be adaptive and produce good long-term economic performance.

Critics of this perspective insist that this is not sensible, and that the specific *direction* in which a strong culture aligns people or a change-promoting culture points people should make a big difference. Their argument is that a culture in which values change, for example, may be very unadaptive, because it could encourage people – even intelligent and non-political people – to change everything, or the wrong things. Similarly, a culture that values leadership may generate leadership in the wrong direction (Kotter and Heskett 1992).

Peters and Waterman (1982) in their book *In Search of Excellence* discuss 'customers' and imply that if a culture values customers strongly, and creates change to serve customers' needs, it will help make an organization adaptive. Kotter and Heskett (1992) offered a variation on this theme. They emphasized the importance of all the constituencies that support a business, especially customers, stockholders and employees. Kotter and Heskett did not state explicitly why a managerial culture needs to care about all of its key constituencies, but the implicit logic is this: only when managers care about the legitimate interests of stockholders do they strive to perform well economically over time, and in a competitive industry that is only possible when they take care of their customers, and in a competitive labour market, that is only possible when they take care of those who serve customers, i.e. employees. In other words, the relevant environment to which a management must adapt consists of its key constituencies.

Strong and weak cultures

The strength of organizational culture is often defined as the extent to which the members have 'internalized' the beliefs, attitudes and values that exist within the organization. In a cultural context, internalization is the reasoning process whereby individuals come to accept and agree with the beliefs, attitudes and values of other members. Strong cultures are characterized by dedication, spontaneity and co-operation in the service of common values. Internalization of the organization's values results in increasing 'identification'. To identify with the organization means to have a positive attitude towards it.

There is evidence to suggest that the stronger the culture the better the performance in terms of efficiency and productivity. Precisely how a strong culture leads to exceptional performance is not always spelled out by commentators, but three key elements are discernible here. Brown (1998, p. 227) identified them as follows.

(*a*) A strong organizational culture facilitates goal alignment. The idea is that because all employees share the same basic assumptions they can agree not just on what goals to pursue but also on the means by which they should be achieved. As a result employee initiative, energy and enthusiasm are all channelled in the same direction. In these organizations there are few problems of co-ordination and control, communication is quick and effective, and resources are not wasted in internal conflicts. This all means that organizational performance is likely to be healthy.

(*b*) A strong culture leads to high levels of employee motivation. There are two main arguments here. First, it has been suggested that there is something intrinsically appealing about strong cultures that encourage people to identify with them – in short, that employees like to be part of an organization with a distinctive style and ethos with its own peculiarities and idiosyncrasies, and with others who share their view on how an organization should work. Second, it is sometimes thought that strong culture organizations incorporate practices which make working for them rewarding. These practices tend to include employee participation in decision making and various recognition schemes. High levels of motivation among employees, so the argument states, translate into high organizational performance.

(c) A strong culture is better able to learn from its past. The idea is that strong cultures characteristically possess agreed norms of behaviour, integrative rituals and ceremonies, and well known stories. These reinforce consensus on the interpretation of issues and events based on past experience, provide precedents from the organization's history which help decide how to meet new challenges, and promote self-understanding and social cohesion through shared knowledge of the past. The suggestion here is that an organization which is able to reflect on its development and which is able to draw on a stock of knowledge encoded in stories, rules-of-thumb and general heuristics is likely to perform better than competitors unable to learn from their past successes and failures.

Culture and company performance

The Kotter and Heskett study

The study by Kotter and Heskett (1992) into corporate culture and the performance of large service companies between 1987 and 1991 is particularly interesting. They conducted four studies to determine whether a relationship exists between corporate culture and long-term economic performance, to clarify the nature of and the reasons for such a relationship, and to discover whether and how that relationship can be exploited to enhance a firm's performance. In particular, they were interested in the potential impact of *corporate* culture (*not* sub-unit cultures). Their first inquiry was focused on the largest ten firms in 22 different US industries. They attempted to test the most widely accepted theory linking corporate culture to long-term economic performance. In the second study, two more culture/performance theories were tested, this time by examining in more depth a small subset of 22 firms. The third study examined 20 firms that appear to have had cultures that hurt their economic performance. The last project focused on ten firms that seemed to have changed their corporate cultures within the recent past and then benefited economically.

In their study, strong culture was defined by the extent to which managers and employees share the same set of relatively consistent values and methods of doing business. Firms with a strong culture were seen as having a certain 'style' with deep roots. Company performance was measured using the firms' net income growth and the return on average investment. Their studies strongly suggest that the early corporate culture looks were very much on the right track, although they failed in some important ways – not unusual in the case of pioneering work. More specifically, their studies found the following.

(a) *Corporate culture can have a significant impact on a firm's long-term economic performance*. They found that firms with cultures that emphasized all the key managerial constituencies (customers, stockholders and employees) and encouraged leadership from managers at all levels outperformed firms that did not have those cultural traits by huge margins. Over an 11-year period, the former firms increased revenues by an average of 682% versus 166% for the latter, expanded their workforces by 282% versus 86%, grew their stock prices by 901% versus 74%, and improved their net incomes by 756% versus 1%.

(b) *Corporate culture will probably be an even more important factor in determining the success or failure of firms in the next decade*. Performance-degrading cultures have a negative financial impact for a number of reasons, the most significant being their tendency to inhibit firms from adopting necessary strategic or tactical changes. In a world that is changing at an increasing rate, one would predict that unadaptive cultures would have an even larger negative financial impact in the coming decade.

(c) *Corporate cultures that inhibit strong long-term financial performance are not rare; they develop easily, even in firms that are full of reasonable and intelligent people*. Cultures that encourage inappropriate behaviour and inhibit change to more appropriate strategies tend to emerge slowly and quietly over a period of years, usually when firms are performing well. Once these cultures exist, they can be enormously difficult to change because they are often invisible to the people involved, because they help support the existing power structure in the firm, and for many other reasons.

(d) *Although tough to change, corporate cultures can be made more performance enhancing*. Such change is complex, takes time and requires leadership, which is something quite different from even excellent management. That leadership must be guided by a realistic vision of what kinds of cultures enhance performance – a vision that is currently hard to find in either the business community or the literature on culture.

As for the cultural factors that contributed to company success, Kotter and Heskett found that leadership quality was one of the significant factors that had influenced the economic conditions of the companies they studied. They noted that cultural traits helped the firms to do well in a changing business environment. In other words, they saw a causal link from cultures that value leadership to superior company performance – an assessment that is entirely consistent with the adaptive cultures viewpoint. Evidently, those companies that developed and maintained an adaptive culture (i.e. adaptive to external environment) performed well financially. When the data were analysed, the adaptive cultures at these companies all seem to have originated around a small number of people, often just one individual. These individuals and their management teams developed strategies that fitted the business environments in which they operated, that worked well and, as a result, became embedded in the cultures of their firms. The same was seen for most, if not all, of the lower performers. What seemed to differentiate the two groups is this: in the cases of the better performers, the leaders got their managers to buy into a timeless philosophy or set of values that stressed both meeting constituency needs and leadership or some other engine for change – values that cynics would liken to motherhood, but that when followed can be very powerful. Those people and their successors then perpetuated the adaptive part of their culture (the values/philosophy part relating to constituencies and leadership) because they worked at it. Within the constraints of their methodology, Kotter and Heskett stated:

In the firms with more adaptive cultures, the cultural ideal is that managers throughout the hierarchy should provide leadership to initiate change in strategies and tactics whenever necessary to satisfy the legitimate interests of not just stockholders, or customers, or employees, but all three. In less adaptive cultures, the norm is that managers behave cautiously and politically to protect or advance themselves, their product, or their immediate work groups.

Accordingly, they constructed the following dimensions to differentiate between adaptive and unadaptive corporate cultures.

	Adaptive corporate cultures	**Unadaptive corporate cultures**
Core values	Most managers care deeply about customers, stockholders, and employees. They also strongly value people and processes that can create useful change (e.g. leadership up and down the management hierarchy)	Most managers care mainly about themselves, their immediate work group, or some product (or technology) associated with that work group. They value the orderly and risk-reducing management process much more highly than leadership initiatives

	Adaptive corporate cultures	Unadaptive corporate cultures
Common behaviour	Managers pay close attention to all their constituencies, especially customers, and initiate change when needed to serve their legitimate interests, even if that entails taking some risks	Managers tend to behave somewhat insularly, politically and bureaucratically. As a result, they do not change their strategies quickly to adjust to or take advantage of changes in their business environments

The Peters and Waterman Study

In their study of 62 American companies with outstandingly successful performance, Peters and Waterman (1982) identified eight basic attributes of excellence which are related to 'organization culture' and appear to account for success:

- a bias for action, i.e. being action-oriented and with a bias for getting things done
- close to the customer, i.e. listening and learning from the people they serve, and providing quality, service and reliability
- autonomy and entrepreneurship, i.e. innovation and risk-taking and an expected way of doing things
- productivity through people, i.e. treating members of staff as the source of quality and productivity
- hands-on, value driven approach, i.e. having well-defined basic philosophies and top management keeping in touch with the 'front lines'
- stick to the knitting, i.e. in most cases, staying close to what you know and can do well
- simple form, lean staff, i.e. simple structural forms and systems, and its top-level staff
- simultaneous loose–tight properties, i.e. operational decentralization but strong centralized control over the few, important core values.

The companies were marked, above all, by the 'intensity itself' which stemmed from their strongly held beliefs. From their research, Peters and Waterman reported that:

Any intelligent approach to organising had to encompass, and treat as interdependent, at least seven variables: structure, strategy, people, management style, systems and procedures, guiding concepts and shared values (i.e. culture), and the present and hoped-for corporate strengths or skills. We defined this idea more precisely and elaborated what came to be known as the McKinsey 7-S Framework. With a bit of stretching, cutting and fitting, we made all seven variables start with the letter S and invented a logo to go with it.

A key factor in organisational effectiveness is the successful management of change. Diagnosing and solving organisational problems involves the inter-action of a multiplicity of factors influencing an organisation's ability to change and its proper mode of change.

A common thread among the successful companies is innovation. A common characteristic of excellently managed companies is that they tend to have a flexible organisation structure. In contrast to bureaucracies, the attributes of successful, well-managed companies included open communications, infor-mality, participative decision-making and freedom of expression. The flexible nature of organisation led to a bias for quick action rather than inertia, and emphasis was placed on risk-taking and innovation.

The logo mentioned by Peters and Waterman is shown in Fig. 7.8. When looking at management excellence itself, they chose a double meaning for 'innovation':

In addition to what might normally be thought of – creative people developing marketable new product and services – ... innovative companies are especially adroit at continually responding to change of any sort in their environment.

When their environments change, innovative companies change too. As a whole culture, they innovate to meet changes in the needs of their customers, the skills of competitors, the mood of the public, forces of international trade or government regulations. The concept of innovation defined the task of the truly excellent manager or management team.

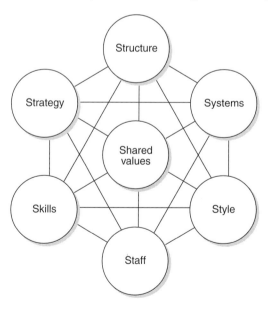

Fig. 7.8.   The McKinsey 7-S Framework (from Peters and Waterman (1982))

Companies that appeared to have attained that kind of innovative performance were the ones Peters and Waterman labelled 'excellent companies'.

Summary

The chapter deals with the concept of organizational culture. Culture is defined as the common beliefs, patterns of behaviour, norms, values and rules that are exercised among members of an organization. There are four types of culture – power, role, task and person – and each of these types should mirror the type of structure formed for the organization.

Culture has certain distinguishing characteristics. In particular, culture is dynamic in nature and can be influenced by the external environment, company strategy and the leadership style. The developed culture can be either strong or weak. The strength of culture is the extent to which the members have 'internalized' their beliefs and values that exist within the organization. It is evident that a strong culture can have a significant impact on a long-term economic performance.

References

Ansoff, I. *Corporate Strategy*. London, Penguin, 1987, revised edn.

Brown, A. *Organizational Culture*, Pitman Publishing, 1998, 2nd edn.

Deal, T. and Kennedy, A. *Corporate Culture: The Rites and Rituals of Corporate Life*. Reading, Massachusetts, Addison-Wesley, 1982.

Gowler, D., Legge, K. and Clegg, C. (Editors) *Case Studies in Organisational Behaviour and Human Resources Management*. London, Paul Chapman (part of Sage Publishing), 1998.

Handy, C. *Understanding Organizations*. London, Penguin, 1998, 5th edn.

Harrison, R. Understanding your organization's character. *Harvard Business Review*, **50**, May–June, pp. 119–128.

Johns, G. Transaction Costs, Property Rights and Organizational Culture. *Administrative Science Quarterly*, **29**, No. 3, 1983.

Kotter, J. and Heskett, J. *Corporate Culture and Performance*. London, Macmillan, 1992.

Latham, M. *Trust and Money*. London, HMSO, 1993.

McGregor, L. *The Human Side of Enterprise*. London, Penguin, 1960.

Mullins, L. *Management and Organizational Behaviour*. Boston, MA, Pitman, 1999, 5th edn.

Peters, T. and Waterman, R. *In Search of Excellence*. New York, Harper & Row, 1982.

Scholz, C. Corporate culture and strategy – the problem of strategic fit. *Long Range Planning*, **20**(4), 1987, pp. 78–87.

Watson, T. A business and its beliefs. *McKinsey Foundation Lecture*. New York, McGraw-Hill, 1963.

WILLIAMS, A., DOBSON, P. and WALTERS, M. *Changing Culture – New Organisational Approaches*. London Institute of Personnel Management, 1993, 2nd edn.

WOODWARD, J. *Industrial Organization*. Oxford University Press, 1965.

Case study. Culture change and quality improvement in British Rail (from Gowler *et al.* (1998, pp. 126–132))

Background to the case

Like many other organizations, British Rail has been trying to change its culture. There are a number of features of the kind of organization British Rail is hoping to become, but one consistent theme is the need to improve the quality of service provided to both internal and external customers. There has therefore been a major investment in programmes to improve quality. However this is only one of a number of changes underway in British Rail as it responds to market pressures and, more especially, to the government's drive for greater cost effectiveness and better quality of service.

British Rail has always been a highly centralized formal bureaucracy. This has been reflected in a complex and extensive hierarchy, considerable attention to rules and regulations and a rather rigid autocratic style of management. This does not sit easily with the typical approach to quality improvement, which emphasizes greater flexibility, considerable devolvement of responsibility to those who interact with customers and therefore encouragement of local initiative, perhaps through a sense of empowerment. If this logic is pursued, British Rail has to change both the attitudes and behaviour of its staff, long used to a hierarchical system of control, and change the system of control.

The system of control has been changing. For many years British Rail had a powerful headquarters organization, six geographical regions, a number of divisions within the regions and a number of areas within the divisions. At all levels within the organization there were a number of powerful functional hierarchies for engineering, finance, operations and personnel management. In the 1980s, this system was overlaid by a marketing structure, including, for example, InterCity and Network South-East while the divisional level was removed.

A further reorganization, completed during 1991, has moved British Rail towards a kind of holding company for a number of businesses. These businesses include Network South-East, which is responsible for almost all passenger traffic within the South East of England; InterCity, which operates main-line trains throughout the country; Regional Rail, which operates suburban and rural routes throughout the country other than the South East; and Railfreight, which is responsible for movement of goods in wagons. The reorganization, which was called 'Organizing for Quality' in an attempt to maintain a general focus on quality, reintroduced divisions instead of regions. Therefore, for example, the Southern Region has disappeared and been replaced by three divisions, known as the South-East, Central and South-West Divisions. Each divisional manager has considerable autonomy over railway operations within a defined budget.

One of the important elements of the reorganization has been the appointment of an infrastructure manager within each division. He is responsible for all aspects of engineering. This may help to bring together the previously highly autonomous groups of civil, mechanical and signals and telecommunications engineers. The importance of this is reflected in the fact that 45 per cent of operating costs are attributable to infrastructure. Equally important, the reorganization attempts to remove the traditional power bases of the regions and the functions, representing operating and professional power, and to subordinate these to the 'business' of Network South-East.

The reorganization, like those before it, has been highly disruptive, involving thousands of job changes, and has absorbed a great deal of time and energy. It is only one of a number of changes designed to make the railway more business-like in the possible lead up to privatization. Preparations for Channel Tunnel operations have provided an additional competing priority for some senior managers. The aftermath of the Clapham disaster, in which many passengers died following a signalling maintenance failure, has been more widely felt. It has necessitated a major focus on safety including tightening up of procedures and an attempt to reduce hours of overtime work, This in turn has implications for a range of human resource policies ranging from selection and training to work rostering and reward systems. In the midst of all these changes, the onset of economic recession in 1990 created additional pressures for British Rail as for many other organizations.

As noted above, the use of the term 'Organizing for Quality' reflected a deliberate attempt to give coherence and direction to the variety of changes underway within the railway. The increased attention to safety can also be fitted comfortably under the rubric of quality. Perhaps the key integrating factor, and the main pressure for quality improvement, has been the move towards greater commercialization and the recognition that, if British Rail is to sell a service in a competitive market, that service must improve in quality. Certainly that message has been picked up by its competitors, such as the airlines and the motor industry.

When the concept of quality is discussed in British Rail, it means first and foremost improving quality of service to external customers. As market research has shown, for passengers this means a clean and comfortable service running on time and operated by polite and helpful staff. However, to meet the needs of external customers, the needs of a whole host of internal customers have to be considered and additional factors, of which external customers may be only dimly aware, must also be taken into account. These include the maintenance of the infrastructure, such as track and signalling, the complex co-ordination of weekend repair work and the quality of personnel systems to monitor and control absenteeism. On a railway that has generally been starved of investment, much attention has to be paid to these 'hidden' factors before it is possible to have a major impact on quality of service as defined by external customers.

While the reorganization provides a framework within which to improve quality, the main method of obtaining quality improvements has been through training, the intention being to use training on a massive scale to change the attitudes and behaviour of staff. This was initially channelled through a centrally organized training programme known as 'Leadership 500'. This was a week-long off-the-job training course for the top 500 managers in the whole of British Rail. These courses were followed by 'Leadership 5000'. These were training programmes for the next 5000 senior and middle managers. Both courses gave some emphasis to experiential learning through analysis of relationships and problem-solving styles. In addition, 'Leadership 500' provided top management with an insight into total quality management (TQM), and explored company-wide strategies for its implementation. 'Leadership 5000' focused more on local strategies for implementing TQM and also gave more emphasis to problem-solving skills. Furthermore, the organization and implementation was delegated initially to the five British Rail regions.

The training programme for nearly 1000 Southern Region managers was virtually complete when the regions were abolished in April 1991. Responsibility for the final courses and for all subsequent quality improvement programmes passed to the businesses that, in the case of almost all managers who had worked in the Southern Region, meant Network South-East.

The organization and implementation of the quality programmes, initially in each region and subsequently in business units, was the responsibility of a team of quality managers, largely appointed from within British Rail. The training was conducted by external consultants chosen by the region and business unit. On Southern Region the officially stated aim of the course was 'to introduce into the Region both the principles and practices of Total Quality Management'. This was achieved through a series of inputs and exercises designed to inculcate an awareness of the importance of TQM and provide the competencies necessary to act to improve quality. According to the official statement, managers should leave the programme with

- a clear set of objectives in relation to TQM
- a strategic action plan that involves all employees
- the confidence and competencies to implement the plan.

It was expected that by the end of the whole programme there would be 'an observable improvement in the Quality of service provided within the Region to both Internal and External Customers'.

These courses were run on a regular basis over a period of 18 months and were completed by mid-1991. Evidence from end-of-course reactions and from subsequent follow-up discussions indicates that the training programme was highly regarded by participants. As noted above in the statement of course outcomes, course teams were expected to develop programmes to improve quality in their work areas. The course teams were led by quite senior functional managers who had already attended 'Leadership 500'. These functional managers were team leaders for their immediate subordinates in their sections. Often this meant a team of about six managers. Where there were 12 to 14 managers reporting to the same boss, as occasionally happened, they would be split into two teams. Some teams not only drew up general programmes but also identified a specific quality-improvement project. Sometimes these led to the formation of a formal quality improvement team to pursue the project when they had returned to their workplaces. Whether a specific project was actually taken up after the course seemed to depend partly on the reaction of senior management in the area and partly on the level of enthusiasm of members of the potential team.

A fairly typical example of how this was interpreted and acted upon by a course team is a small plant project. This project examined the use of small hand-held power tools, such as saws, drills and impact wrenches, by the Permanent Way Department, which is responsible for maintaining the track. Traditionally, these had been supplied to the Permanent Way Department by the Regional Engineer's Plant Section. The 'Leadership 5000' team decided to look at this customer–supplier relationship. During the course they devised a system whereby the Permanent Way Department hired the equipment directly from the external supplier, thus reducing overall plant holdings and improving service. Authority to proceed with this project was subsequently given by senior local management and a quality improvement team was set up, after the training course, to implement the plan.

While the courses were still in progress, and as part of the activity to promote quality, the quality managers on Southern Region decided to hold a quality fair. In this it was following a pattern adopted by such organizations as Rank Xerox with a well-established reputation for quality improvement. A quality fair is an exhibition at which those responsible for quality projects display the projects, usually through a combination of media and sometimes including models and demonstrations, and explain them to an invited audience. The fair may last from half a day to three days. There were several advantages in holding a quality fair. It provided an opportunity to monitor the quality improvement projects that should have emerged from the training programme. It would make managers at all levels more aware of the issue of quality – in some cases it would prick their consciences and perhaps goad them into action if they had been slow to follow up their training. The successful cases would provide models and lessons for others to emulate. It should reward, enthuse and motivate those who had undertaken successful projects by providing praise, recognition and an opportunity to explain to an interested audience what they had achieved. And finally, it was useful publicity both within British Rail and with a wider audience of the progress British Rail was making in improving quality.

The fair was held in November 1990. (It should be borne in mind that while the reorganization described earlier, which would abolish Southern Region, was in the offing, at the time of the fair Southern Region still existed and was responsible for managing the quality programme.) Thirty-five exhibits were presented, a large number of senior executives attended and the exercise was judged to be a considerable success. The exhibits ranged from those publicizing the staff-suggestion scheme (called 'On Winning Lines') and those dealing with the trackside environment, including how to make it attractive, maintain visibility and care for flora and fauna, to more technical issues of track care and rolling stock and train maintenance. The co-ordinating group of quality managers within British Rail had decided to hold a national quality fair and those attending this Southern Region fair were asked to judge which exhibits they thought were the most successful and should therefore go forward to the national fair.

The problem

As part of a wider evaluation of the impact of the quality programme, it was decided to look more closely at those projects that had been judged the most successful by those attending the fair. It was thought that some general lessons about the way in which these projects had originated and been implemented might emerge. Ten highly rated projects from six locations were selected for closer inspection. The aim was to identify how the projects originated, what outcomes had emerged in terms of discernible quality improvements and other benefits, and how the process of change and implementation was handled.

People and organizational management

There was considerable variety of project. One sought to produce a Filofax for supervisors. Another was concerned to devise new ways of dealing with graffiti. Two looked at ways of providing improved training. Another explored a specific computer link. Finally, three were concerned with the development of systems that would attract BS 5750, the British Standards quality accreditation based on the writing and monitoring of procedures to ensure quality. It is perhaps worth emphasizing that several of the projects focused on the development of processes to monitor quality rather than on substantive quality issues.

The origins of the projects

Four of the projects emerged directly from the local quality training programmes, but five had been initiated by more senior managers and one by an outside organization. This occurred despite the intention to use the quality fair to follow up the training. One partial explanation is that some of the projects ostensibly presented as follow-ups to the training were put together hurriedly when the request for participation in the fair was issued and reflected an obligation to show some sort of training follow-up rather than any deep commitment to the project.

The outcomes of the projects

All the projects were successful to the extent that they had developed solutions that had been accepted as feasible by senior management. Authorization to proceed with implementation had been given in eight of the ten projects and six had actually been implemented. All of the implemented projects were judged by senior management to be successful in improving quality. The concrete evidence to support this claim could not be provided in most cases, partly because this was the first attempt at systematic evaluation. On the other hand supervisory and junior management staff, while generally positive, were rather less enthusiastic about the outcomes, largely because the projects for which they felt particular ownership had often made little progress. They remained very positive towards the general idea of improving quality but felt let down in particular by poor communications, lack of resources and especially the lack of senior management support.

The process of change

Comparing the projects that were and were not implemented at the time of the fair, the key factor appears to be the process of authorization by senior management and the requirement for some sort of feasibility study. Three of the implemented projects entailed achievement of BS 5750 certificates for particular procedures. Although another was a very

190

specific computer link, it does appear the projects concerned with developing processes and procedures had a greater chance of success than those dealing with more concrete topics. In contrast, the four non-implemented projects have run up against delays within the bureaucracy, usually related to resource shortages and the need to determine priorities, and have fallen victim to poor communication and a lack of urgency. One, for example, has been in train for 18 months and is still at the early-trials stage.

All the non-implemented projects originated in the training pro-grammes. In contrast, the implemented projects were all devised by senior management. There appears to be a link between the source from which the project originated and the speed of authorization and implementation. It may well be that senior managers more wisely identify and select projects with a better chance of implementation. However, far and away the most highly rated project at the quality fair was one emerging from training and it is one that has not been authorized for implementation. The graffiti project originated at a 'Leadership 5000' course and was handed on to a voluntary team of staff to develop and implement. They conducted an extensive survey of all interested parties to diagnose the problem and spoke to all those who had to deal with it including police, contractors and chemical companies. They tested out for themselves various chemicals and various approaches to cleaning graffiti. They took extensive photographs and videos of the results and compiled detailed statistics and graphs. In conducting such a detailed and enthusiastic analysis, they went well beyond their brief. Presentations were made to their steering group, to their colleagues and to the general manager. Despite an apparently compelling case, reflected in support for the project at the quality fair, authorization to proceed with implementation had not been received.

Evidence from the evaluation of the projects raises some questions about the training. On the one hand it is resulting in some promising and highly rated projects; but the projects are facing difficulty in being implemented. On the other hand, quality is clearly on the managerial agenda and a number of encouraging initiatives are being undertaken. However, their chances of success, judged by implementation, are greater if they originate and are controlled and implemented within the traditional bureaucratic hierarchy.

Chapter 8

Leadership

A good leader needs to have charisma and style.

The organization is founded to perform specific tasks through people. The person who leads the organization needs to have vision and be responsible to direct, plan, control, motivate and co-ordinate between the people and the tasks of the organization. The leader needs to be decisive and a risk taker. The personal characteristics of the leader together with his/her style must be selected appropriately, depending upon the situation at hand.

Previous chapters focused on the relationship between the variables of environment, corporate strategy, organizational structure and the changing culture. The relationships between these variables are cyclic in nature and are based on an input–output principle. In other words, executive managers develop a new strategy, which in turn influences the structure and culture. A new culture will then generate new leaders and the cycle continues. This chapter tackles some key leadership questions. Who is the leader? Why is leadership necessary? Who can be leaders? Are leaders born or made? Is there a role model for leadership? Is there a technique or a style that makes effective leaders? The chapter explains the meaning of leadership and discuss the main theories of leadership. It will also present the factors that can influence the style of leadership both at organization and project level. The discussion is supplemented with examples and case studies related to construction. Figure 8.1 summarizes the overall principles of the chapter (also see Fig. 1.1).

Learning objectives

To:

- ➢ understand the nature and importance of leadership activities
- ➢ understand the difference between a leader and a manager

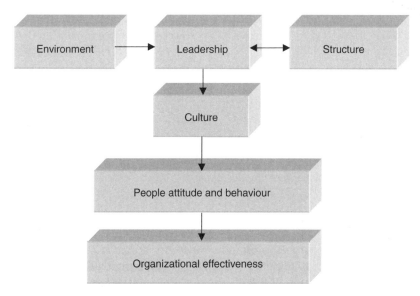

Fig. 8.1. Overall principles of chapter 8

> ➢ identify the various styles of leadership
> ➢ evaluate the main factors which are to be considered in the choice of
>   a leader
> ➢ recognize the relationship between leadership styles and organiza-
>   tional effectiveness.

The nature of leadership

The subject of leadership has been written about very widely and it is very
crucial towards achieving success (at industry, organization and project
levels). A good leader tends to have the ability to integrate people,
motivate them and get them to do things willingly. There are more specific
definitions of leadership which have been cited but most depend on the
theoretical orientation of the writer. Besides influence, leadership has
been defined in terms of group processes, personality, compliance, particular behaviours, persuasion, power, goal achievement, interaction, role
differentiation, initiation of structure, and combinations of two or more
of these. Luthans (1998, p. 380) gave the following definition:

Perhaps as good a definition as any, comes from a Fortune *article, which states:*
'When you boil it all down, contemporary leadership seems to be a matter of
aligning people toward common goals and empowering them to take the
actions needed to reach them (Sherman 1995)'.

> *A good definition of leadership is implied in hockey great Wayne Gretzky's famous quote: 'I don't go where the puck is; I go to where the puck is going to be.' But, as Bennis recently pointed out, 'the issue is not just interpreting and envisioning the future, or knowing where the puck is going to be, but being able to create the kind of meaning for people, the values that make sense to them, where there's enough trust in the system so it's going to stick.'*

Fiedler (1967) defined leadership within the context of the contingency theory. He stated:

> *Leadership depends as much on the organization as on the leader's own attributes. Except perhaps for the unusual case, it is simply not meaningful to speak of an effective leader and an ineffective leader; we can only speak of a leader who tends to be effective in one situation and ineffective in another.*

Therefore, whatever specific definition is used is not important. What is important is to interpret leadership in terms of the specific theoretical framework and to realize that leadership, however defined, does make a difference. There are three distinct theoretical bases for leadership effectiveness:

- trait theory
- style theory
- contingency theory.

The first theory considers a leader as having a set of trait or attributes which are not possessed by others. These traits are also called characteristics or qualities, such as intelligence, confidence and decisiveness. The premise of trait theory is whether a leader is born with these characteristics or is made for them. The second theory looked into the leadership style and studied whether the leader approaches the job to be done, or the people, or both. In other words, does the leader have a task-oriented style of leadership or people-oriented style of leadership or a combination of both? The third leadership theory looked into the contingency factors which determined the best type of leadership towards success. In other words, is there a best way to lead the workforce? These theories are discussed in more detail later in this chapter.

Leadership versus management

The terms 'leaders' and 'managers' are often used interchangeably, although there are fundamental differences between the two. The meaning of management was discussed in some detail in chapter 2. Briefly, management is an activity which deals with short-term problems and takes place within the internal hierarchical structure of the organization. The role of the manager is to establish clear targets, define standards, encourage staff development, undertake appraisals, analyse short-term problems and make short-term decisions.

A 'leader', on the other hand, is usually viewed as a person who has the ability and personality to direct and guide people, influence their thoughts and behaviour, motivate them and control them to work towards goals that are regarded by the group and the organization as desirable and achievable. Leadership can take place within the internal and external hierarchical structure of the organization. A leader is usually viewed as a charismatic person who is prepared to take risks and brings about long-term changes in peoples' attitudes, behaviour and culture. The following quote from Adair (1988) clarifies the difference between a leader and a manager.

Leadership is about a sense of direction. The word 'lead' comes from an Anglo-Saxon word, common to north European languages, which means a road, a way, the path of a ship. It's knowing what the next step is. Managing is a different image. It's from the Latin manus, *a hand. It's handling a sword, a ship, a horse. It tends to be closely linked with the idea of machines. Managing had its origins in the 19th century with engineers and accountants coming in to run entrepreneurial outfits. They tended to think of them as systems.*

But there are valuable ingredients in the concept of management that are not present in leadership. Managing is very strong on the idea of controlling, particularly financial control and administration. Leaders are not necessarily good at administration or managing resources.

There are other specific differences between the characteristics of a leader and a manager. For example, Bennis (1989) identified the differences shown in Table 8.1. As shown in the table, there are scientifically

Table 8.1. Some characteristics of managers versus leaders in the 21st century (from Bennis (1989, p. 7))

Manager characteristics	Leader characteristics
Administrates	Innovates
A copy	An original
Maintains	Develops
Focuses on systems and structure	Focuses on people
Relates on control	Inspires trust
Short-range view	Long-range perspective
Asks how and when	Asks what and why
Eye on the bottom line	Eye on the horizon
Imitates	Originates
Accepts the *status quo*	Challenges the *status quo*
Classic good soldier	Own person
Does things right	Does the right thing

derived differences between the characteristics of a leader and a manager, but it is also safe to say that not every manager can be a leader and not every leader can be manager.

Leadership theories

There are a number of studies and a considerable knowledge base on leadership theories. This section will review the well known classical studies on leadership which can help to link the traditional and modern theories of leadership. In general, the subject of leadership is examined in terms of three approaches:

- trait theories (also known as the characteristics or qualities approach)
- style theories (also known as the behavioural approach)
- contingency theories (also known as the situational approach)

Trait theories

Since the 1940s, a number of studies have attempted to answer the question 'what makes a good leader and who is a bad leader?' The aim of these studies sought to investigate 'whether a good leader is born or made, presuming that leadership characteristics are either inherited or learned'. The trait studies produced a variety of trait lists such as those of Byrd (1940) and Jennings (1961). Large numbers of attributes were used in these lists to describe a successful leader; the most common ones are as follows:

- *Vision*. Good leaders display an ideological vision that is congruent with the deeply held values of followers, a vision that describes a better future to which the followers have a moral right.
- *Intelligence*. Good leaders should be above average but not of genius level. They should be particularly good at solving complex and abstract problems.
- *Decisiveness*. Good leaders should have the ability to make calculated decisions and act swiftly according to the situation.
- *Confidence*. This implies that good leaders should be confident in themselves and in the ability of their followers to meet a high-performance outcome.
- *Supervision*. Good leaders should have the ability to watch and direct individuals and the group.
- *Individuality*. Individual leaders can have there own ways of doing things. It might appear weird sometimes but it helps to give the leader a degree of uniqueness which can pay off when managing people; think, for example, of Gandhi's way of living.

- *Integrity.* Good leaders having the quality of being honest and upright in their character.
- *Image building.* Outstanding leaders are self-conscious about their own image. They recognize that followers must perceive them as competent, credible and trustworthy. This image building will set the stage for effective role modelling because followers identify with the values of role models who are perceived positively.
- *Inspirational communication.* Outstanding leaders often, but not always, communicate their messages in an inspirational manner using vivid stories, slogans, symbols and ceremonies.
- *Sociability.* This refers to good leaders who have the ability of mixing with their people and have a social relationship with them.

As to the question of whether a leader is born with these characteristics or made for them, previous studies of trait theories were not consistent in their conclusions. While some writers believe that people are born with leadership qualities, other writers have stated that leadership cannot be created or promoted and cannot be taught or learned. It is safe then to say that there are certain characteristics which a good leader can learn by experience throughout his/her professional career, such as the ability to have a vision or planning an effective company strategy. These can be called interpersonal characteristics. On the other hand, there are other characteristics which a leader is born with and which are difficult (though not impossible) to learn, such as intelligence or integrity. These could be called personnel characteristics. An outstanding leader needs to have a combination of these two types of characteristics. However, the degree of need depends on the situation that he/she is dealing with at the time, such as the task and the people to be led.

Trait theories were challenged during the 1940s. The main criticisms are listed below.

(a) There has not been enough empirical evidence to prove that there is a significant relationship between trait attributes and a successful leader. Perhaps the study of Seligman (1992) into Emotional Maturity and the EQ concept was an exception. Seligman suggested that EQ may be an overlooked diminution of predicting effective leadership. High EQ leaders would seem to have empathy and graciousness as well as the uncanny ability to read a social situation (the great majority of emotional communication is non-verbal). Such characteristics may be more associated with effective leaders than are raw intelligence and technical skills.

(b) Trait theories did not take into account the situational factors that face the leader at the time he/she is leading the workforce. For example, no considerations were made of the various characteristics of the organization and its people. At project level, this means that trait theories did not take into account the type of project, its complexity and the characteristics of the tasks to be performed.

Style theories

Around the 1940s, trait theories were challenged by the style (or behavioural) theories, which hypothesize that leaders' characteristics can be considered prerequisites for becoming a leader. A leader should also have a style of leadership which distinguishes him/her from other managers and can influence the people to do the specific task willingly. The styles are usually referred to as a continuum between 'autocratic' and 'democratic' dimensions. With an autocratic leadership, the power of making a decision is placed in the centre by the leader who alone exercises this authority. In a democratic leadership system, the power is shared among members of the working group. These two extremes were then classified differently by other theorists and various terminologies were used alongside the leadership styles. Figure 8.2 shows the major studies on leadership style together with the continuum between extremes of styles.

The Ohio State leadership study

The first major challenge to trait theories came in 1945 from a study undertaken at the Ohio State University into leadership behaviour. The rationale for the Ohio study started with the premise that no satisfactory definition of leadership exists and the term leadership is often used synonymously with *good* leadership. The research team designed a leader behaviour description questionnaire to establish the independent behavioural characteristics of a leader. By the use of factor analysis,

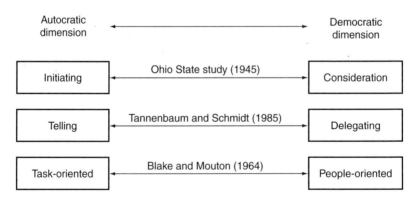

Fig. 8.2. Leadership style theories and their continuum

results of the questionnaire revealed that a leader could fall between two behavioural dimensions. One dimension was labelled an *initiating structure* because leaders in this category were more task-oriented, authoritarian in nature, and concentrated on the structuring of subordinates' roles to achieve organizational goals. The other dimension was labelled a *consideration structure* (or people-oriented) because leaders in this category were more democratic and concerned with subordinates' feelings; they showed respect for subordinates' ideas.

The Ohio study revealed an interesting correlation between a subordinate's performance and the manager's style of leadership (see Fleishman and Bass (1974)). Subordinates who were working for managers with high scores in both dimensions (i.e. highly task- and highly people-oriented) were more satisfied with their jobs and achieved a better performance than those who were working for managers with high scores in either of the two dimensions. In other words, managers scoring high in the initiating structure and low in the consideration structure lead to a decrease in job satisfaction for their subordinates. Conversely, managers scoring high in the consideration structure and low in the initiating structure give the impression of weak leadership and this results in a loss of confidence by the subordinates. Leaders should therefore maintain the right balance between the two dimensions and that balance will depend on the situation at hand. The outcome of the Ohio study fitted very well with the contingency theories which emerged in the 1940s to narrow the gap between the scientific approach and the human relations approach.

The Tannenbaum and Schmidt model of leadership

The model designed by Tannenbaum and Schmidt (1973) demonstrates a continuum of leadership styles. At the extreme left of the continuum there is a boss-centred autocratic style and at the extreme right there is a subordinates-centred democratic style. The five styles of leadership along the continuum were described as follows (see Fig. 8.3).

(a) *Tells.* This is located at the extreme left-hand side of the continuum. Managers who fall under this category identify the problem, make a decision alone, announce it to subordinates and expect them to obey. Clearly, in the tells style of leadership, the subordinates have no responsibility for decision making.

(b) *Sells.* This is located slightly away from the left-hand side of the continuum. In this case, managers make the decision on their own as in the previous style, but then make attempts to sell it to the subordinates.

(c) *Consults.* This style of leadership moves away from the selling position to a more participative approach. In this case, managers

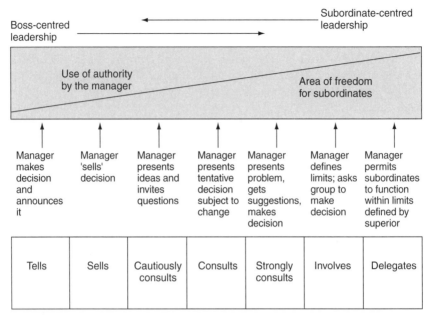

Fig. 8.3. The Tannenbaum and Schmidt (1958) continuum of leadership styles

do not make a decision without first consulting the subordinates. Here, the subordinates know that the decision rests ultimately with the leader but they have the opportunity to influence the decision.

(d) *Involves*. In this case, the manager identifies the problem and defines the limits within which the group has to decide.

(e) *Delegates*. This is located at the extreme right-hand side of the continuum. In this case the manager defines the limits as in the involves style but allows the subordinates to make and implement the decision within these limits.

The factors that determine the appropriate style of leadership are discussed later in this chapter.

The Blake and Mouton (1964) managerial/leadership grid

One of the best known works on leadership style is that by Blake and Mouton on the managerial/leadership grid which was first published in 1964, then 1985 and re-published in 1991 by Blake and McCanse. As shown in Fig. 8.4, the grid is two-dimensional with 'concern for people' on the vertical axis and 'concern for task' on the horizontal axis. The term 'concern for' does not indicate how much concern, but it refers to the

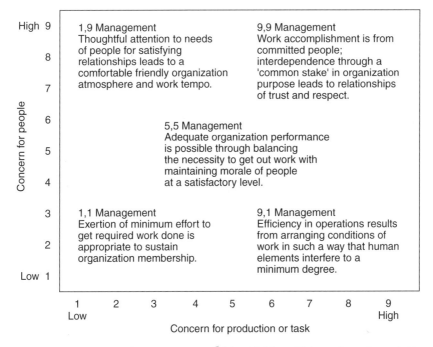

Fig. 8.4. The Blake and Mouton managerial grid (from Blake and McCanse (1991, p. 29))

character and strength of assumptions which underline the manager's own basic attitudes and style of management. The question is *how* the manager expresses concern about production or about people. Each axis is on a scale of 1–9 representing various degree of concern that the manager has for either production or for people. At the corners are the four extreme leadership positions with a middle-of-the-road position at the centre. The different types are explained more fully in the following.

- *The impoverished manager*. This is a poor leadership position, rated (1,1), with low concern for production and low concern for people. Managers and subordinates that fall in this category are lazy with minimum effort expended to achieve production in order to avoid dismissal. Poor human relations are commonplace, resulting in conflict.
- *Authority leadership*. This style is classified as a task-oriented style, rated (9,1), with a high concern for production and low concern for people. People in this category are perceived as machines in order to get the work done. Production is high but motivation is low.

- *Country club leadership*. This is a people-oriented style, rated (1,9), with a low concern for production and high concern for people. Organizations showing this type of leadership have a very comfortable working environment with little conflict among staff. Although innovation may be encouraged, managers tend to reject ideas if they are likely to affect harmony among staff.
- *Team leadership*. This style is classified as a unified system, rated (9,9), with a high concern for people and a high concern for production. Production and organization goals are achieved from an integration of task and people. In this leadership style, managers identify the problem, consult with subordinates, seek their ideas and give them freedom of action. This position will maintain interdependence and mutual trust among people.
- *Middle-of-the-road leadership*. This style, fair but firm and rated (5,5), swings between concern for production and concern for people. Under pressure, this style of leadership is likely to swing more towards a task management style but when the situation is calm and stable, the leader adopts a compromise approach.

Blake and McCanse concluded that the 9,9 (team) leadership style appears to be the best style, though there can be no universally applicable 'best style' as discovered later by research into contingency theory.

Leadership style theories came under investigation by subsequent researchers. For example, Larson *et al.* (1976) challenged the managerial grid model by pointing out that it does not provide clues as to how we may characterize leaders. Indeed, whilst the 9,9 leadership style may be the most effective in certain situations, there would appear to be little evidence to support their conclusion that this style is the most effective in all situations. Langford *et al.* (1995, p. 75) demonstrated this point in the following:

> *Imagine a resident engineer being informed that the ready-mix concrete lorries have arrived in readiness for the pouring of a structural slab in which the reinforcement fixers have only just finished their work. At this point a decision has to be made as to whether the reinforcement has been placed properly and the framework has not been disturbed by the steel fixer's operations. There is no time for a discussion with other members of the construction team, an immediate decision is needed. In this situation we might quite reasonably expect the resident engineer to become completely task-oriented (i.e. utilising a 9,1 style of leadership). When the slab is poured and the pressure is off, the selfsame engineer may well return to being more people-oriented in his approach. Whilst accepting crucial aspect of leadership is the ability to make last minute and immediate decisions, Black and McCanse (1991) argue that in this case the resident engineer (through ongoing inquiry and critique) will be able to assume the responsibilities of team members. This, however, does not remove the likelihood of short term task orientation.*

Handy (1998) provided evidence that supportive styles of leadership:

- are related to subordinate satisfaction
- are related to lower turnover and grievance rates
- result in less intergroup conflict
- are often the preferred styles of subordinates.

There are also many instances where supportive styles of leadership were found to be associated with higher producing work groups. But the following points were also noted.

(*a*) On average, over all the studies, the productivity differential has only been 15 per cent – a figure well below what some theorists would lead one to expect.

(*b*) It has been suggested that it could be more effective working that leads to (or permits) more supportive styles, i.e. the causal relationships might be the other way round than that supposed.

(*c*) Experimental studies, where the style of leadership has been deliberately manipulated as an experimental variable, have failed to reproduce the evidence on improved productivity. Out of six available studies, four report no difference in productivity between the styles, one reports the structuring style to be more effective and one reports the supportive style to be more effective.

(*d*) It has been shown that some people prefer to be directed and structured – in particular individuals with low needs for independence and in cultures where participation with the leader is not 'legitimate'.

(*e*) In repetitive or routine work, a structured style of leadership leads to higher productivity in the short term, although usually accompanied by lower morale. (It is arguable, but unproven, that this lower morale will eventually lead to reduced productivity.)

In conclusion, the research findings into leadership styles suggest that style alone is not the answer to effective leadership, nor indeed would many of its principal advocates today maintain that it was. However, there are good indications that, where the psychological contract encourages it, a supportive style of management will lead to a higher degree of contentment and to greater involvement with the work group. This is not necessarily the cause of higher productivity but it is a good base to build on. Overall effectiveness, however, is clearly dependent on more than style alone. Hence, what are called contingency theories (Handy 1998).

Contingency theories

The trait theories and the style theories discussed above fall short in establishing a significant relationship between leadership behaviour and successful performance. Neither theory takes into account the 'situational factors' which the leader is likely to face at the time. This led theorists to apply the concept of contingency theory into leadership effectiveness. Contingency theory states that there is no one best way to organize or to manage the organization. Effective management is contingent upon the purpose that the organization is seeking to fulfil and upon the nature of the tasks that have to be managed. Among the most well known studies of leadership effectiveness is that by Fiedler (1967). Other contingency models of leadership were devised by House (1971), Vroom and Yetton (1973), Hersey and Blanchard (1977) and others. These are discussed later in this chapter.

Fiedler's model

Fiedler's research presented a theory of leadership effectiveness which takes account of the leader's 'style' as well as the 'situational' factors. His theory was that the same type of leadership style or leadership behaviour will not be suitable for all situations. Fiedler made an attempt to specify in more precise terms the conditions under which one leadership style or another would be more conducive to group effectiveness. The theory thus reconciles the sometimes conflicting claims and results which would favour one style of leadership over another. Fiedler's model proposed four main variables:

- leader's style
- leader–member relations
- the task structure
- position power.

The *leader's style* was measured by developing an attitudinal scale called 'Least Preferred Co-worker' (LPC) Questionnaire. It included 16 factors and each of these factors was given a single rating of between one and eight points, with eight points indicating the most favourable rating. A detailed questionnaire was designed and sent to workers in various industries in order to express their views about their leader's characteristics. The questionnaire is shown in Fig. 8.5.

From the questionnaire responses, the LPC score was calculated as the total sum of the numerical ratings on all the items on the question list. Fiedler argued that a low LPC score indicates a task-oriented style of leadership and a high LPC score indicates a relationship-oriented style of leadership.

After identifying the leadership style from the above LPC questions, Fiedler suggested that there are three 'situational variables' which determine the leadership condition situation and which affect the leader's role and influence. These factors can either be favourable to the leader or unfavourable, as follows.

Think of the person with whom you can work least well. He may be someone you work with now, or he may be someone you knew in the past. He does not have to be the person you like least well, but should be the person with whom you had most difficulty in getting a job done. Describe this person as he appears to you.

The LPC questionnaire included the following factors.

	8	7	6	5	4	3	2	1	
Pleasant	8	7	6	5	4	3	2	1	Unpleasant
Friendly	8	7	6	5	4	3	2	1	Unfriendly
Rejecting	1	2	3	4	5	6	7	8	Unpleasant
Helpful	8	7	6	5	4	3	2	1	Frustrating
Unenthusiastic	1	2	3	4	5	6	7	8	Enthusiastic
Tense	1	2	3	4	5	6	7	8	Relaxed
Distant	1	2	3	4	5	6	7	8	Close
Cold	1	2	3	4	5	6	7	8	Warm
Co-operative	8	7	6	5	4	3	2	1	Unco-operative
Supportive	8	7	6	5	4	3	2	1	Hostile
Boring	1	2	3	4	5	6	7	8	Interesting
Quarrelsome	1	2	3	4	5	6	7	8	Harmonious
Self-assured	8	7	6	5	4	3	2	1	Hesitant
Efficient	8	7	6	5	4	3	2	1	Inefficient
Gloomy	1	2	3	4	5	6	7	8	Cheerful
Open	8	7	6	5	4	3	2	1	Guarded

Fig. 8.5. Fiedler's Least Preferred Co-worker (LPC) questionnaire

- *Leader–member relations* are measured by the degree to which the leader is trusted and liked by group members, and their willingness to follow the leader's guidance.
- *The task structure* is measured by the degree to which the task is clearly defined for the group and the extent to which it can be carried out by detailed instructions or standard procedures.
- *Position power* is measured by the power of the leader through which he can exercise authority and influence. Particularly, this is related to hiring and firing, promotion and demotion, disciplinary matters, etc.

Based on these three situational variables, Fiedler constructed eight combinations of group–task situations through which to relate leadership style. The results are summarized below and in Table 8.2.

Table 8.2.   *Results of Fiedler's leadership effectiveness study (from Fiedler (1967))*

	I	II	III	IV
Leader–member relations	Good	Good	Good	Good
Task structure	Structured	Structured	Unstructured	Unstructured
Position power	Strong	Weak	Strong	Weak
Effective leader's style	Task-oriented	Task-oriented	Task-oriented	Relations-oriented
	V	VI	VII	VIII
Leader–member relations	Poor	Poor	Poor	Poor
Task structure	Structured	Structured	Unstructured	Unstructured
Position power	Strong	Weak	Strong	Weak
Effective leader's style	Relations-oriented	Relations-oriented	Either	Task-oriented

(a) *A task-oriented leadership style* works best when the situation is either very favourable or very unfavourable to the leader. For example, when there are good leader–member relations and a well structured task with a strong position power, then a task-oriented style of leadership can be most effective. This type of leadership style is also known as a 'structuring' or 'directive' approach.

(b) *A relations-oriented style* works best when there is a mix of situational variables that are moderately favourable to the leader. For example, when there are good leader–member relations coupled with an unclear task and a weak position, then a relations-oriented style of leadership can be most effective. This style of leadership is also known as a 'participative', 'supporting' or 'consideration' approach.

Fiedler's approach to leadership effectiveness was undoubtedly very original and in particular it draws attention to the concept of the contingency theory for leadership effectiveness. However, his research was criticized on the ground that the situational variables were limited and the model was tested only on a limited group of industries.

Vroom and Yetton model

Vroom and Yetton developed a decision tree model which included five styles of leadership (called management decision styles) that needed to match seven situations (called decision rules). Mullins (1999) summarized the five main management decision styles as follows.

- *Autocratic*
  A.I   Leader solves the problem or makes the decision alone using information available at the time.
  A.II Leader obtains information from subordinates but then decides on solution alone.
- *Consultative*
  C.I   The problem is shared with relevant subordinates, individually. The leader then makes the decision which may or may not reflect the influence of subordinates.
  C.II The problem is shared with subordinates as a group. The leader then makes the decision which may or may not reflect the influence of subordinates.
- *Group*
  G.I   The problem is shared with subordinates as a group. The leader acts as chairperson, rather than an advocate. Together the leader and subordinates generate and evaluate alternatives and attempt to reach group consensus on a solution.

The seven questions, which could be set out like a decision tree, are shown below. The first three rules protect the quality of decisions. The last four rules protect the acceptance of decisions.

(a) Is there a quality requirement such that one solution is likely to be more rational than another?
(b) Is there sufficient information to make a high-quality decision?
(c) Is the problem structured?
(d) Is acceptance of the decision by subordinates critical to effective implementation?
(e) If you were to make the decision yourself is it reasonably certain that it would be accepted by subordinates?
(f) Do subordinates share the organizational goals to be obtained in solving the problem?
(g) Is conflict among subordinates likely in preferred solutions?

These rules indicate decision styles that the manager should avoid in a given situation and indicate the use of others. Decision tree charts can be produced to help in the application of the rules and to relate the situation to the appropriate leadership style.

House's model

House (1971) developed and tested a model that linked (1) leadership style, (2) subordinates' perceptions and motivations and (3) organization outcomes. In his model, the situational variables were (1) subordinates' characteristics and (2) environmental forces.

House identified four leadership styles, namely directive, supportive, participative, and achievement-oriented. He tested the model on a sample of 19 large organizations and his research concluded the following.

(a) From studies of seven organizations, it was found that directive leaders (i.e. those who give clear guidance) are (i) positively related to the satisfaction and expectations of subordinates engaged in ambiguous tasks and (ii) negatively related to satisfaction and expectations of subordinates engaged in clearly defined tasks.
(b) From studies of ten other samples of employees, it was found that supportive leaders (i.e. those who are friendly and express concern for people's needs), will positively affect the satisfaction of subordinates who work on stressful, frustrating or dissatisfying tasks.
(c) From a major study of a large manufacturing organization, it was found that participative leaders (i.e. those who ask for suggestions from subordinates) can make employees more satisfied if they are working on non-repetitive, ego-involving tasks.

(*d*) From a study of three separate organizations, it was found that for subordinates performing ambiguous, non-repetitive tasks, the higher the achievement-orientation of the leader, the more subordinates were confident that their efforts would pay off in effective performance. An achievement-oriented leader was defined as one who gets the subordinates to accept full responsibility for their work and sets challenging goals for them.

Hersey and Blanchard model

Another contingency model of appropriate leader behaviour was developed by Hersey and Blanchard (1977) who based their theory on the maturity of followers. The model of this approach also identified the two typical dimensions of leadership behaviour – task behaviour and relationship behaviour. Hersey and Blanchard suggest that there are four combinations of task and relationship behaviour which determine the style of leadership; these are as follows.

(*a*) *Telling*. This position suggests that if a follower is unable and lacking willingness to perform the task, a leader should be task-oriented and guide their behaviour. In other words, the leader should provide specific instructions and closely supervise performance.

(*b*) *Selling*. This position suggests that if a follower is unable but willing to perform the task, a leader should sell ideas by being high in task behaviour *and* high in relationship behaviour. In other words, the leader should explain decisions and provide opportunities for clarification.

(*c*) *Participating*. This position suggests that if a follower is able but unwilling to perform the task, a leader should encourage participation by being high in relationship and low in task. In other words, the leader should share ideas and facilitate in making decisions.

(*d*) *Delegating*. This position suggests that if a follower is both able and willing to perform the task, a leader should be delegate the work by being low in task and low in relationship. In order words, the leader should turn over responsibilities for decisions and implementation.

These four basic positions of leadership correspond very closely with the continuum model of Tannenbaum and Schmidt shown in Fig. 8.3. The validity of the contingency models of leadership styles depends on other factors such as the complexity of human motivation, work groups and other organizational contexts. An outstanding leader is one who has tolerance and the conceptual ability to cope with a multi-dimensional situation.

Conceptual model of leadership effectiveness in organizations

This section summarizes the variables that are associated with leadership styles and which dictate the success of an organization. Considerations of these variables and their causal relationships are crucial areas for research in the construction industry and a conceptual model, such as that shown in Fig. 8.6, would be useful for predicting the efficiency and success of various leadership styles in construction. The following seven variables are parameters in the conceptual model.

(*a*) Operation characteristics:
    (i)   nature and complexity of task
    (ii) technology involved.
(*b*) Subordinates characteristics:
    (i)   personality
    (ii) ability and willingness
    (iii) group development and maturity.
(*c*) Organizational variables:
    (i)   size and structure
    (ii) strategic control.
(*d*) Leadership style:
    (i)   directive versus supportive
    (ii) structured versus unstructured
    (iii) initiating versus consideration
    (iv) task oriented versus people-oriented.
(*e*) Motivation:
    (i)   morale
    (ii) job satisfaction.
(*f*) Culture:
    (i)   norms
    (ii) internal environment.
(*g*) Effectiveness:
    (i)   productivity/efficiency
    (ii) profit
    (iii) growth.

As shown in Fig. 8.6, the model is designed in a systematic way with the contingency theory in mind. The variable characteristics of the operation and its subordinates are seen as primary independent variables (i.e. the inputs). To operate the model one would start with an assessment of the characteristics of these two variables. In response to this, the next intervening variable of organizational control and leadership style (i.e. the process) is selected in order to achieve the needs of the subordinates

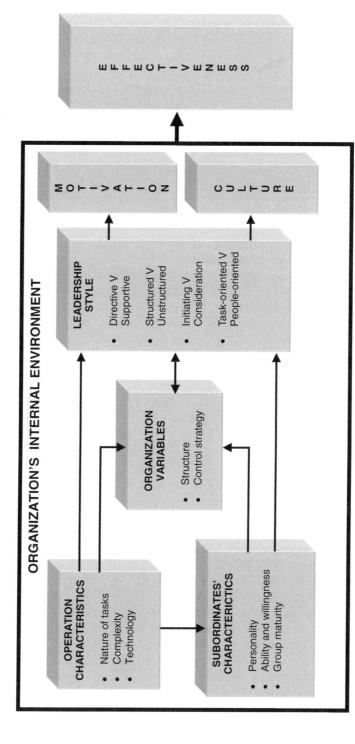

Fig. 8.6. Leadership model of organizational effectiveness

and to create a strong culture and highly motivated employees: the object being to achieve optimum results on the seven dependent variables of effectiveness. These seven variables, including effectiveness, are all subject to the influence of the environment (internal and external).

It should be noted that there is a two-way arrow from the organization variable variable to the leadership style variable in Fig. 8.6. This indicates that the process of leadership is dynamic in nature and, at a particular stage of organization/project development, the chosen leader might decide to change the goals and determine a new strategy and management structure.

Operation characteristics

Nature of task

Leadership style can be determined by the nature of the task, i.e. is the extent to which it is routine and structured, or non-routine and unstructured. For example, when a task is highly structured, the objectives are clear and the subordinates are able and confident to perform the task, attempts by the leader to further explain the task or to provide specific instructions are likely to be viewed as unacceptable behaviour. Therefore, this situation requires a 'delegating' leadership style. On the other hand, when a task is highly unstructured, the objectives are not clear and subordinates are inexperienced, then a more directive style of leadership behaviour is likely to be welcomed and more appropriate – this situation requires a 'telling' style of leadership.

Technology

The increasing use of technology in the construction industry has meant that leadership characteristics and style need to fit the situation. The Kuala Lumpur City Centre project is a good example of technologically complex projects where a participative style of leadership was exercised in a highly technologically complex project. This project marked a process of technology transfer on an unprecedented scale, with many Malaysian companies working alongside overseas partners, whether product manufacturers or consultants. Malaysian project managers trained on the job under the supervision of Bovis subsidiary, Lehrer McGovern (Malaysia), whose managers worked alongside their Malaysian equivalents. Watch, listen, learn – and they did, before being assigned other parts of the project to manage under their own steam. As training was part and parcel of the process, the level of supervision on site worked out at about one supervisor for every six workers, compared with a ratio of one to ten or more in Western construction.

Working alongside overseas advisors, the Malaysian management was very much in charge, able to assert the cultural courtesies and traditions associated with their way of working, yet embracing Western influences, such as site safety procedures and contract bids based on drawings and specifications, rather than a full bill of quantities. One aspect of the local management culture is that decisions are rarely left to any one person, but involve committees and organizational hierarchies. Slow? Maybe, but the Malaysian philosophy focuses very much on taking decisions based on the best possible sources of opinion and expertise (i.e. a participative leadership style).

Subordinates' characteristics

The characteristics of the people working on the task are very important in deciding what type of leadership is practicable and appropriate for them. Characteristics of subordinates are continuously changing either because of changes in the task or movement of people in and out of the group. Some of the important characteristics of subordinates and groups are as follows.

- *Ability and competence*. How much direction and control is needed from the leader? Highly able and competent subordinates need more freedom at their work but they also require high control.
- *Knowledge and experience*. How experienced are the subordinates to deal with the problem? Experienced subordinates are more likely to need a 'structuring' style of leadership than inexperienced ones. For example, professionals such as engineers may have so much experience, ability and training that they do not need task-oriented leadership to perform well and be satisfied.
- *Tolerance*. What is the degree of tolerance for ambiguity or what is their need for structure?
- *Culture*. How are subordinates used to doing things? Are subordinates used to being involved in decision making? How fragile are they to accepting changes by the leader?
- *Maturity and responsibility*. How ready are the subordinates to assume responsibilities? Highly matured and responsible subordinates tend to allow greater freedom of action by the leader. With immature subordinates, a structured, task-oriented style of leadership tends to be more appropriate.

Organizational variables

Size and structure

In chapter 5 the view was put forward that the size of organization is a crucial factor in influencing the structure, which in turn affects the style of leadership. Large organizations tend to be more formal and to develop specialized groups that require systematic co-ordination. This formalization will facilitate both an increase in delegation and a reduction in close supervision, pushing the organization towards a task-oriented style of leadership.

As organizations grow in size and as their operational complexity develops with diversification and technological advance, a heavily centralized approach to control becomes increasingly difficult to sustain. The sheer size and diversity of many large organizations today, and their consequently attenuated lines of communication, enforce a degree of decentralization in which control parameters are established with some reference to objectives and/or operating standards generated in sub-units such as divisions. In large, complex organizations, top managers do not have the time to be immersed in details since, as the leaders of prominent organizations, they will find many external demands on their time. In the development of an organization, a combination of factors will move their management away from personal centralized control towards bureaucratic control and output control (Child 1984).

Heron and Friesen (1976) examined the relative use of three structural control dimensions over a period of college growth and development. The three structural control dimensions were identified as being centralization–delegation, formalization–informality and the degree of supervisory emphasis. They found that as the colleges grew in size:

(*a*)   their degree of formalization increased fairly steadily
(*b*)   their degree of delegation increased overall, but was reduced for a while during growth
(*c*)   their 'supervisory emphasis' (low first-line supervisory span of control and high percentage of managers to total employees) at first rose in step with delegation and subsequently tended to fall.

These relationships point to a number of tentative conclusions. First, the difference between small–young and larger–older organizations was marked. The small–young organization tended to be highly centralized, to have little formalization and not a great amount of close supervision. As growth proceeded, delegation increased, but this was accompanied by a rise in close supervision and, after a while, by a rise in formalization. Then a crisis of *control* appears to have been reached in which formalization was increased sharply, delegation decreased, but supervisory emphasis declined.

Strategic control

Another important organizational factor that has an impact on leadership style is the way in which subordinates are brought into the decision making process. If, as a result of a new strategy and structure, high executives in an organization decide that they need to change the way for subordinates to get involved in decision making, this information will probably permeate through the organization quickly, and also act as a guide for subordinate managers in choosing their own immediate leadership style. In previous sections, it was reported that there is a continuum where at one end the leader makes all the decisions, announces them to subordinates, and tells them to execute their portions of these decisions. At the other end of the continuum is the condition where the leader points to a situation and allows the subordinates to define the problem and develop and adopt their own solutions. Needless to say, there are many points between these extremes, involving a partial involvement of the subordinates in the decision making activities.

A possible outcome will be that the leadership practices within the organization will probably tend to be homogenous. True, there will be individual variations but, taken as a whole, we cannot but be impressed with the uniformity of leadership practices usually found within organizations. Thus, we can see that even within the range of factors that would normally expect the leader to control, in regard to the needs of subordinates the leader does not act as a completely free agent. Rather, many of the decisions will be guided or moulded by general properties of the organization in which the leader finds himself/herself. Hence leadership quite properly has to be considered primarily as an organizational matter (Litterer 1967).

Child (1984) identified four strategies of control in organizations: (1) personal centralization; (2) bureaucratic; (3) output and (4) cultural control. These four strategies can have an impact on the style of leadership for the organization. The four strategies of control and their more common constituents are described below.

(a) *Personal centralized control.* This approach is often found in the small owner-managed enterprise. It is also a form of control which used to be associated very much with the internal subcontractor in building and civil engineering, the 'butty' in coalmining, and comparable arrangements in engineering and iron and steel making. From the perspective of top management, however, internal subcontracting is a form of output control. The fundamental characteristics of personal centralized control are:
   (i)   centralized decision taking
   (ii) direct supervision
   (iii) personal leadership – founded upon ownership or charisma, or technical expertise
   (iv) reward and punishment to reinforce conformity to personal authority.

215

(b) *Bureaucratic control strategy.* This approach is familiar in public service organizations and in many larger organizations of all types. Its rationale is an attempt to ensure predictability through the specification of how people in the organization shall behave and carry out their work. For instance, formal job descriptions and procedures are introduced, tasks are broken down into constituent tasks and standard methods for the performance of each task are specified. A bureaucratic control strategy permits delegation of routine decision making within formal limits. The fundamental characteristics of the bureaucratic approach are:

(i) the breaking down of tasks into easily definable elements
(ii) formally specified methods, procedures and rules applied to the conduct of tasks
(iii) budgetary and standard cost-variance accounting controls
(iv) technology designed to limit variation in the conduction of tasks, pace, sequence and possibly physical methods
(v) routine decision taking delegated within prescribed limits
(vi) reward and punishment systems to reinforce conformity to rules.

(c) *Output control strategy* depends upon having the ability to identify tasks which are complete in themselves in the sense of having a measurable output or criterion of overall achievement. Output in this sense does not have to be an end-product – it could be a piece-part manufactured to agreed standards, a batch production or a sub-assembly. Once outputs or criteria for overall achievement have been identified, it is possible for management to specify output standards and targets. The fundamental characteristics of output control strategy are:

(i) jobs and units designed to be responsible for complete outputs
(ii) specification of output standards and targets
(iii) use of 'responsibility accounting' systems
(iv) delegation of decisions on operational matters: semi-autonomy
(v) reward and punishment linked to attainment of output target procedures.

(d) *Cultural control strategy.* This approach is exercised by organizations which offer professional services and are heavily staffed by professional people. The rationale of this strategy is very much one of maintaining control by ensuring that members of the organization accept as legitimate, and willingly comply with, managerial requirements. A strong professional identification is one example. As with an output control strategy, subordinates who are subject to an effective cultural control can be given considerable freedom to decide on how to go about their work, assuming that they possess the necessary skills and abilities. The difference is that there is not necessarily any reliable or valid way of assessing the quality of their output, at least in the short term. The fundamental characteristics of the cultural control approach are:

(i)   development of strong identification with management goals
(ii) semi-autonomous working: few formal controls
(iii) strong emphasis on selection, training and development of personnel
(iv) rewards oriented towards security of tenure and career progression.

Leadership style versus culture

In chapter 7 the view was put forward that the choice of leadership style and the issue of culture (at industry, organizational and project level) is crucial towards effectiveness. Culture can affect the style of leadership and the leader can influence the culture in the workplace. Hestbaek (1995) suggests that the gaining of a better understanding of how industries differ, would help managers in all industries to decide on how best to manage organizational culture, power within cultures and in the designing of structures that are likely to be most successful in their particular industry. If the leader is a great person, then inspiring ideas will permeate the corporation's culture. If the leader is mundane, then the guiding beliefs may well be uninspired. Strong beliefs make for strong cultures. The clearer the leader is about what he/she stands for, the more apparent will be the culture of that company (Davis 1984).

Research studies have repeatedly demonstrated that the absence of top leadership support for a project is often a key factor in that project's ultimate failure. The successful management of culture also requires the backing of top managers, especially the most senior executive in any organization. New leadership brings with it new ideas, recipes for success, visions for the future and experience. Allen and Kraft (1987) claimed that 'the very definition of successful leadership is the ability to bring about sustained culture change'. The leader of an organization establishes a sense of crisis or need for change, and then creates a new direction for the firm based on a philosophy and contextually appropriate business strategies. Indeed, results of the case studies by Kotter and Heskett (1992) into corporate culture and performance have shown that leaders who provide effective leadership through communication with their people and by motivating others to implement the vision and strategy, lead firms with a high level of performance. This in turn influences the values and behaviour of the firm's employees.

Leadership style versus subordinates' motivation

Chapter 6 emphasized the importance of work groups in relation to company performance. An important ingredient in achieving good performance is the style of leadership in motivating subordinates. The issue of motivation will be discussed in detail in chapter 9. However, here it is essential to quote the well known study by Likert (1961) into managerial/leadership effectiveness:

> *As the importance of group influence has been recognised and as more precise measurements have been obtained, there is increasing evidence which points to the power of group influences upon the functioning of organisations. In those situations where the management has recognised the power of group motiva-tional forces and has used the kind of leadership required to develop and focus these motivational forces on achieving the organisational objectives, the performance of the organisation tends to be appreciably above the average by other methods of leadership and management. Membership of groups which have common goals to which they are strongly committed, high peer-group loyalty, favourable attitudes between superiors and subordinates, and a high level of skill in interaction clearly can achieve far more than the same people acting as a mere assemblage.*

Leadership effectiveness of construction projects

Figure 8.6 showed that the variables of client characteristics and project characteristics are primary independent variables (i.e. the inputs) to the building process. Based on these two characteristics, the intervening variable of contractual arrangement influences the next intervening variable of leadership style (i.e. the process): the objective being to achieve optimum results in the dependent variable of project per-formance. These variables, including effectiveness, are all subject to the influence of the project and organization environments. There are four fundamental factors which can have an impact on the leadership style in construction projects:

(*a*) client characteristics
(*b*) project characteristics
(*c*) contractual arrangement
(*d*) stage of contract.

Client characteristics

The characteristics of the client organization differ with respect of the type of business, its size and the experience that the client has of the construction industry. This will generate different expectations and criteria for achieving satisfaction with respect to time, cost and quality and consequently influence the selection of the contractor type. For instance, property developers and commercial clients are likely to place great emphasis upon speed of construction because of the necessity to borrow money. Yet the quality will be equally important as the building cannot be sold or let if the quality is not appropriate to the market. For a factory, a successful outcome might be completion of the building on time in order to commence scheduled production needs. In contrast, the public sector client, because of public accountability, is likely to focus upon cost prediction and will be more concerned about the level of certainty associated with the tender sum.

Evidently, these variables, together with the organizational structure of the client in terms of the nature of the decision making process, will influence the client's selection of the contractual arrangement for the project and subsequently affect the type of leadership expected on site. The issue of contractual arrangement/procurement method is discussed below. It refers to the ways in which the building teams are related to one another to deliver the project, with specific attention to the proportion of subcontracting against direct labour employed by the contractor.

Project characteristics

Building projects also vary in their type (commercial, industrial, housing, etc.), size of project, nature of task, level of constructional complexity and technology. Large capital projects coupled with high complexity can require a wide range of services and expertise. These features can impress a greater managerial pressure upon the design and construction teams and can require different styles of leadership in order to optimize success in the building of the project. Moreover, large and complex projects are expected to take longer to build than small and simple projects, and a participative style of leadership with bureaucratic organization is expected to be more appropriate than a directive style.

A study of leader orientation of construction site managers was carried out by Bresnen *et al.* (1986). Their work studied 43 site managers in England and Wales, taking Fiedler's contingency model as the point of departure. The main questions and findings were as follows.

Research questions

(*a*) What is the range of patterns of observable leader behaviour found among site managers, and is this affected in any way either by the characteristics of the individuals concerned, or by the characteristics of the situation in which they operate?

(*b*)   To what extent, and in what ways, do site managers' approaches to managing work on site have implications for performance?

(*c*)   To what extent do the characteristics of the situation facing site managers influence or moderate the approaches that they adopt and their effects?

The main findings of the research related to project size and duration

(*a*)   Performance, particularly on projects of more extensive duration and greater size, allows site managers an opportunity to broaden their focus away from the immediate concerns of the task in hand and to turn their attention towards the development of relationships on site. This indeed would be consistent with the central finding that better performing contracts are more likely to have site managers with a stronger relationship-orientation. However, caution must be taken here as the project situation changes throughout the duration of the contract and project leaders must change course accordingly.

(*b*)   The orientation of site managers does appear to have implications for performance but this is critically dependent upon certain key characteristics of the situation in which they are operating, namely project size, project duration and characteristics of the labour force employed on site. On small, shorter, and mainly sub-contract projects, variability in site managers' orientations appears to have little effect; on larger, longer, and mainly direct labour sites, variability in site managers' orientations appears to be more critical.

(*c*)   The findings have suggested that the degree of transience or temporaries of project cycles may have a bearing upon an understanding of leadership in construction and its effects. Only on longer duration projects was an orientation towards the development and maintenance of interpersonal relationships found to be significantly associated with performance levels achieved. On shorter projects, no such association was found. More extended accounts given by construction managers support this interpretation. For instance:

> *You get different styles of management. I think in a fast job, when there's no room for messing about, you get a much more directive style of management. I think if you get time on the job, it's a much more consultative style of management, you are more willing to get blokes in to sort the thing out, be together, you've got time for a joint approach.*

It may therefore be the case that the more immediate pressure stemming from the need to respond to short-term project objectives coupled with the shorter time horizon for the development of stable working relationships among members of the site team, may constrain the options that site management have in developing interpersonal relationships on site, and make such an approach less critical to performance.

(*d*) The impact of leadership becomes more critical on larger projects, and performance on such projects is enhanced by site management being more relationship-oriented in their dealings on site. However, it should be noted that the results allow for no such conclusions with respect to smaller contracts; in such situations leader orientation appears to have no association with performance. The conclusion to be drawn here is that caution should be exercised in extrapolating findings derived from studies of large projects to smaller ones within the industry.

Leadership style on construction sites is also determined by the nature of the task in terms of repetitiveness and the technology involved in operating the tasks. Non-routine and unstructured tasks with unclear goals and objectives require a more directive style of leadership (tight) than structured and routine tasks.

The impact of task on leadership styles in construction was researched by Quinnless (1986). In his study, Quinnless compared Handy's best fit model on design and construction teams which suggests that, in any situation that confronts a leader, there are four sets of influencing factors that he or she must take into consideration:

- the leader
- the subordinates
- the task
- the environment.

Quinnless administrated a questionnaire for 10 architects practices, 12 construction firms and 7 local authority teams. The research sample was categorized by 14 design team organizations and 19 construction managers. His two hypotheses were:

a relatively structured task like construction will exhibit a structured type of leadership with subordinates who prefer structured leadership, and an organization environment which is mechanistic in nature.

While a relatively unstructured task like design work will have a participate style of leadership, subordinates who prefer the participative approach and an organization environment which is organic in nature.

The results of Quinnless supported the above two hypotheses in that construction managers tend to achieve a best fit nearer the tight (structured) end of the scale, while design team leaders tend to achieve a best fit nearer the flexible (unstructured) end of the scale. However, his results also produced some other interesting findings. In particular, task-oriented construction managers worked best with independent mature sub-ordinates; and the organization environment appeared to be 'organic' rather than 'mechanistic', as predicted.

Contractual arrangement/procurement method

The contractual arrangement for procuring the project is another factor that can have an impact on the leadership style of projects. After the client organization establishes its needs and priorities, and identifies the characteristics of the project (usually with a professional), it will then decide on a suitable method to procure the building. Among the most popular procurement methods are:

- traditional contracting
- management contracting/construction management
- design and build
- project management.

The extensive use of sub-contracting by main contractors has become the norm in the majority of contracts. This indeed suggests a different role for site management, an emphasis rather more upon the planning organization, and co-ordination of work undertaken by contracted personnel, than upon the traditional 'man-management' associated with work on site, i.e. the directive or initiating aspects of leader behaviour. The main issue that concerns the relationship between procurement method and leadership style is the proportion of sub-contracting against direct labour employment on project sites. The results of Bresnen *et al.* (1986) indicated that:

> *leader orientation is important only in those situations in which members of the site team are largely directly employed, and consequently where relationships are more direct and continuous. Where subcontract labour forms the bulk of the workforce, it appears that variability in leader orientation has little effect. Naturally, where subcontract labour is employed, it is employed indirectly via contracts with firms of subcontractors or labour-only gangs. Individual links with those supervising work on site on behalf of the main contractor are less direct and are based fundamentally upon a contractual exchange between organisations or gangs, as opposed to an internal, hierarchical chain of command. In such circumstances, 'man management' may become less relevant to the site manager (it being displaced onto the subcontractor) and the emphasis be placed upon more instrumental, task-oriented forms of leader behaviour. One site manager commented on the difference between the management of direct and subcontract labour:*

'With the subcontractors, you've got to adopt a fairly hard line and be seen to adopt that line, and be seen to stick to that line. With direct labour ... especially on quality control, you can let it slip a bit, you can also foresee a problem much quicker and put it right before it happens.

On the question of familiarity with subcontractors, one site manager commented:

'We've got some 'tame' subcontractors that we use on all our sites, so you know the people before they come here, and that's a great help. You know the style and, hopefully, you know what sort of work they did on the last job, and they are almost direct labour in that instance. But then our main mechanical contractor here, we've never worked with him before. In that respect you've got to just keep it going straight down the program line.'

Stage of contract

Different styles of leadership can also be more appropriate at different stages in the development of a project. For example, a project manager may need to adopt different styles of managerial leadership, such as the innovator, the commander or the housekeeper, at various stages of the contract:

- *The initiator (pre-construction stage).* As a new venture develops into a project, it needs an innovator to initiate and define the project for the client. The initiating leader (an architect or a project manager) must be able to drive a group of professionals and engineers to put the project pieces together, provide a wide range of management skills, and have the authority and power to deal with a range of different matters. At this stage, project aims and objectives are not clear and the leader needs to adopt a 'task-oriented' style of leadership with a centralized decision making structure.
- *The commander (construction stage).* As the project enters its realization stage the project manager needs to create a friendly atmosphere, develop supportive team and have leadership qualities to be able to accomplish tasks though people. At the early stages of construction, the project is defined and the leader needs to control the people through a 'people-oriented' style of leadership.
- *The housekeeper.* As the project progresses, the leader has to keep his/ her hand on the pulse in order to ensure the efficient and productive running of the project. When the project faces obstacles, then the leader needs to adopt a 'task-oriented' style of leadership. When the problem is smoothed out, then the leader needs to turn back to a 'people-oriented' style of leadership.

Leaders may thus have to switch from one style of leadership to another or combine elements of different styles until the right balance between concern for tasks and concern for people is reached.

Summary

This chapter deals with the issue of leadership. The term 'leader' is usually used interchangeably with the term 'manager'. Although there is a close relationship between these two terms, they are different in their context. A leader is viewed as a person with long-term vision, who has the ability and personality to direct and guide people, influence their thoughts and behaviour, motivate them and control them to work towards goals willingly. The role of the manager, on the other hand, is to establish clear targets, define standards, encourage staff development, undertake appraisals, analyse short-term problems and make short-term decisions.

There are three main leadership theories – trait, style and contingency. Trait theory deals with the characteristics and quality of the leader, such as intelligence, integrity and decisiveness. Style theory deals with a continuum between two leadership orientations: a task-oriented or a people-oriented leadership style and a democratic or autocratic style. Contingency theory deals with the premise that there is no one best way to lead a group or an organization – it is dependent on the situation at the time. The situation includes factors such as the nature of the task and characteristics of the subordinates. Research work has shown that the leader can have a significant impact on changing the culture of the organization as well as its effectiveness.

References

ADAIR, J., Interview. In the *Director*, September 1988.

ALLEN, R. and KRAFT, C. *The Organizational Unconscious*. Morristown, NJ. Human Resource Institute, 1987.

BENNIS, W. Managing the dream: leadership in the 21st century. *Journal of Organizational Change Management*, **2**(1), 1989, p. 7.

BLAKE, R. and MECANSE, A., *Leadership Dilemmas – Grid Solutions*. Houston, Gulf Publishing, 1991.

BLAKE, R. and MOUTON, J. *The Managerial Grid*. Gulf Publishing Company, 1985.

BRESNEN *et al.* Leader orientation of construction site managers. *American Society of Civil Engineers, Journal of Construction Engineering*, **112**(3), September, 1986, pp. 370–386.

BYRD, C. *Social Psychology*. New York, Appleton-Century-Crofts, 1940.

CHILD, J. *Organization – A Guide to Problems and Practice*. New York, Harper & Row, 1984, 2nd edn.

DAVIS, S. *Managing Corporate Culture*. San Francisco, Ballinger, 1984.

FIEDLER, F. *A Theory of Leadership Effectiveness*. New York, McGraw-Hill, 1967.

FLEISHMAN, E. and BASS, A. The Ohio study. In *Studies in Personnel and Industrial Psychology*. Dorsey, 1974, 3rd edn.

HANDY, C. *Understanding Organizations*. London, Penguin, 1998, 5th edn.

HERON, R. and FRIESEN, D. *Organizational Growth and Development*. University of Alberta, Edmonton, Working Paper, March 1976.

HERSEY, P. and BLANCHARD, K. *Management of Organizational Behaviour*. Englewood Cliffs, NJ, Prentice-Hall, 1977

HESTBAEK, E. *Chord & Discord (Leadership Culture in the Construction and Touring Musical Entertainment Industries)*. Unpublished MSc dissertation, University of Bath, 1985.

HOUSE, R. A path-goal theory of leadership effectiveness. *Administrative Science Quarterly*, **16**, 1971, pp. 32–38.

JENNINGS, E. The anatomy of leadership. *Management of Personnel Quarterly*, **1**(1), Autumn 1961, p. 2.

KOTTER, J. and HESKETT, J. *Corporate Culture and Performance*. New York, The Free Press, 1992.

LANGFORD, D., HANCOCK, M., FELLOWS, R. and GALE, A. *Human Resources Management in the Construction Industry*. London, Longman, 1995, p. 75.

LARSON, L., HUNT, J. and OSBORN, R. The great Hi–Hi leader behaviour myth: a lesson from Occam's Razor. *Academic Management Journal*, December 1976, pp. 628–641.

LIKERT, R. *New Patterns of Management*. New York, McGraw-Hill, 1961.

LITTERER, J. *The Analysis of Organization*. New York, Wiley, 1967.

LUTHANS, F. *Organizational Behaviour*. New York, McGraw-Hill, 1998, 8th edn.

NEWCOMBE, R. and HANCOCK, M. *A Change of Project Manager*. Case study. Management and People. Construction management by distance learning, Work Book 2, 1996, pp. 7-24, 7-25.

QUINNLESS, P. *Leadership Styles in the Construction Industry: an Empirical Examination of Handy's 'Best Fit' Concept*. Unpublished dissertation, Brunel University, 1986.

SELIGMAN, M. *Learned Optimism*. New York, Pocket Books, 1992.

SHERMAN, S. How tomorrow's best leaders are learning their staff. *Fortune*, 27 November 1995, pp. 91–92.

TANNENBAUM, R. and SCHMIDT, W. How to choose a leadership pattern. *Harvard Business Review*, March–April 1973, pp. 162–175, 178–180.

VROOM, V. and YETTON, P. *Leadership and Decision-Making*. University of Pittsburgh Press, 1973.

Case study. A change of project managers (from Newcombe and Hancock (1996, pp. 7-24–7-25))

As project manager in charge of the Budgerigar Wharf project (a five-year docklands development), Ralph Jones had the reputation of being a tough boss who demanded strict adherence to his instructions and placed great emphasis on the use of formal, as well as informal, control methods. When he was first appointed as project manager two years ago, by

Project Management Consultants Ltd, a considerable amount of discord developed in the project team as a result. During the first six months of his appointment, eight of the fourteen site management, engineering and technical personnel on the project either transferred to other projects within the company or left because of dissatisfaction with his methods. However, just about the time that John Bradley, director of the project management division, was considering removing Jones as project manager, the problems on site subsided as the remaining members and those he appointed accepted his style of leadership. Although he encouraged participation by his subordinates during the planning stage of a project, once he made procedure and scheduling decisions he expected strict compliance on the part of the project personnel.

During his tenure as project manager, Ralph Jones reduced project construction costs by 10% while meeting all time schedules for programme completion set by the director of the project management division and by clients and architects. He had the reputation of running a tight and efficient operation. Largely because of this record of accomplishment, he was offered what he described as an irresistible managerial opportunity with a competing firm in the construction industry and after four weeks' notice left the company to accept that position. This was three months ago.

At first John Bradley assumed that he would promote someone from within the project team. However, he found that no one had really been Jones' assistant or understudy, and that no one on the site seemed particularly keen to go into project management. After two weeks of searching, Mr Bradley was able to arrange the transfer of Tom Yarborough, then chief surveyor, to the vacated position. In turn, Yarborough had one of his subordinates take over management of the surveying division. Yarborough was regarded as a highly competent manager and although this transfer did not represent a promotion for him, he saw it as an opportunity to gain a greater diversity of experience.

Tom Yarborough was a strong proponent of management by objectives (MBO). He believed in defining all task assignments in terms of the objectives to be accomplished and leaving it up to the personnel involved to formulate the necessary procedures and methods. He was available for consultation regarding job problems; but the personnel on the project found that he avoided becoming involved in the detail of the work. After Yarborough's first month as project manager, it was obvious to John Bradley that things were not going well on the site. Two scheduled completion times for project tasks had been missed, and the progress on one or two other project phases was possibly behind schedule. In discussing the situation with two or three of the key employees on the project during site visits, the divisional manager learned that it was the consensus of the team that Tom Yarborough did not understand the work he was supervising and was not acting as a manager. He refused to specify how goals were to be accomplished and then held individual employees responsible when specific tasks were not completed on time. As a result, the personnel in the section were frustrated by the very absence of direction on his part and doubted that Yarborough was capable of providing the direction – even if he wanted to do so.

Source: A change of project managers, Management and People, Construction Management by distance learning, Work Book 2, 1996, pp. 7-24 and 7-25.

Chapter 9

Motivation and job satisfaction

Individual behavioural patterns are the result of many complex factors and represent an integral and important part of the social subsystem within an organization. There must be some type of 'motive' which pushes people to behave in certain way. It could be their personal desires, their individual characteristics, the environment in which they work, or many more factors. The means that management should take to satisfy its employees can vary from incentives and bonuses to making them feel involved and part of the company.

The study of motivation is of fundamental importance in the management of people. It is concerned with understanding 'why' people behave they way they do. This chapter explains the meaning of motivation and discusses the main theories of motivation. It also presents the factors that can influence the motivation of people at work and their consequences on job satisfaction and productivity. The discussion is supplemented with examples and case studies related to construction. Figure 9.1 summarizes the overall principles of the chapter (also see Fig. 1.1).

Learning objectives

To:

➤ appreciate the importance of motivating people at work
➤ evaluate the various theories of motivation
➤ identify the main factors which influence motivation at work
➤ understand the relationship between motivation, job satisfaction and productivity.

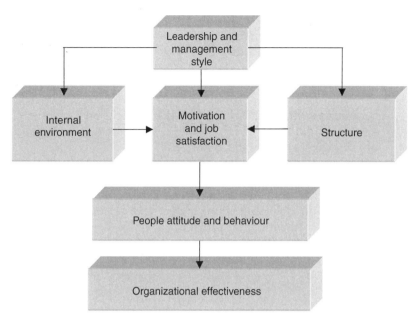

Fig. 9.1. Overall principles of chapter 9

The meaning of motivation

The concept of motivation is very complex and has been mentioned in almost all of the previous chapters of this book. For many years, psychologists have been studying the behaviour of people in order to understand why people behave as they do. What motivates them to work? Why do some people work harder than others? Over the years, various psychologists arrived at the following assumptions.

(*a*) There is a 'cause' for all human behaviour, which itself is the consequence of the combined effects of heredity and environment.

(*b*) There are 'needs' at the root of human behaviour.

(*c*) There are 'objectives' which people try to achieve in order to satisfy their needs.

(*d*) Achievements of needs and goals are related to job satisfaction and performance.

On the basis of these assumptions, the following definitions emerged.

(*a*) Buchanan and Huczynski (1991) defined motives as 'learned influences on human behaviour that lead us to pursue particular goals because they are socially valued. Motivation on the other hand is a decision-making process through which the individual chooses desired outcomes and sets in motion the behaviours appropriate to acquiring them'.

(b) Kast and Rosenzweig (1985) defined motive as 'what prompts a person to act in a certain way or at least develop a propensity for specific behaviour. This urge to action can be touched off by an external stimulus, or it can be internally generated in individual physiological and thought processes'.

(c) Ballachey *et al.* (1962) defined motivation as 'the direction and persistence of action. It is concerned with why people choose a particular course of action in preference to others, and why they continue with a chosen action, often over a long period, and in the face of difficulties and problems'.

(d) Kempner (1987) defined motivation as 'the process of initiating and directing behaviour. Individuals produce and sustain behaviour when they find it rewarding to do so; that is, when the behaviour accomplishes an objective that satisfies a need'.

Mitchell (1982) identified the following four characteristics which underlie the definitions of motivation.

- Motivation is typified as an individual phenomenon.
- Motivation is described, usually, as intentional.
- Motivation is multi-faceted.
- The purpose of motivational theories is to predict behaviour.

Various theories and philosophies have been offered in relation to motivation and what motivates an individual. These theories can be classified into various groups. Choosing the more contemporary views of motivation, the following groups have been selected in order to classify and understand motivation.

- Content theories of motivation (also known as need theories) – they place emphasis on 'what motivates?'.
- Process theories of motivation (also known as goal theories) – they place emphasis on 'how to motivate?'.

Content theories of motivation

Content theories focused on the needs that motivate behaviour. In some publications, content theories have been referred to as 'need theories'. Content theories attempt to explain those specific issues, which actually motivate the individual at work. These motivating issues are concerned with identifying people's needs and their relative strengths, and the goals they pursue in order to satisfy these needs. Among the most well known content theories of motivation are:

- the hierarchy of needs (Maslow 1943)
- existence, relatedness and growth (ERG) theory (Alderfer 1972)
- achievement theory (McClelland 1961)
- two-factor theory (Herzberg *et al.* 1959).

Maslow's hierarchy of needs

The need hierarchy concept was developed by Abraham Maslow (1943) as an alternative to viewing motivation in terms of a series of relatively separate and distinct drives. His concept stressed a hierarchy with certain 'higher' needs becoming activated by the extent that certain 'lower' needs become satisfied. Figure 9.2 illustrates the steps in the hierarchy of needs. Maslow suggests:

- each lower order need must be satisfied before the next higher order need assumes dominance
- when an individual need becomes satisfied, it declines in importance and the need at the next level of the hierarchy increases in importance
- when the individual moves up to the highest level of need, satisfaction of this need increases in importance (self-actualization)
- the number and vanity of needs increases as an individual's psychological development takes place.

Although Maslow argued that most people have the basic needs in about the order indicated in Fig. 9.2, he also made it clear that the hierarchy is not necessarily a fixed order. One need does not have to be 100% satisfied before the next level becomes potent. However, there are a number of problems in relating Maslow's theory to the work situation, of which Mullins (1999) cites the following:

- People do not necessarily satisfy their needs, especially higher level needs, just through the work situation.
- There is doubt about the time which elapses between the satisfaction of a lower level need and the emergence of a higher level need.
- Individual differences mean that people place different values on the same need.
- Some rewards or outcomes at work satisfy more than one need.
- Even for people within the same level of the hierarchy, the motivating factors will not be the same.
- Maslow viewed satisfaction as the main motivational outcome of behaviour, but job satisfaction does not necessarily lead to improved work performance.

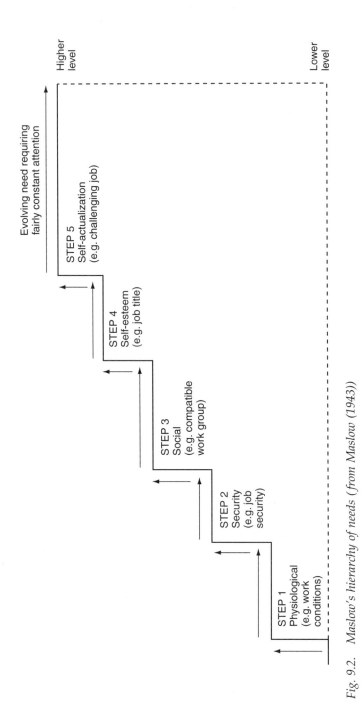

Fig. 9.2. Maslow's hierarchy of needs (from Maslow (1943))

Existence, relatedness and growth (ERG) theory

The ERG theory was developed by Professor Clayton Alderfer in 1972 (see Fig. 9.3). It started with the concept that people strive to meet a hierarchy of existence, relatedness and growth needs and if efforts to reach one level of needs are frustrated, individuals will regress to a lower level. For example, if growth needs are blocked, then relatedness needs become more important. If relatedness needs are frustrated, then a person may revert to the level of existence needs. Equally, once relatedness needs are satisfied, then the importance of growth needs increases.

The ERG theory relates closely to Maslow's hierarchy of needs in that existence is similar to Maslow's physiological and safety needs, related-ness is similar to Maslow's social needs and growth is similar to Maslow's esteem and self-actualization needs. However, Alderfer makes the following three important points:

(*a*) The less a need is satisfied, the more important it becomes.
(*b*) The more a lower level need is satisfied, the greater the importance of the next higher level need.
(*c*) The less the higher level need is satisfied, the greater the impor-tance the lower need assumes.

McClelland's achievement motivation theory

McClelland (1961) argued that all healthy adults have a reservoir of useful energy. The means by which energy is released depend on:

(*a*) the strength of the basic motive or need involved
(*b*) the individual's expectation of succeeding
(*c*) the incentive value of the goal.

McClelland indicated that a strong need for achievement and the desire to succeed or excel in competitive situations is related to how well individuals are motivated to perform their tasks. McClelland defined three types of socially acquired needs: (1) the need for achievement; (2) the need for affiliation; (3) the need for power. The need for achievement reflects the desire to meet task goals. The need for affiliation reflects the desire to develop good interpersonal relationships. The need for power reflects the desire to influence and control other people.

Herzberg's two-factor theory

The American psychologist Frederick Herzberg proposed a theory of motivation at work which divides the factors of the work environment

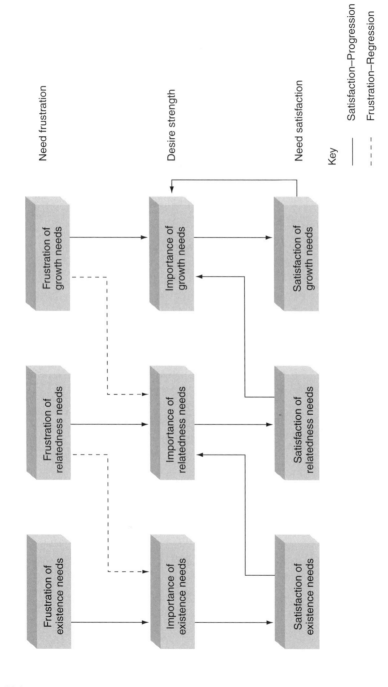

Fig. 9.3. Existence, relatedness and growth theory (from Alderfer (1972))

into two categories:

- factors that create satisfaction – the motivators
- factors that prevent dissatisfaction – the hygiene or maintenance factors.

Herzberg *et al.* (1959) engaged in extensive research concerning the attitudes of people toward their work. In their well known research was testing of the hypothesis in the medical health service which states that 'maintaining good standards of hygiene can help prevent illness, but will never improve the physical state of health'. Relating this hypothesis to the workplace, hygiene factors will not lead to job satisfaction but will predominantly prevent dissatisfaction. Hygiene factors (also known as maintenance factors) include essential elements such as:

- salary
- working conditions
- company policy
- supervision
- interpersonal relations.

These hygiene factors deal with the question 'why work here?', while motivation factors deal with the question 'why work harder?' The motivation factors (also known as growth factors) include essential elements such as:

- a sense of achievement
- recognition
- the rewards of the work itself
- responsibility
- opportunities for achievement.

Herzberg interviewed 203 accountants and engineers and asked them to recall times when they felt exceptionally good or exceptionally bad about their work. Figure 9.4 illustrates the relative importance of various hygiene factors and motivation factors with regard to 'good feelings' about work and shows:

- 40% of cases cited a sense of achievement
- 35% of cases put it down to recognition
- 25% put it down to the work itself.

The factors mentioned most often in connection with *reduced* job satisfaction were:

- company policy (33%)
- supervision (20%)
- salary (20%)

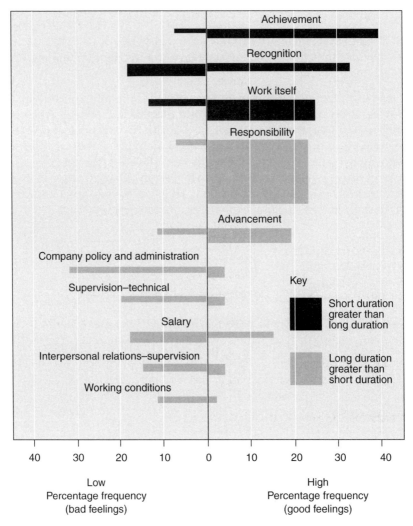

Fig. 9.4. Herzberg's two-factor theory (from Herzberg et al. (1959))

- interpersonal relations (15%)
- working conditions (12%).

There are, however, two common general criticisms of Herzberg's theory. One criticism is that the theory has only limited application to 'manual' workers. The other criticism is that the theory is 'methodologically bound'. Previous research showed that the boundaries between these two definitive categories are much more vague than Herzberg proposed. However, his work has drawn attention to the importance of 'job design' in order to bring about 'job enrichment'. This will be discussed

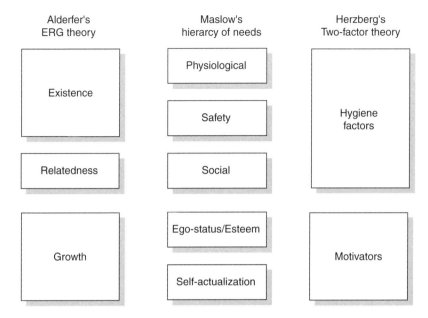

Fig. 9.5. Similarities between the content theories of Herzberg, Maslow and Alderfer

in detail later in this chapter. The content theories discussed so far appear to overlap each other. Figure 9.5 show the relationship between the three needs-driven theories of Herzberg, Maslow and Alderfer.

Process theories of motivation

Process theories attempt to identify the 'relationships' among the dynamic variables which make up motivation. They provide a further contribution to our understanding of the complex nature of work motivation. While content theories explain 'what motivates', the process theory of motivation attempts to explain 'how to motivate'. Among the most well known original process theories of motivation are:

- expectancy theory (Vroom 1964)
- equity theory (Adam 1965)
- goal-setting theory (Locke 1968).

Expectancy theory

Expectancy theory emphasizes the relationship between 'effort' and 'reward'. It is based on the principal that people are influenced by the expected results of their actions. Here, motivation is seen as a function of the relationship between 'expended' and the 'perceived' likely

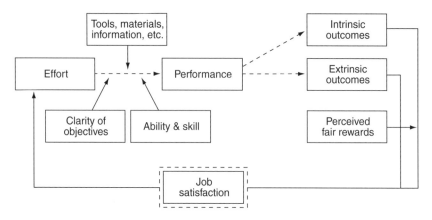

Fig. 9.6.   Basic model of expectancy theory (from Vroom (1964))

outcomes, and the expectation that reward will be related to performance. In other words, the achievement of high performance depends upon the perceived likelihood of being rewarded and that the reward will be worth the effort. Vroom (1964) was the first to propose an expectancy theory which was aimed specifically at work motivation. The original model by Vroom has been modified by a number of researchers such as Porter and Lawler (1968), and Fig. 9.6 illustrates a typical model of the expectancy approach. The following terms are now commonly used to describe expectancy theory.

- *Valence*. Relates to the strength of a person's preference for a particular reward or outcome. It can be positive (desired) or negative (not desired).
- *Outcome*. A consequence or result of one's actions.
- *Job outcome (also known as first-level outcome)*. This is the immediate effect of one's action, e.g. improved job performance. The first-level outcome is often the outcome of concern to the organization.
- *Personal outcome (also known as second-level outcome)*. This is divided into two types of outcomes, namely:
  - extrinsic outcomes which are related to material benefits, such as salary and other benefits.
  - intrinsic outcomes which are generally related to 'growth', such as a sense of belonging and promotion.
- *Expectancy*. The probability that behaviour (particular level of effort on the job) will result in a particular first-level outcome (improved job performance).
- *Instrumentality*. The strength of the causal relationship between the first-level outcomes and the second-level outcomes, e.g. pay rise and/or increase in status and authority.

Equity theory

The equity theory of motivation was first developed by Adam (1965). It focuses on people's perceptions of how fairly they have been treated in comparison with other colleagues. The equity theory suggests that job performance and satisfaction depend upon the extent to which individuals feel they are equally treated at work in terms of pay and promotion. The principle of Adam's model is that people evaluate their social relationships in the same way as buying or selling an item. People expect certain outcomes in exchange for certain contributions or inputs. Most exchanges involve a multiple of inputs and outcomes. According to equity theory, people place weighting on these various inputs and outcomes according to how they perceive their importance. When the ratio of a person's total outcomes to total inputs equals the perceived ratio of other people's total outcomes to total inputs there is equity – the result is job satisfaction. When the ratios compare unequally the person experiences a sense of inequity and the result is disenchantment. Generally, a person experiencing a state of inequity they will behave in one or more of following ways.

(a) Change the inputs or efforts – a person will decrease or increase the level of productivity, the quality of work, absenteeism, etc.

(b) Change the outcomes, e.g. demands for more pay, working conditions, equipment, etc.

(c) Distort their perception of inputs and outputs to achieve the same results. This could be done by rationalizing the value that they place on effort and reward.

(d) Leave the field.

(e) Act on others by making changes to alter their inputs.

(f) Change the objective of comparison by shifting the attention on to somebody else whom they feel offers a more direct comparison into the output–input ratio.

Goal-setting theory

Goal-setting theory can be applied to the performance of individuals and organizational systems. Locke (1968) was the first to apply goal-setting theory to individuals. This theory assumes that people's goals or intentions play an important part in determining their behaviour. This theory highlights the importance of values and value judgements and suggests that these values influence emotions and desires. People's intentions and goals are strongly associated with their emotions and desires which will in turn guide them to respond and act accordingly. Goals will direct work behaviour and performance, and lead to certain consequences or feedback.

Application of goal-setting theory to organization performance is traditionally known as Management By Objectives (MBO). It follows a series of systematic steps, these are:

(*a*) setting overall objectives and action plans
(*b*) developing organizational strategy
(*c*) setting individual objectives and action plans
(*d*) implementing the plan
(*e*) conducting periodic appraisal, providing feedback on progress and making adjustments
(*f*) conducting final appraisal of results
(*g*) setting new goals.

There are a number of criteria that need to be considered when setting goals (see Fig. 9.7 for a goal-setting example). The goal should:

(*a*) be clear
(*b*) be realistic

Using stretch goals

Goal setting is widely recognized as a technique to improve performance. However, there are a number of problems associated with the indiscriminate use of ambitious goals. Steven Kerr, a noted organizational behaviour researcher and now chief learning officer for General Electric, has noted that many organizations fail to effectively use what can be called 'stretch goals'. The goals are set very high, but the support needed to accomplish them is often missing. For example, top management may ask their people to increase output by 25 percent but fail to provide them with the knowledge, tools and means to reach such an ambitious goal. As a result, the only way that people can meet these new and demanding challenges is by working longer – often on their time. In fact, notes Kerr, everywhere in America people are working evenings and weekends in order to meet the goals that the organization has set for them.

This is not necessary, however, if the enterprise carefully examines what needs to be done and how it has to occur. Kerr recommends three rules that can help organizations create stretch goals and reach them without exhausting and burning out their human resources. These include (1) do not set goals that overly stress people; (2) if goals require people to stretch, do not punish them if they fail; and (3) if they are being asked to do things that they have never done before, give them whatever tools and help are available.

How should goals be set? Kerr believes that easy goals are too simple and do not improve performance and that difficult goals may be *so* difficult that people cannot attain them – so they give up. Stretch goals force them to go beyond what they are accustomed to doing, and thus improve performance, but, importantly, they are also attainable. At the same time, the organization has to be willing to reward the personnel for attaining the stretch goals. How can this be done? One way is with money. Financial rewards are very direct and encourage individuals to continue their efforts. However, if management decide that they will give back to those involved one-third of the performance gain (i.e. gain sharing), they must stick to this and not back down when big gains are realized. If organizations follow these simple suggestions of using stretch goals and pay for performance, they can increase their productivity and employees can be challenged and rewarded for their efforts.

Fig. 9.7. An example of goal setting (adapted from Luthans (1995, p. 211))

(c) be specific
(d) allow for use of the appropriate equipment/tool
(e) be acceptable to individuals
(f) consider the ability of individuals
(g) be interesting to individuals.

Factors influencing employees' motivation within an organization

In this book there have been many discussions which are related to employee satisfaction and motivation and the term motivation has taken part in almost every chapter. Figure 9.8 summarizes the factors that influence employee motivation under four broad headings:

(a) employee characteristics
   (i) needs and expectations
   (ii) age and maturity
(b) management factors
   (i) management/leadership style
   (ii) personnel (human resource) management
(c) organizational factors
   (i) job characteristics
   (ii) structure and job design
   (iii) quality of work environment
   (iv) communication (group cohesiveness)
(d) outcome
   (i) task performance/goal achievement
   (ii) employee job satisfaction

Individual characteristics

Needs and expectations

Most content theories of motivation (such as those of Maslow, Herzberg, Alderfer and McClelland) gave reference to individual needs and expectations. Briefly, individuals differ in their needs for the following:

- Material or intrinsic needs such as:
  - money
  - other material benefits, e.g. car or company pension
- Organizational or extrinsic related needs such as:
  - power
  - responsibility and achievement
  - having a challenging job

241

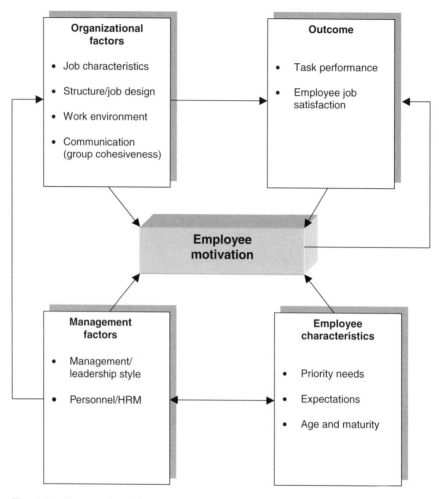

Fig. 9.8. Factors that influence employee motivation

  - feeling of belonging and part of the company
  - being aware of what is going on
  - being involved in decision making
  - feeling important
  - getting promotion
  - having a secure job.
- Task-related needs such as:
  - good equipment
  - good working relationships
  - good supervision.

Age and maturity

Naturally, the above needs and expectations fluctuate with maturity and age of the person. For example, the needs of a newly graduated engineer are different from those of a mature contract manager and the desire of these needs changes with age. Levinson (1978) believes that there are four identifiable stable periods of an individual's career life:

- entering the adult world (ages twenty-two to twenty-eight)
- settling down (age thirty-three to forty)
- entering middle adulthood (age forty-five to fifty)
- culmination of middle adulthood (age fifty-five to sixty).

Levinson hypothesized that there is a great variability in work attitude and values during 'transitional' periods of the above stages. Hall (1968) took Levinson's theory and developed a career stage model (see Fig. 9.9). In his model, Hall identified four stages of a person life: (1) exploration (i.e. searching for identity); (2) establishment (i.e. settling down); (3) maintenance (i.e. personal legacy); and (4) decline. Hall's model corresponds very closely with Luthans and Thomas' (1989) model of age and job satisfaction. Their research showed that as individuals get older their job satisfaction increases, but with a downturn in satisfaction on approaching retirement age. This decline was explained by the assumption that unmet expectations, downsizing and 'merger mania' can leave old-term employees feeling unwanted and with no sense of loyalty or belonging.

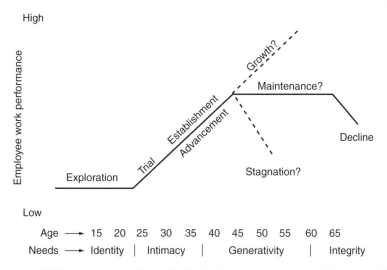

Fig. 9.9. Hall's career model (from Hall (1968) cited in Luthans (1998), p. 135)

Management factors

Management/leadership style

The impact of the characteristics and management style of a leader/manager on motivating employees in the workplace were clearly identified in chapter 8 (see Fig. 8.7). In a study by Luthans (1998), the leader/manager role was researched by observing 248 real managers. Leader/manager effectiveness was measured by a combined effectiveness index that represented the two major and generally agreed upon criteria of both leadership theory/research and practice: (1) getting the job done through high quantity and quality standards of performance, and (2) getting the job done through people, requiring their satisfaction and commitment.

In particular, an organizational effectiveness questionnaire to measure the unit's quality and quantity of performance, a job satisfaction questionnaire and an organizational commitment questionnaire were used. This multiple-measures index was employed in the study to answer the most important question of 'what do effective managers do?'

Luthans found that communication and human resource management activities made by far the largest relative contribution to managers' effectiveness and traditional management activities, especially networking, made by far the least relative contribution. In other words, if effectiveness is defined as the perceived quantity and quality of the performance of a manager's unit and his or her work group members' satisfaction and commitment, then the biggest relative contribution to leadership effectiveness comes from the human-oriented activities – communication and human resource management.

Personnel (human resource) management

The subject of personnel management is discussed in some detail in chapter 10. Briefly, personnel management is that part of the management function which is concerned with people at work and their relationships within the organization. It is also concerned with the human and social implications of change in the internal organization and in methods of working, and of economic and social changes in the community. Here, the responsibilities of the personnel manager are:

(a) to ensure that the firm's reward system is competitive with other companies
(b) to devise remuneration systems to stimulate workers into enhanced effort and efficiency
(c) to administrate the superannuating schemes (in conjunction with finance department) and advise employees about their pension and other entitlements

(d) to prepare accurate job descriptions and other recruitment aids
(e) to implement health and safety regulations, accident prevention and first-aid facilities
(f) to provide training and staff development programmes.

The above activities will motivate employees by providing them with jobs which are satisfying in themselves and by offering them financial and other rewards. For example, an employee who has been selected and has been well trained for his or her job will be more motivated than someone who has been carelessly selected and untrained. The use of consultation and participation, besides motivating employees, will often show how they can be better utilized. A well designed and safe working environment will enable better use to be made of people's abilities and will in most cases help to provide satisfaction of human needs.

Organizational factors

Job characteristics

The characteristics of the job and associated tasks is an area on which managers can also have a great impact. The relationship between job characteristics and motivation was better understood after Herzberg introduced his two-factor theory (see p. 233).

Hackman and Oldham (1980) developed a job characteristics model of work motivation. The model recognized that certain job characteristics contribute to certain psychological states and that the strength of employees' need for growth has an important moderating effect. The principle of the model is illustrated in Fig. 9.10.

The core job characteristics included five dimensions:

- *skill variety* refers to the extent to which a job entails the employee to draw from different activities and involves a range of knowledge, skills and abilities
- *task identity* refers to the extent to which the job has an identifiable beginning and visible completion
- *task significance* refers to the extent to which a job is important and its impact to people inside and outside the organization
- *autonomy* refers to the extent to which a job is independent – how much freedom and control do employees have to plan their work and determine how to accomplish its objectives?
- *feedback* refers to the extent to which the tasks result in direct and clear information about progress and effectiveness of job performance.

The critical psychological states included three dimensions:

- *meaningfulness* – the job characteristics of skill variety, task identity and task significance can influence the degree to which employees

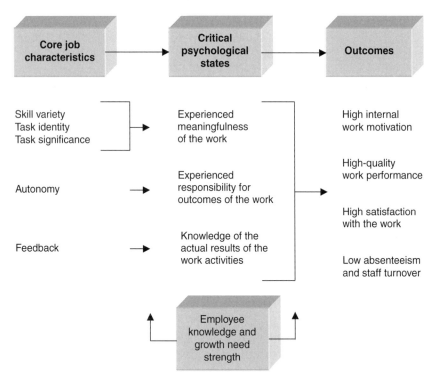

Fig. 9.10.   The job characteristics model of work motivation used in job design (from Hackman and Oldham (1980, p. 90))

perceive their work as making a valued contribution, as being important and worthwhile
- *responsibility* – job autonomy can influence the extent to which employees feel a sense of being personally responsible or accountable for the work being done
- *knowledge of results* – the extent to which employees understand how they are performing in the job (feedback).

The outcome included four dimensions:

- high internal work motivation
- high-quality work performance
- high satisfaction with the work
- low staff turnover and absenteeism.

Hackman and Oldham tested their model by designing a questionnaire known as a Job Diagnostic Survey (JDS). Their questionnaire contained questions on job characteristics, such as:

- How much variety is there in your job?
- To what extent does your job involve doing a whole and identifiable piece of work?
- In general, how significant or important is your job?
- How much autonomy is there in your job?
- To what extent does doing the job itself provide you with information about your work performance?

Each respondent had to give a score of between 1 and 7 to each question. The overall measure of job enrichment was then calculated using the Motivating Potential Score (MPS) formula:

$$\text{MPS} = \left(\frac{\text{skill variety} + \text{task identity} + \text{task significance}}{3} \right) \times \text{autonomy} \times \text{feedback}$$

Hackman and Oldham's studies concluded the following.

(a) People working in enriching jobs with high score levels on the JDS are definitely more motivated and satisfied and, although the evidence is not as strong, may also have better attendance and performance effectiveness records.
(b) The core job characteristics of skill variety, task identity and task significance combine to predict the level of meaningfulness experienced in the work.
(c) The core characteristics of autonomy and feedback did not relate so clearly to experienced responsibility and knowledge of results.

In another large longitudinal study by Hackman *et al.* (1975), the long-term impact of the results of the Hackman–Oldham model was tested and the results were fairly encouraging. Using about a thousand tellers from 38 banks of a large holding company, the following results were obtained from a job redesign intervention.

(a) Perceptions of changed job characteristics increased quickly and were held at that level for an extended period. Thus, employees perceive meaningful changes that have been introduced into their jobs and tend to continue to recognize those changes over time.
(b) Satisfaction and commitment attitudes increased quickly, but then fell back to their initial levels.
(c) Performance did not increase initially but did increase significantly over the longer time period. The implication here is that managers and researchers need to be more patient in their evaluation of work redesign interventions.

Structure and job design

Structuring or restructuring the organization can have a significant impact on work groups and job design or redesign. This in turn will influence employee motivation and job satisfaction. The issues of organizational structure and work groups were discussed in some detail in chapters 5 and 6.

Job design, however, is particularly concerned with the relationship between individuals and the nature and content of jobs and their task functions. It attempts to meet people's personal and social needs at work through reorganization or restructuring of work. Mullins (1999) identified two major reasons for attention to job design:

- to enhance the personal satisfaction that people derive from their work
- to make the best use of people as a valuable resource of the organization and to help overcome obstacles to their effective performance.

There are three fundamental mechanisms associated with redesigning or restructuring a job (see Fig. 9.11): (1) job rotation; (2) job enlargement; (3) job enrichment.

Fig. 9.11. Job design model (from Mullins (1999, p. 646))

Job rotation. Job rotation is the most basic form of individual job design. Job rotation involves moving a person from one job or task to another in an attempt to add some variety and help remove boredom, at least in the short term. However, if the tasks involved are all very similar and routine, then once the person is familiar with the new task the work may quickly prove boring again. Job rotation may lead to the acquisition of additional skills but does not necessarily develop the level of skills. Strictly, job rotation is not really job redesign because neither the nature of the task nor the method of working is restructured. However, job rotation may help the person identify more with the completed product or service. It can also be used as a form of training.

Job enlargement. Job enlargement involves increasing the scope of the job and the range of tasks that a person carries out. It is usually achieved by combining a number of related operations at the same level. Job enlargement is horizontal job design – it makes a job structurally bigger. It lengthens the time cycle of operations and may give the person greater variety. Job enlargement, however, is not always very popular and may often be resisted by workers. Although it may give the person more to do, it does little to improve intrinsic satisfaction or give a sense of achievement. Workers may see job enlargement as simply increasing the number of routine, boring tasks they have to perform. Some workers seem to prefer simple, routine tasks which they can undertake almost automatically, and with little thought or concentration. This enables them to daydream and to socialize with colleagues without affecting their performance.

✒ *Job enrichment.* This is an extension of the more basic job rotation and job enlargement methods of job redesign. Job enrichment arose out of Herzberg's two-factor theory. It attempts to enrich the job by incorporating motivating or growth factors such as increased responsibility and involvement, opportunities for advancement and the sense of achievement.

Job enrichment involves vertical job enlargement. It aims to give the person greater autonomy and authority over the planning, execution and control of their own work. It focuses attention on intrinsic satisfaction. Job enrichment increases the complexity of the work and should provide the employee with a more meaningful and challenging job. It provides greater opportunities for psychological growth. The main methods of achieving job enrichment include:

- permitting workers greater freedom and control over the scheduling and pacing of their work, as opposed to machine pacing
- allowing workers to undertake a full task cycle, build or assemble a complete product or component, or deliver a complete service

- providing workers with tasks or jobs which challenge their abilities and make fuller use of their training, expertise and skills
- giving workers greater freedom to work in self-managing teams with greater responsibility for monitoring their own performance and the minimum of direct supervision
- providing workers with the opportunity to have greater direct contact with clients, consumers or users of the product or service.

Quality of work environment

The quality of the working environment of the organization can influence the quality of work, productivity and employees' motivation to work. This idea is also known as Quality Work Life (QWL). The concept of QWL was formed in the 1970s as an important ingredient in job design or when restructuring a job. The philosophy behind improving the quality of working life is that employees will normally be more productive if they actively enjoy the work experience, rather than just tailoring their lives at work. The main principle of a QWL is to change the climate or the culture of the workplace by:

- allowing people to be more involved in the production process by participating in problem solving and decision making
- improvement of environmental conditions
- increasing the flow of communication within the organization
- employee involvement in target setting
- introduction of staff development systems
- having employees solve workplace problems
- better leadership styles and interpersonal relationships
- stress-reduction programmes.

Communication (group cohesiveness)

This issue is discussed in chapter 6 (see pp. 132–134, 141–142).

Outcome

It is a well known fact that success leads to high satisfaction for the people involved in achieving the task. It is also axiomatic that success depends on many critical factors, including planning, organizing, co-ordinating and controlling. Within this context, it is safe to say that a well planned and resourced organization can achieve a high level of performance which in turn affects people's attitude and motivation. In order words, individuals that are working in a successful organization feel more motivated to work harder than those working within an organization that suffers from decline in profit, loss of clients, uncertainty and low growth. The diagram below shows a simple illustration of the relationship between performance and motivation.

Productivity model of a construction site

The subject of productivity and its relationship to motivation is very crucial to contracting organizations. The definition of productivity ranges from industry-wide economic parameters to the measurement of crews and individuals. In this section, the term 'productivity' is referred to as individual productivity and is defined as the amount of goods and services produced by a productive factor in a spell of time. It is usually expressed in terms of unit rate such as productivity output/cost or work-hours. In the construction industry, the relationship between productivity factors and the production process has been modelled in an attempt to analyse the cause and effect analogy.

The model in Fig. 9.12 shows the interrelationship between the factors that can significantly affect productivity on a construction site. The purpose of the model is to represent or explain the phenomenon of productivity. In this way, managers can predict what needs changing to improve the productivity level on a construction site and develop a strategy for achieving the change. Executive managers' responses can either reinforce and identify the productivity problem, or create pressures to change it. Much depends upon how sophisticated a diagnostic model the manager uses. For instance, one of the factors that can influence productivity is motivation of the workforce. Achieving high motivation depends on the working environment where financial or psychological rewards can be regarded as an incentive for the efforts needed in achieving high productivity. In order to assure a good working environment, the management of resources needs to be highly effective, as demonstrated by previous research (Stukhard 1987). For the purposes of this chapter, three main factors are selected for discussion: (1) management factors; (2) employee motivation; (3) experience/training.

Management factors and productivity

The level of productivity attained by a firm is determined by a variety of organizational, technical and human factors, many of them

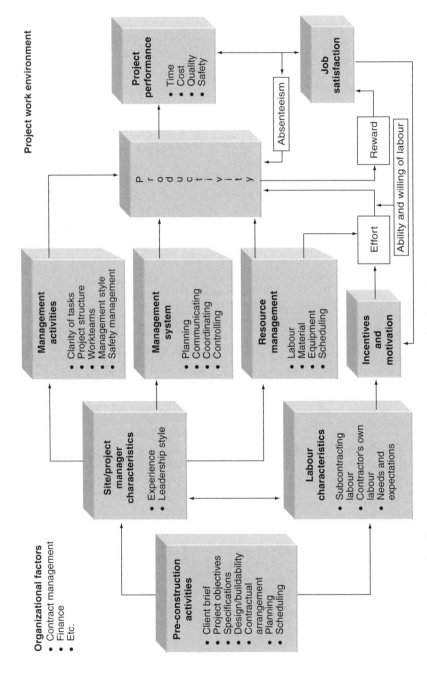

Fig. 9.12. Process model of motivation and productivity on a construction site

directly controlled or influenced by management decisions. Previous works have identified two main HQ decisions that have the greatest input to the site manager's performance. These are: the site managers' involvement at the contract stage and the delegation of responsibilities. Laufer and Jenkins (1982) examined various approaches to motivate construction workers and found that construction management would benefit from a general move toward a more participative decision-making style of leadership. Bresnen *et al.* (1987) identified site management involvement in planning as a very important factor because of their input at an early stage in developing an understanding of, and preparedness for, their job. It has been suggested that site managers should have a major say in setting the original targets, planning the process and organizing the resources. In terms of good atmosphere to boost performance, a better atmosphere on site has been associated with increased decentralization of decision making authority within the firm, and a greater level of site manager influence over operations and decisions on site. Olomolaiye (1990) found that good supervision was the most significant variable influencing percentage productive time and that fluctuations in productivity are primarily the responsibility of on site management. This suggests that site managers have a powerful influence on the behaviour of site employees. At project level, management relations with the site can be a source of dissatisfaction or motivation.

Other researchers regarded the management information system (MIS) as the linking mechanism of the above factors, i.e. decision making, site supervision, communication and morale. For example, Reinschmidt (1976) argued that the productivity of firms depends on the management's access to accurate information to aid in faster decision making. Information which does not flow promptly from one group to another will cause delays, rework, low motivation and, hence, decrease productivity. Sanvido and Paulson (1992) empirically tested the possible utilization of practical tools (from a productivity improvement viewpoint) that can support various theoretical decision-making phases. He demonstrated that jobs where the planning and control functions were performed at the right level in the site hierarchy, were more profitable, finished sooner and were better constructed than those where the functions were performed at the wrong level.

Several other studies have emphasized the importance of utilizing effective resources in order to improve productivity. For example, Stukhard (1987) suggested that the ability to achieve good project performance hinges, primarily, on the attainment of forecasted productivity and manpower levels. Equally essential to project success are the minimization of construction interferences, effective field co-ordination and proper control of activities.

Employee motivation and productivity

As mentioned earlier in this chapter, since the 1940s there has been a tremendous amount of work carried out to investigate the relationship between the individual and the company, coupled with intrinsic motivation within the individual. In construction, the empirical study by Nicholls and Langford (1987) tested the hypothesis that Herzberg's two-factor theory of motivation is an accurate way of determining the motivation of construction site engineers. The two factors are hygiene and motivators. Hygiene factors such as money, supervision, status, security, working conditions, policies and interpersonal relations prevent dissatisfaction but do not motivate; they do not produce output but prevent a decay in performance. Motivators such as work itself, recognition, advancement, possibility of responsibility and achievement can have a positive effect on job satisfaction which will lead to an increased output. Nicholls and Langford's conclusion was an overall agreement with Herzberg in that site managers consider the most important factor to be the work itself. However, some doubts were cast about the hygiene factors, particularly supervision and working conditions. Some site engineers are motivated by these factors and, as such, should not directly contribute to motivation. Moreover, some hygiene factors can motivate construction employees, in particular, site managers who value responsibility and autonomy as powerful motivators.

Other researchers such as Maloney (1990) found that quality of work life includes the autonomy people are granted in the performance of their work, the participation they are allowed in making decisions that affect them, and the social interactions allowed by the job. A positive quality of work life leads to a positive organizational outcome, e.g. reduced absenteeism and staff turnover, greater job satisfaction, etc. Therefore, the quality of work life is a major determinant of an organization's ability to recruit, motivate and retain skilled workers.

A review of the empirical findings of work investigating the relationship between financial incentives, motivation and productivity suggests that there are disparities in conclusions (see Laufer and Borcherding (1981) and Olomolaiye (1990)). Financial incentives can motivate construction workers to put more effort and produce more, but money by itself is not the only determinant. Within the framework of motivation, productivity is also dependent on the ability and willingness of the labour as well as the clarity of the goals, training and the quality of the equipment to be used in executing the work.

Experience, training and productivity

Formal education and training programmes have been considered substitutes for leadership, by developing individuals to work independently or with minimal supervision. Evidence that the worker orientation of a construction worker may act as a substitute for leadership was investigated by Stinchombe (1959) who stated that 'Craft Institutions are a method of administering work. Craft administration differs from bureaucratic administration by substituting professional training of manual workers for decentralized planning of work'. Productivity is, therefore, closely related to skill – without skill there is no way for a worker to be productive. In some crafts the workers may be skilled and willing to produce, while in other crafts the skill or willingness may be absent. Workers today are comparatively well educated, so training or teaching job skills is a necessity, as expressed by the hypothesis: 'In order to grow specialisation in the construction process, a multi-skilled professional to effectively manage construction projects is seriously required' (Bresnen *et al.* 1987). The essential ingredient for success in a first line supervisor's role is the ability to communicate with experience, planning and goal setting, all of which play roles in communication. Hinze and Kuechenmeister (1981) concluded that people who took advantage of these factors were found to be the most productive. This ability is even more important on a 'super project' in which the workers are essentially lost without the careful guidance of a foreperson.

Considerable organizational behaviour research has been conducted with the first line supervisor because of the link between management and workmen. Horner (1989) suggested that management must bear the burden of controlling the rapidly changing technological and social conditions, and that training programmes and methods of assessment must be relevant and appropriate to the needs of the organization – they must be designed and implemented in joint ventures between academia and industry.

A productivity survey

Naoum (1996) conducted a survey to find out if there are significant differences in perceptions between head office personnel and site managers with regard to factors that impair construction productivity. The information was obtained through use of a structured questionnaire containing a list of productivity factors. The questionnaire was first tested by interviewing five different contractors. The suitability of the form and areas of particular interest to each participant were highlighted and the set of factors evolved from these interviews. Some modifications were made to the original questionnaire and the final version was completed by 36 construction contractors (19 from contract managers working at head office and 17 from experienced site managers who had worked in the construction industry for over ten years). The firms involved were large companies which meant that the survey is totally confined to large organizations. However, the nature of the projects that the site managers were involved in varied in type (commercial and industrial) and in size (over £2 million to £20 million).

The questionnaire was designed using the rating system. The productivity factors were assigned scores for high importance (3 points), medium (2) and low (1). The results were statistically analysed and the following section discusses the results.

The results

There was overall agreement regarding the factors that can affect productivity rates on a construction site. Both types of respondents identified 'ineffective project planning' as the most crucial factor likely to impair construction productivity. This finding supported the notion (Borcherding and Ganer 1981) that:

> *the planning/design level is probably the key communication link in the hierarchy model between the 'realities' of the site construction level and the 'abstract' of the policy and programme management levels. The planning/ design level becomes the controlling element in the industry's effort to translate productivity information from above into a common language with a terminology meaningful to the desired audience.*

Another high scoring factor within this section was 'lack of inter-unit integration of project information', which is a factor related to the site information system. This emphasizes the importance of focusing on the information required to drive the building process to the technical information for design-related problems. In addition to the above, three factors were moderately scored by both site managers and head office. These were: (1) exclusion of site management from contract meetings; (2) under-direction of employees; (3) poor scheduling of project activities.

Differences in perception between the two groups were noted in the areas of 'poor selection of project personnel' and 'lack of consultation in decision-making'. Head office personnel assigned a high score to these factors while site managers gave low scores. On the other hand, site managers attached more importance to 'ineffective delegation of responsibilities' as well as 'lack of shared beliefs between head office and site'.

The factors that seemed to be of importance to both groups in matters related to resource management effectiveness were 'difficulties with the procurement of materials' and 'disruption of site programme'. As far as material mismanagement is concerned, comments from site managers indicated that the most acute problems arise from material supply and storage, which have a great impact on the sequence of work and rework due to disruptions. This finding corresponds closely with the studies of Thomas *et al.* (1989, 1992) who found that the average daily productivity for non-disrupted days was 0.44 work hours/m², while disrupted days had an average productivity of 2.16 work hrs/m², an increase of 388%. This finding demonstrates that productivity improvements can be achieved through better managerial control.

With regard to 'disruption of site programmes', this factor can cause delay in executing the work and prevent optimizing utilization of available resources. Timely input from all levels of management can reduce the risk of overlooking activities necessary to complete the project. Therefore, delays contributing to lowering a worker productivity can be reduced by planning the work to utilize manpower efficiently.

There was disagreement between the groups on 'discrepancies with technical information' and 'ignorance of project technology'. Head office personnel do not regard them as highly important, while site managers do. It was noted by site managers that waiting time due to discrepancies with technical information can be reduced by providing adequate supervision at the workplace.

In reviewing the results described by previous researchers, there would appear to be a difference in views as to whether workforce motivation can effect construction productivity. Several behavioural and psychological researchers have indicated that the expenditure of effort by a worker is the physical manifestation of motivation – the greater a worker's motivation, the greater his/her expenditure of effort. Ranking of questions related to motivation shows that there was 'moderate' support to questions related to 'promotion', 'rewards', 'exercising skills', 'grievances' and 'career prospects'. The statement that 'constraints on a worker's performance arising from ineffective management will affect their motivation at work and consequently influence worker's productivity' attracted larger agreement from both groups. Major sources of dissatisfaction commonly expressed are problems related to delay and reworking. According to Thomas *et al.* (1989) frequently cited problems included the lack of tools, materials, delayed decisions, late information and changes to orders. The link between satisfaction and improved productivity is based upon the impact that such conditions are assumed to have on the motivation of both workers and supervisors. It can be concluded, therefore, that individual needs for opportunities for advancement as well as the satisfaction from the work itself can be frustrating and, consequently, the potential for significant productivity gains is seen by the respondents as being thwarted by inappropriate or inadequate managerial actions.

Both groups regarded 'lack of experience and training' as highly influential to site productivity. Obviously, each task requires specific skills and knowledge of how to use these skills. This finding ties in closely with earlier results of this research regarding 'ineffective planning' and 'material management'.

Summary and conclusions

This chapter deals with the issue of motivation and its effect on individual and organizational outcomes. Motivation is a topic of continuing psychological significance, and is also one which continues to attract the attention of those who try to influence and manage the motivation of other people in organizations. Motivation is a complex concept and cyclic in nature. It has been difficult for psychologists to describe the urge behind behaviour. The motivation of any organism, even the simplest one, is only partly understood. An extract from Handy (1998), gives an indication of the problems associated with motivation:

> *We should perhaps be relieved that no guaranteed formula of motivation was founded. But there is now a much better understanding of the process by which the individual reaches decisions on the apportionment of his or her ambitions, time, energy and talent. The decision is often unconscious or instinctive, physical as when we go in search of food, or more psychological as when we seek security under threat; or it may be a conscious and deliberate decision to leave or join a firm, to satisfy or to optimize.*

Contemporary thinking in the area of motivation combines some 'constants' (issues that have not changed much) with some 'variables' (issues that have evolved and changed their shape through time). In putting together this chapter, many competing theories were investigated, all of which attempt to explain the nature of motivation. The majority of these theories, if not all, are practically true, and all help to explain the behaviour of certain people at certain times. Differences in patterns of motivation are illustrated by, for example Hunt (1986), who developed average 'goal profiles' showing the relative importance of different categories of needs for people in different occupations, and changes in profiles at different stages for an average manager. The complex nature of motivation is supported by the work of Vroom (1964) who cites a tremendous amount of research investigations and concludes that there is no all-embracing theory of motivation to work. It is dependent on the individual and the organization.

The theoretical models offered in this chapter are classified under two main categories: content and process theories of motivation. The content theories attempt to answer the question 'what motivates?' and the process theories attempt to explain 'how to motivate'. The systems approach seems to support the social concept of motivation. There is a direct relationship between effort–performance–satisfaction and this relationship is affected by many variables, such as individual needs, abilities, perceptions, job characteristics, work environment, organizational structure and job design.

The balance of both intrinsic and extrinsic rewards and their perceived equity to the individual are also crucial. The match between individual needs and expectations, and factors such as work conditions, relationships, salary, job design and the manner in which these factors are balanced, can lead to high or low levels of motivation amongst individuals.

Finally, motivation is a vitally important concern to both the employee and employer within an organization. Its importance arises from the simple but powerful truth that poorly motivated people are likely to perform poorly at work and gain little satisfaction from their job. As offered by the great Aristotle himself:

All men seek one goal: success and happiness. The only way to achieve true success is to express yourself completely in service to society. First, have a definite, clear, practical ideal – a goal, an object. Second, have the necessary means to achieve your ends – wisdom, money, materials, and methods. Third, adjust your means to that end.

Aristotle, 384–322 B.C.

References

ADAM, J. Towards an understanding of inequity. *Journal of Abnormal Psychology*, **67**, 1965, pp. 422–436.

ALDERFER, C. *Existence, Relatedness and Growth.* London, Macmillan, 1972.

BALLACHEY, E., CRUTCHFIELD, R. and KRECH, D. *Individuals in Society.* New York, McGraw-Hill, 1962.

BORCHERDING, I. and GANER, D. Work force motivation and productivity on large jobs. *Journal of the Construction Division, ASCE*, **107**, 1981, pp. 443–456.

BRESNEN, M., BRYMAN, A., BREADSWORTH, A. and KEIL, T. Effectiveness of site managers. *Chartered Institute of Building*, Technical Paper No. 85, 1987, pp. 1–7.

BUCHANAN, D. and HUCZYNSKI, A. *Organisational Behaviour.* Englewood Cliffs, NJ, Prentice-Hall, 1991, 2nd edn.

HACKMAN, J. and OLDHAM, G. *Work Redesign.* Reading, MA, Addison-Wesley, 1980.

HACKMAN, R., OLDHAM, R., JANSON, R. and PURDY, K. A new strategy for job enrichment. *California Management Review*, Summer, 1975, pp. 55–71.

HALL, D. An examination of Maslow's need hierarchy in an organisational setting. *Organisational Behaviour and Human Performance*, **3**, February 1968, pp. 12–35.

HERZBERG, F., MAUSNER, B. and SYNDERMAN, B. *The Motivation to Work.* London, Chapman and Hall, 1959, 2nd edn.

HINZE, J. and KUECHENMEISTER, K. Productivity foremen characteristics. *Journal of the Construction Division, ASCE,* **107**, New York, 1981, pp. 627–639.

HORNER, R. Labour productivity. *CIB-W65, Proceedings on Organization and Management of Construction.* Dubrovnik, Yugoslavia, 1989.

HUNT, J. *Management of People at Work.* New York, McGraw-Hill, 1986, 2nd edn.

KAST, F. and ROSENZWEIG, J. *Organization and Management.* New York, McGraw-Hill, 1985, 5th edn.

KEMPNER, T. *The Penguin Management Book.* London, Penguin, 1987.

LAUFER, A. and JENKINS, D. Motivating construction workers. *Journal of the Construction Division, ASCE,* **108**, 1982, pp. 531–545.

LEVINSON, D. *The Seasons of a Man's Life.* New York, Knopf, 1978, p. 49.

LOCKE, E. Towards a theory of task motivation and incentives. *Organisational Behaviour and Human Performance,* **3**, 1968, pp. 157–189.

LAUFER, A. and BORCHERDING, J. Financial incentives to raise productivity. *Journal of the Construction Division, ASCE,* **107**, 1981, pp. 745–756.

LUTHANS, F. *Organizational Behaviour.* New York, McGraw-Hill, 1998, 8th edn.

LUTHANS, F. and THOMAS, L. The relationship between age and job satisfaction. *Personnel Review,* **18**, No. 1, 1989, pp. 23–26.

MALONEY, W. Framework for analysis of performance. *Journal of Construction Engineering and Management, ASCE,* **116**(3), 1990, pp. 399–415.

MASLOW, A. A theory of human motivation. *Psychological Review.* 1943, pp. 370–396.

McCLELLAND, D. *The Achieving Society.* Cambridge: Cambridge University Press, 1961.

MITCHELL, T. Motivation: new directions for theory, research and practice. *Academic Management Review,* **7**(1), January 1982, pp. 80–88.

MULLINS, L. *Management and Organizational Behaviour.* Boston, MA, Pitman, 1999, 5th edn.

NAOUM, S. Do site managers and the head office perceive productivity factors differently? *Journal of Engineering, Construction and Architectural Management,* **3**(1), March 1996, pp. 147–160.

NICHOLLS, C. and LANGFORD, D. Motivation of site engineers. *Technical Information Service,* CIOB (1987).

OLOMOLAIYE, P. An evaluation of the relationships between bricklayers' motivation and productivity. *Construction Management and Economies,* **8**, 1990, pp. 301–313.

POTER, L. and LAWLER, E. *Managerial Attitudes and Performance.* Irwin-Dorsey, 1968.

REINSCHMIDT, K. Productivity in the construction industry. *Productivity in Engineering Design,* Proceedings of ASCE Conference, Lincoln, IL, 1976.

SANVIDO, V. and PAULSON, B. Site-level construction information system. *Journal of Construction Engineering and Management, ASCE,* **118**(4), 1992, pp. 701–715.

STINCHOMBE, A. Bureaucratic and craft administration of production: a comparative study. *Administrative Science Quarterly,* **4**, 1959, pp. 168–187.

STUKHARD, G. Construction management responsibilities during design. *Journal of Construction Engineering and Management, ASCE,* **113**(1), 1987.

THOMAS, H., SANDERS, S. and BILAL, S. Comparison of labour productivity. *Journal of Construction Engineering and Management, ASCE*, **118**(4), 1992, pp. 635–650.

THOMAS, H., SANVIDO, V. and SANDERS, S. Impact of material management on productivity – a case study. *Journal of Construction Engineering and Management, ASCE*, **115**(3), 1989, pp. 370–384.

VROOM, V. *Work and Motivation.* New York, Wiley, 1964 (also published by Krieger, 1982).

Chapter 10

Personnel management

Personnel management is the part of management that deals with the administration and welfare of the human resources. It can be regarded as the agent for implementing the organizational strategies that are set by its leaders. Hence, the personnel function becomes as important a part of practising construction organizations as the marketing and finance functions.

This chapter provides the reader with an appreciation of the function of the personnel department and recognizes its importance for improving organizational effectiveness. The first part of this chapter explains the nature of the personnel function and analyses personnel policies and activities. The second part deals with the 'soft' issues of human resource management (HRM), namely interviewing, recruitment, training, staff development and management development. Figure 10.1 summarizes the overall principles of the chapter (also see Fig. 1.1).

Learning objectives

To:

> ➢ explain the nature of the personnel function and contrast personnel management and human resource management
> ➢ understand the process of recruitment
> ➢ recognize the importance of training and staff appraisal
> ➢ understand the meaning and importance of management development.

The meaning of personnel management

Personnel management is another essential management function within the overall make-up of the organization. It deals with the administration

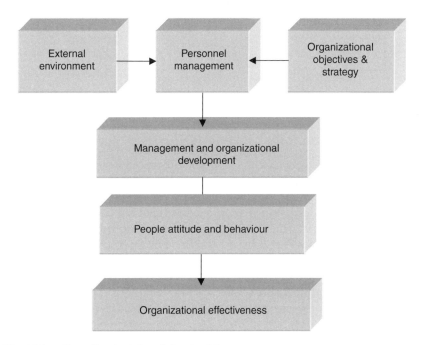

Fig. 10.1.   Overall principles of chapter 10

and welfare of the human resources within the organization. The Institute of Personnel Management has defined the term personnel management as:

> *that part of management which is concerned with people at work and their relationships with an enterprise. Its aim is to bring together and develop into an effective organization the men and women who make up an enterprise and, having regard for the well-being of the individual and of working groups, to enable them to make their best contribution to its success'*

Personnel management is therefore concerned with the following functions.

- (*a*) Staffing:
    - (i)   manpower planning or human resource planning
    - (ii) recruitment and selection of staff
    - (iii) contracts of employment.
- (*b*) Staff appraisal and development:
    - (i)   administrating staff appraisals
    - (ii) staff training
    - (iii) management development.
- (*c*) Health and safety:
    - (i)   administrating health and safety
    - (ii) welfare.

    (*d*) Industrial relations:
        (i)   trades unions
        (ii)   strikes.

It is important to emphasize here that the term human resource management (HRM) is usually used interchangeably with personnel management – however, there are some differences in the meanings of these two terms. Graham and Bennett (1995) noted the following relationships and differences between HRM and personnel management.

    (*a*) Personnel management is practical, utilitarian and instrumental, and mostly concerned with administration and the implementation of policies. Human resources management, conversely, has strategic dimensions and involves the total deployment of human resources within the firm. Thus, for example, HRM will consider such matters as:
        (i)   the aggregate of the organization's labour force in the context of an overall corporate plan (how many divisions and subsidiaries the company is to have, design of the organization, etc.)
        (ii)   how much to spend on training the workforce, given strategic decisions on target quality levels, product prices, volume of production and so on
        (iii) the desirability of establishing relations with trades unions from the viewpoint of the effective management control of the entire organization
        (iv) human asset accounting, i.e. the systematic measurement and analysis of the costs and financial benefits of alternative personnel policies (e.g. the monetary consequences of staff development exercises, the effects of various salary structures, etc.) and the valuation of the human worth of the enterprise's employees.

The strategic approach to HRM involves the integration of personnel and other HRM considerations into the firm's overall corporate planning and strategy formulation procedures. It is proactive, seeking constantly to discover new ways of utilizing the labour force in a more productive manner, thus giving the business a competitive edge. Practical manifestations of the adoption of a strategic approach to HRM might include:

        (i)   incorporation of a brief summary of the firm's basic HRM policy into its mission statement
        (ii)   explicit consideration of the consequences for employees of each of the firm's strategies and major new projects
        (iii) designing organization structures to suit the needs of employees rather than conditioning the latter to fit in with the existing form of organization
        (iv) having the head of HRM on the firm's board of directors.

More than ever before, human resource managers are expected to contribute to productivity and quality improvement, the stimulation of creative thinking, leadership and the development of corporate skills.

(b) HRM is concerned with the wider implications of the management of change and not just with the effects of change on working practices. It seeks proactively to encourage flexible attitudes and the acceptance of new methods.

(c) Aspects of HRM constitute major inputs into organizational development exercises.

(d) Personnel management is (necessarily) reactive and diagnostic. It *responds* to changes in employment law, labour market conditions, trade union actions, government Codes of Practice and other environmental influences. HRM, on the other hand, is *prescriptive* and is concerned with strategies, the initiation of new activities and the development of fresh ideas.

(e) HRM determines general policies for employment relationships within the enterprise. Thus, it needs to establish within the organization a *culture* that is conducive to employee commitment and co-operation. Personnel management, on the other hand, has been criticized for being primarily concerned with imposing *compliance* with company rules and procedures among employees, rather than with loyalty and commitment to the firm.

(f) Personnel management has short-term perspectives; HRM has long-term perspectives, seeking to *integrate* all the human aspects of the organization into a coherent whole and to establish high-level employee goals.

(g) The HRM approach emphasizes the need:
   (i)   for direct communication with employees rather than their collective representation
   (ii) to develop an organizational culture conducive to the adoption of flexible working methods
   (iii) for group working and employee participation in group decisions
   (iv) to enhance employees' long-term capabilities, not just their competence at current duties.

A contentious view of the difference between HRM and personnel management is the proposition that the latter is 'pluralistic' in orientation, while HRM is 'unitaristic'.

Despite the above differences, it is perhaps safe to state that the variations between personnel management and HRM are largely of meaning and emphasis rather than substance. As Mullins (1999) put it: 'HRM is really little more than *old wine in new bottles* and associated with personnel managers seeking to enhance their status and influence'.

For simplicity, I shall use the terms personnel management and personnel function throughout the remainder of this chapter.

The personnel function

As personnel management deals mainly with the administrative part of human resources, the personnel function plays an essential role in the overall success of an organization, especially in a highly labour-intensive industry such as construction. Figure 10.2 shows the steps and functions that are associated with personnel management. The following sections discuss the main functions of personnel management.

Manpower (human resource) planning

Manpower planning can be defined as a management technique for forecasting and selecting the type and number of employees required in order to achieve specific objectives. The manner in which personnel management deals with manpower planning depends largely on analyses of the external environment and organizational objectives and needs (see analyses of the environment in chapter 3 and organizational strategy in chapter 4). Atkinson (1985) stated that:

> *under the combined influences of profound economic recession, uncertainty about market growth, technological change in both product and production methods, and reductions in working time, British employees are beginning to introduce novel and unorthodox formations in their development of labour. They mark a significant break with the conventional ... labour markets which dominate manpower management both in theory and in practice. These innovations are intended to secure greater flexibility from the workforce ...*

Moreover, the nature of the product delivered by the construction industry and the manner in which the building team is formed make the selection process of people rather different from other industries. In construction, there is a clear divide between the resourcing of operatives on site and the appointment of professional and management staff at organizational level. This divide implies that there is a need for long-term planning at the organizational level and short-term planning at site level.

Short-term planning is concerned with the day-to-day acquisition and recruitment of manpower at site level (e.g. bricklayers and carpenters). Site recruitment is usually decentralized and is done by the project manager or the site manager. However, with large projects, manpower planning is usually done in consultation with the personnel manager at organizational level.

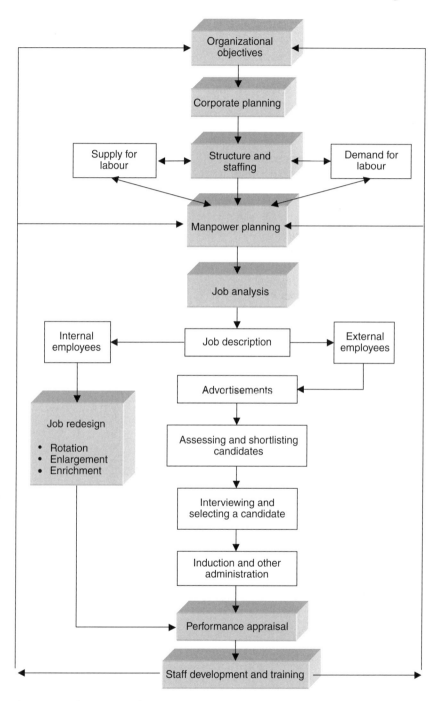

Fig. 10.2.   The process of manpower planning

Long-term planning is concerned with working out a strategic plan for acquiring and utilizing human resources at organizational level (mainly skilled labour, experts, professionals and managers). It is very much linked with organizational objectives and structure and forms part of the firm's corporate planning. In construction, manpower planning is usually done by the personnel manager who acts in consultation with and takes advice from line managers and project managers. Manpower planning is a dynamic process that requires continuous review (see Fig. 10.2).

Pratt and Bennett (1985) listed seven interrelated areas of activity or 'steps' towards creating the 'manpower plan'.

(a) *Manpower objectives as part of the corporate plan.* Any objective regarding the demand or supply of manpower is influenced by issues such as capital expenditure, marketing, reorganization, diversification and financial forecasts. The manpower demand and supply forecasts will in turn lead to manpower polices such as recruitment, training, transfer, promotion, redundancies, etc. These polices will be audited to ensure that the right numbers and type of staff are employed.

(b) *Manpower audit (external).* This is an assessment of the external environment with regard to the supply and demand of the labour markets, etc. The national labour market is extremely dynamic and useful statistical information concerning factors of employment is generally available. In construction, such information is available from employment institutions such as the Construction Industry Training Board (CITB).

However, according to Agapiou *et al.* (1995), much of the information available is unintelligible to companies, and instances abound of large projects being located in areas where there is insufficient labour to satisfy the demand generated. It is difficult to estimate how many trained craft workers are either employed or working in other industries at any one time. The reason being is that there is a high flow rate for workers getting in and out of the industry due to fluctuation of payment. A more thorough analysis of supply and demand of skilled labour can therefore be carried out by an internal audit.

(c) *Manpower audit (internal).* This can be done within the framework of the corporate plan by using management information carried within the company. Analyses need to audit factors such as:
  (i)   age
  (ii) skills
  (iii) promotion and transfer possibilities
  (iv) productivity levels

> (v) costs
> (vi) turnover and wastage.

(d) *Supply forecasting.* Having established the objectives and carried out the external and internal audits, it will then be possible to forecast future needs for manpower and assess the sources available to meet those needs for the life of the plan.

(e) *Demand forecasting.* Manpower demand forecasting will be based upon activity levels indicated by the corporate plan, as well as any shortage indicated by the audits. From this, a forecast of the numbers and types of staff required by various departments or units should be possible. Various techniques are available to forecast manpower demand, e.g. operational research, work study and statistical models.

(f) *Implementation.* The objectives, audits and supply and demand forecasts that contribute to the manpower plan should then be converted into policies that should produce in turn concrete programmes of action. The manpower policies should be formed by considering:

> (i)   recruitment – the numbers and types of employees required over the period of the plan together with details of any potential supply problems
>
> (ii) training – the amount and types of training required for both new recruits and existing staff
>
> (iii) employee development – closely linked to training, this should take account of projected promotions and transfers
>
> (iv) productivity – methods for maintaining or improving productivity including work methods, incentives, productivity bargaining and other methods of improving motivation
>
> (v)   redundancy – specific plans regarding the number of potential redundancies and how these will be dealt with
>
> (vi) accommodation – plans for expansion, contraction or relocation, including buildings, equipment and for improving working conditions.

(g) *Control.* Part of the manpower policy implementation will be a system of manpower control, mainly for cost, productivity and quality.

Recruitment

Site recruitment

Recruitment is that part of the personnel function that deals with the process of filling a vacancy. It includes examination of the vacancy, consideration of sources of suitable candidates, making contact with those candidates and attracting applications from others. As mentioned above, most on site recruitment is carried out by project or site managers who decide the labour requirements for each stage of the construction process and have to plan the order in which events take place. Many construction sites only have one or two contractor's staff permanently present, usually a project manager and possibly a general foreman depending on the size of the job. Larger sites have a site manager and a site agent (Drucker and White 1996).

It is important to point out here that, over the last two decades or so, there have been several employment acts which have affected the use of permanent labour by contracting firms. For instance, the Redundancy Payment Act made a number of firms cautious of their policy to keep labour permanently employed, whilst the Employment Protection Act provides grounds for realizing unfair dismissal. At the present time, because of the way the industry secures its work, continuity of employment is becoming difficult to guarantee. Contractors are looking to minimize fixed costs as much as possible. On average, contractors now provide only around 25% of their employees with steady employment, the other 75% are, to varying degrees, 'casual'. As a result, firms end up appointing different people on various projects. Here, the majority of workers that are appointed on building sites are appointed on a trial and error basis, which makes the satisfactory performance of any individual highly dependent on chance. However, some large companies realize the importance of employing operatives, especially skilled labour, on a permanent basis and try to use the same teams on a series of contracts. The degree to which construction operatives remain in the employment of a single contractor over a period of time depends largely on the type of labour market in which the operative is working.

A decision to use self-employed labour should take full account of the employment law implications and the potential liabilities of self-employment. The professional and technical labour requirements of each site will be decided by the heads of each department (e.g. surveying, planning, contracts managers), and these needs will be met from central pools at either head office or regional office level. The role of the personnel or human resource manager may be to act as conciliator between these different groups and to overcome divisions.

Professional and management recruitment

The main stages in the recruitment process of professionals are as follows.

(a) *Job analysis.* At the implementation of the company strategy new jobs may need to be created and filled by internal or external candidates. Here, each job needs to be examined in turn and a job description will then be written. The process of job analysis is essential to effective staff selection. It also provides the basis for performance review and appraisal, training, reward systems, staff development and career progression, and the design of working methods and practices.

(b) *Job description.* This is a broad statement of the purposes, scope, duties and responsibilities of a particular job. A job description may contain the following:

(i) department name

(ii) job title

(iii) function and scope of job

(iv) main duties and responsibilities

(v) chain of authority (i.e. who the job is responsible to)

(vi) person specifications and job criteria such as qualifications, skill and experience

(vii) salary details.

(c) *Attracting applicants and advertising.* This is an important step in the recruitment process and it requires a specialist person or department to deal with it. It is at this stage when suitable candidates for the job can be found. Potential sources for placing advertisement include: employment agencies and job centres; universities; newspapers such as the *Times* and the *Daily Telegraph*; and trade and professional publishers such as Chartered Institute of Building; *Building Magazine* and *New Civil Engineer*.

(d) *Selection of the right candidate.* Once the personnel department receives application forms from candidates, they can be analysed in order to select the most suitable potential employees. A short list of candidates is normally drawn up and the selection process commences. There is a wide range of techniques for selecting the right candidate for the job. The most popular one is to conduct a face-to-face interview. Here, there are certain guidelines that need to be followed. Pratt and Bennett (1985) suggested the following.

(i) Base the interview upon a thorough job description and person specification that set out clear criteria (e.g. seven-point plan, 'difficulties and distastes', 'critical incidents', etc.)

(ii) Ensure that the interviewer is thoroughly conversant with all data concerning the job and the applicant before the inter-view commences.

(iii) Interviews should be held in comfortable surroundings, free from interruption and allowing enough time for adequate discussion.

(iv) Prepare a criterion-related check list against which to rate the applicant.

(v)   Begin the interview in a conversational manner in order to help the candidate relax.

(vi)   Ask open-ended questions rather than those only requiring yes/no answers.

(vii)   Follow interviewee's lead where possible, and endeavour to probe relevant areas in depth.

(viii)   Be attentive, but do not react in a way that will reveal disapproval or prejudice.

(ix)   Allow the interviewee to talk freely, but endeavour to ensure that all the information you require is obtained.

(x)   Avoid being influenced by 'halo effects' and 'stereotypes'.

(xi)   Leave difficult questions until a rapport has been established, but end on an agreeable note.

(xii)   Note taking is useful, but should preferably be left until immediately after the interview, as it can be distracting.

(e)   *Final assessment and placement.* Once the interview process is completed, a final assessment of all candidates will follow in order to avoid subjectivity or bias. Assuming that a suitable candidate has emerged from the selection process, he or she must then receive a formal offer. Assuming the offer is accepted, the recruitment process is virtually concluded.

Staff appraisal

While the candidate is progressing with the job, the personnel manager should continuously conduct a staff appraisal. The staff appraisal system is a mechanism for gauging the attitude and performance of the employee at the work place. The main purposes of an appraisal are to:

(a)   create two-way communication between management and employees

(b)   establish the strengths and weaknesses of individuals and try to build on the strengths or overcome the weaknesses

(c)   indicate the need for training and staff development

(d)   generate inputs for human resource planning, especially manpower planning, career-path planning and succession planning

(e)   assist managers to determine the future use of an employee, e.g. whether he or she shall remain in his or her present job or be transferred, promoted or dismissed.

Appraisal methods

The six main methods of appraisal are outlined in the following.

(a) *Rating scale.* The appraiser has a scale by which he or she can judge the degree of achievement or non-achievement of the appraisee on a particular factor or issue. The judgements of such factors are called quantifiers: they reflect the intensity of the particular judgement involved. For example, the performance criteria could be:
   (i)   volume of work produced
   (ii)   quality of work
   (iii)   knowledge of job
   (iv)   dependability
   (v)   innovation
   (vi)   staff development
   (vii)   communication skill
   (viii) teamwork spirit.
   The quantifiers could be: (1) high; (2) medium; (3) low; (4) not acceptable.
(b) *Ranking.* The ranking format is used when the manager wants to place a number of subordinates in order of merit, usually on their total ability in the job but sometimes according to a few separate characteristics.
(c) *Semantic differential scale.* Diagrammatic rating scale is another means of measuring intensity of judgement and the semantic differential is the most popular form of this type of scaling. In this method the appraiser indicates his or her judgement on a seven-point bipolar scale defined with contrasting adjectives at each end. It can be best applied when the performance of different groups on a particular matter needs to be compared. Examples could be rating good–bad, strong–weak, satisfied–dissatisfied. The seven-point bipolar scale can be presented in a numerical format, e.g.

$$\text{Good} \; \_\_ \; \_\_ \; \_\_ \; \_\_ \; \_\_ \; \_\_ \; \_\_ \; \text{Bad}$$
$$3 \quad 2 \quad 1 \quad 0 \quad -1 \quad -2 \quad -3$$

(d) *The open-ended method.* In this method, the appraiser creates a free discussion environment with the employee to encourage him or her to express their feelings in their own way. Here, the manager is expected to write a few sentences about the subordinate rather than to make ticks in columns. This method has many varieties, a common one being for the manager to answer the following four questions about the subordinate.
   (i)   What are the employee's strong points in relation to the job?
   (ii)   What are the employee's weak points in relation to the job?
   (iii)   What is the employee's promotion potential?
   (iv)   What are the employee's training needs?

(e) *Behaviourally anchored rating scale (BARS).* This is a relatively recently developed approach which requires the appraiser to select some aspect of a subordinate's behaviour considered by the assessor to be typical of the appraisee's performance in a certain aspect of a job. For example, the superior of an employee being assessed under the heading 'ability to cope with stress' would be asked to complete a form which begins with the words, 'I would expect this employee to (behave in the following way)', followed by a list of statements from which the appraiser must choose. Alongside each statement are a certain number of points indicating the relative desirability of the behaviour. Among the statements in this example might be:

remain calm and collected	5
become frustrated	4
show irritability	3
act erratically	2
fly off the handle	1

(f) *Objective outcome.* This approach – sometimes referred to as Management by Objectives (MBO) – is usually associated with a sophisticated performance appraisal scheme and rating scale. It requires the appraiser to assess a tangible outcome of the employee, e.g. the number of units produced, number of contracts awarded, number of projects delivered on time, etc. The MBO system may follow the process outlined below.

(i) At the outset, the target and objectives of the task must be set clearly and agreed between staff and management. With the MBO system, these targets are established by the subordinates and not by the management. However, the targets must be in line with organizational objectives and special consideration needs to be given to the manager's contribution to improving performance.

(ii) A time span must be set to measure the outcome. Here, there will be a monitoring and review system for appraisal of progress and performance, including self-checking and evaluation.

(iii) At the end of the agreed period, the final outcome will be compared with the target. If targets are achieved, rewards may be given and then new targets will be set for the subsequent period. If targets are not achieved then a new plan should be put in place to undertake the necessary revision.

Criteria for conducting the appraisal

The criteria of a good appraisal system were summarized by Mullins (1999) as follows.

(*a*) The purpose and nature of the appraisal system must be made clear to the assessor and the employee. The system should focus on the strengths and accomplishments of staff, rather than their faults and failures, and it should lead to a plan for the future development and progress of the individual.

(*b*) The system should not be perceived as something which is the prerogative of the personnel department or introduced for its benefit. Top management should be seen to own the system and be fully committed to the concept of appraisal. They should ensure full consultation with trades unions and staff representatives, and all managers and members of staff. Adequate provision will need to be made for the proper training of appraisers and there should be a reasonable time allowance for the activity. An effective administration system should aim to keep form-filling and paperwork to a minimum.

(*c*) The appraisal system should not be viewed in isolation but in relation to the corporate objectives of the organization, and designed to suit its culture and particular requirements. The system should be integrated with related personnel policies and practices such as human resource planning, and training and development programmes. A starting point is the process of job analysis. This identifies the purpose, and main duties and responsibilities of each job. From the job description can be determined the expected outcomes of the job, standards of performance and the criteria against which the appraisal will be based.

(*d*) The system needs to be monitored regularly to ensure that appraisals are being carried out properly and to obtain feedback from managers. The system should be kept under continual review and, where necessary, modified to meet changing environmental influences or the needs of the organization. It is important to ensure that operation of the system and the criteria used for assessment satisfy all legal requirements, for example those defined under the Sex Discrimination Act and the Race Relations Act. The system must be supported by appropriate follow-up action: for example, seeing that work plans or changes in duties and responsibilities actually take place, and that suitable arrangements are made to meet identified training or development needs.

(*e*) As the main purpose of appraisals is to help staff improve their performance, an appeals procedure should only be used in exceptional circumstances. However, in order to help establish the credibility of the system and to maintain goodwill, it is necessary to establish a formal procedure which is clearly understood by all members of staff. Appeals should be made to a manager in a more senior position than the appraiser or sometimes to a representative committee. The appeals procedure should include provision for staff to be assisted, if requested, by a union or staff representative.

Staff training

Training provision and planning is an important function of the personnel manager. Adequate training creates competent employees who can act as a driving force towards organizational development. Training in construction can be divided into two levels – apprentice training and technical training.

Apprentice training

Apprenticeship schemes can suit a range of trainees from graduates to craft apprentices. Training is achieved through a combination of on-the-job and off-the-job training. The latter is usually carried out at a technical college, with knowledge and technical skill usually tested at the end of the training. The training programme must be carried out under the terms and conditions laid down by the National Joint Training Scheme (NJTS) for Skilled Building Occupations.

Technical training

Over the past three decades or so, governments have taken various initiatives on training. The Industrial Training Act 1964 set up the Industrial Training Board (ITB) to encourage the development of training policy. Due to the precarious nature of the construction industry, with a large mobile workforce employed by numerous small firms and the increased use of labour-only subcontracting, skills training in construction has become rather different from that in other industries. As a result, the government launched its special Construction Industry Training Board (CITB) to provide a mechanism for training young people in modern technical skills in construction. Technical training may also be provided by trade associations, private training organizations and internal company training.

Systematic approach to training

A systematic approach to training may take the following steps.

   (a) *Defining training policy*. This policy should include statements such as the link between organizational objectives and training, the type of training available and the person responsible for the training.

(b) *Identifying training needs.* This includes organizational and individual needs and identification can be carried out by diverse means, e.g. via staff appraisal, productivity indices available to the organization, or informal meetings with staff to identify their training needs.

(c) *Preparing a training programme and plan.* The training programme should be an integral part of the management of human resources and must be planned carefully. Consideration should be given to the priority, loading and pacing of information; timing and sequence; common or related items; variety of subject matter and methods of presentation; review and consolidation.

(d) *Deciding on the methods of training.* These may include apprenticeships, assignments or projects, job rotation or job instructions, lectures and seminars, case studies, role-playing, internal and external courses, films and videos, computer simulation and distance learning.

(e) *Evaluating training.* There should be a proper system of evaluation in order to determine whether the training programme actually resulted in the planned intention to increase skill or knowledge or modify employee's attitude and behaviour, as well as to determine whether training has actually achieved organizational goals.

Management development

Management development is a process towards developing managerial skills in order to achieve the needs of both employees and the organization. Langford *et al.* (1995) defined management development as:

the process whereby the construction organization's managerial resources are nurtured to meet the present needs of the organization. This process involves the interaction of the needs of the organization and the needs of the individual manager in terms of development and advancement.

The term 'management development' is sometimes confused with the term 'organizational development'. In short, management development focuses on individuals through the provision of training opportunities and morale building, whereas organizational development aims to make changes to the organization's internal environment or culture. Harrison (1992) stated:

employee development as part of the organization's overall human resource strategy means the skilful provision and organization of learning experiences in the workplace in order that performance can be improved, that work goals can be achieved, and that, through enhancing skills, knowledge, the learning ability and the enthusiasm of people at every level, there can be continuous organizational as well as individual growth. Employee development must, therefore, be part of a wider strategy for the business, aligned with the organization's corporate mission and goals.

Investors in People (IIP) initiative

The IIP initiative was commissioned by the Department of Employment in 1990. Its aim was to raise the level of commitment to training and development among British employees by providing the opportunity for them to audit their existing practices against a national standard (IDS (Income Data Services) 1993). This enables gaps to be identified in existing provision, and focuses attention on the strategic benefits of linking training to business objectives. It also helps organizations in demonstrating the achievement of total quality management along with attainment of the BS 5750 quality standard.

The IIP initiative is defined by Drucker and White (1996) as 'a planned approach to setting and communicating business goals and developing people to meet these goals, so that what people can do, and are motivated to do, matches what the business needs them to do.' There are four IIP principles, namely commitment, planning, action and evaluation. According to Drucker and White (1996, pp. 135–136), the benefits of IIP can be wide ranging and may include:

- improved earning, productivity and profitability through benefiting from more skilled and motivated employees
- reduced costs and wastage because employees are committed to such objectives
- enhanced quality because investment in people can add considerable value to 'kite mark' schemes such as BS 5750 and ISO 9000
- improved motivation because greater involvement, personnel development and recognition can lead to higher morale, reduced absenteeism, readier acceptance of change, and greater identification with the organization beyond the confines of the job
- customer satisfaction because employees become more customer-focused in their work
- public recognition, which itself may attract the best-quality job applicants
- an improvement in competitive edge to secure future prosperity for the organization.

Health and safety

Due to several forces such as public concern and increasing statutory pressure, the issue of health and safety (H&S) at work is becoming a major concern in many construction organizations. It is now regarded as an integral part of the personnel function. The first active H&S committee was formed in 1970, under the chairmanship of Lord Robens. It was commissioned to consider occupational health and safety law and practice. Its findings provided a basis for the Health and Safety at Work etc. Act 1974 (HSWA). The 1974 act consists of four parts:

Part I: Health, Safety and Welfare at Work
Part II: The Employment Medical Advisory Service
Part III: Building Regulations
Part IV: Miscellaneous.

The main objectives of the HSWA are to:

* secure the H&S of persons at work
* protect persons other than persons at work against risks to H&S, arising out of, or in connection with the activities of persons at work
* control the keeping and use of explosive or highly inflammable or dangerous substances; prevent people acquiring, possessing or illegally using such substances
* control the emission of noxious substances from any area.

The HSWA led to an action plan by employers to ensure, so far as is reasonably practical, the health, safety and welfare at work of all employees. The action plan included the following.

(a) *'Provide and maintain plant and systems of work that are safe and without risks to health.'*
(b) *'Arrange for ensuring the safe use, handling, storage and transport of articles and substances.'*
(c) *'Provide such information, instruction, training and supervision necessary to ensure their health and safety at work.'*
(d) *'Maintain any place of work under the employer's control, in a safe condition, without risk to health, and maintain a means of access to and egress from that is safe and without risk.'*
(e) *'Provide and maintain a working environment that is safe, without risk to health and adequate as regards facilities and arrangements for welfare at work.'*

Employer's Statement of Policy. *'Except in such cases as may be prescribed, it is his duty to prepare and revise as necessary a written statement of general policy with respect to the health and safety at work of employees, and the organisation and arrangements made to carry out the policy, and to bring the statement and any revision to the notice of all employees.'* It is usual practice to issue a copy of the general Statement of Policy to every member of the staff, and every time-book paid employee upon joining the company. A more detailed description of the safety organisation including the name of the Director with particular responsibility for health and safety policy and training, should be made available at Head Office and on each contract site. Provision may be included for the addition of any particular site hazards, the precautions to be taken, and duties of persons responsible, to be inserted by site management.

Summary

This chapter deals with the function of the personnel manager. Personnel management is the part of the management system that deals with the administration and welfare of human resources within the organization. Personnel management is sometimes confused with the term human resource management (HRM). In principle they are both the same. However, HRM is more concerned with the strategic part of the company and is integrated into the firm's overall corporate planning and strategy formulation procedures. In short, personnel management is 'pluralistic' in orientation, while HRM is 'unitaristic'.

The main roles of the personnel function are to undertake manpower planning, recruit, conduct staff appraisal, provide training programmes, monitor staff development and ensure the implementation of health and safety policies within the organization.

References

AGAPLOU, A., PRICE, A. and McCAFFER, R. Forecasting and supply of construction skills in the UK. *Construction Management and Economics*, **13**, 1995, pp. 353–364.

ATKINSON, J. The changing corporation. In *New Patterns of Work*, Clutterbuck, D. (ed.), Cowes, 1985.

DRUCKER, J. and WHITE, G. *Managing People in Construction*. London Institute of Personnel Management, 1996.

GRAHAM, H. and BENNETT, H. *M&E Handbook, Human Resources Management*. London, Longman, 1995, 8th edn.

HARRISON, R. *Employee Development*. London Institute of Personnel Development, 1992.

LANGFORD, D., HANCOCK, M., FELLOWS, R. and GALE, A. *Human Resources Management in the Construction Industry*. London, Longman, 1995.

MULLINS, L. *Management and Organizational Behaviour*. Boston, MA, Pitman, 1999, 5th edn.

PRATT, K. and BENNETT, S. *Elements of Personnel Management*. New York, Van Nostrand Reinhold, 1985.

Case study. Investors in People at Shepherd Construction (from Drucker and White (1996, pp. 139–148))

Shepherd Construction is part of the York-based Shepherd Building Group, one of the largest privately-owned building businesses in the UK. The Group includes three divisions: construction (five companies), manufacturing (Portakabin Ltd and Portasilo Ltd), and housing, commercial and industrial development (Shepherd Development Co. Ltd and Shepherd Homes Ltd). Shepherd Construction Ltd was founded as a family business in 1890, and still is, for members of the Shepherd family are involved in the management of the company today. It operates throughout the UK and has regional offices in York, Manchester, Northampton, Birmingham, Nottingham, London, Leeds, Cardiff and Darlington. The company is known as a pioneer in Design and Build techniques and has successfully met the exacting demands of clients in the public sector (e.g. hospitals, universities, law courts, prisons) and the private sector (factories, shopping centres, hotels and office developments). The company has worked for such companies as Glaxo, ICI, Coca-Cola, Vickers, Panasonic, Nestlé, Boots, Asda and W H Smith. It recently completed the new hotel at Alton Towers theme park.

The Group as a whole employs around 2500 people, of whom 1400 are employed in Shepherd Construction. The company is unusual for the construction industry in that it employs a substantial direct workforce of operatives (around two-thirds of the workforce). This commitment to direct labour is based on a number of factors – not least the ability of the company to find a succession of projects for its operatives, enabling them to be employed continuously. Another factor stated by the company in support of direct labour is that such operatives do not have to be retrained for each job and know the company's quality standards. The investment in specialist skills training therefore provides a payback over the longer term. The directly employed need less supervision because the job security provided is an incentive to work productively and to high standards. According to the company, directly employed labour is not more costly than self-employment if it is managed correctly, because the workers can be more productive, although there may be higher administrative costs. The company says that its reputation for employing operatives on a longer-term basis than elsewhere in the industry means that it attracts many adult job applicants and young people looking for career opportunities.

Company philosophy

The company has a well established reputation for reliability and integrity and, as a privately-owned family business, is able to take a long-term view.

In the words of the managing director, Paul Shepherd, the company thinks 'long-term rather than in terms of quick profit'. This applies as much to its employment policies as to other business matters. The company has had a strong commitment to training and developing its employees for around 35 years, from the time Sir Peter Shepherd helped to develop construction industry training through the Chartered Institute of Building and the Construction Industry Training Board. Today the company has highly developed personnel, training and safety policies. These include an appraisal system for all staff, including site-based operatives. The company has a strong belief in the competitive advantage of good human resource management policies, especially in the training and development of its work-force. The aim is to seek constant and continuous incremental improvement which can be measured. The company mission statement includes commitments to personal involvement, constant improvement, quality management, the measurement of progress, and the selection of sub-contractors and suppliers on the grounds of excellence. The chairman and managing director, Paul Shepherd, believes that the company 'is not just here for the boom times, nor are we going to disappear when things get tough'. He says that 'long-term progress is more likely to come from continual action in a small way rather than by occasional great leaps forward'. The company's mission is to be 'not the biggest but the best' building company.

The personnel department

The Construction Division personnel function is centralized in York and serves the four companies nationally. The department consists of the chief personnel services manager, the training and development manager, the health and safety manager, the security manager and four personnel managers. Each of the personnel managers has responsibility for a region or company. There are also three health and safety officers. The training and development manager has an assistant plus two training administrators, one of whom was employed recently to help with Shepherd's external training courses provision.

The company has employee handbooks for both staff and operative employees. The company states that it 'places a high value on good staff relations and believes that effective communication plays an important part in this'. For operatives the company follows the NJCBI working rule agreement and contributes to the national holiday and lump sum retirement schemes for its employees. It has good relations with the local UCATT trade union officials but does not have any formal collective relationships at company level. Subscriptions are deducted at source where employees choose to belong to a union. Staff employees are not unionized and are not covered by collective bargaining.

The company's commitment to good employee relations manifests itself in the low turnover and length of service of employees. Almost 55 per cent of the operatives and 60 per cent the salaried staff have been with the company for six years and over. Around 70 per cent of the salaried staff have had a substantial promotion since they joined the company, and about 40 per cent started with the company as apprentices, students or graduate trainees.

Training and development

Shepherd's training activities are organized by the training and development manager and his staff. Policy statements cover the broad approach to training and development. The company 'encourages members of staff to develop their abilities in order to improve efficiency in their present positions and, where appropriate to equip themselves for more senior positions'. In the view of the managing director, Paul Shepherd, it takes time to produce results – in the case of middle management training up to five years before a payback is seen. However, in his view, 'Training is rather like breathing – you have to keep breathing to stay alive, and you have to keep training to remain successful commercially.' The company has won two national training awards over the last four years. In addition, it became the first national contractor to achieve the Investors in People (IIP) standard in 1992, and was successfully reassessed in 1995.

Staff are encouraged to study for relevant qualifications: continuous personal development is seen as very important. Each employee, including operatives, has an annual appraisal to set training needs and development plans. This appraisal system is designed to focus on the concept of continuous development and improvement as a route towards higher-quality delivery to the customer. At present, some 126 employees are currently attending external courses which lead to vocational qualifications, in addition to the company's 80-plus annual in-house training courses.

The company provides a wide range of training programmes, both internal and external. Craft training is seen as very important and the chief executive, Paul Shepherd, has encouraged greater attention in this area. There are around 60 craft apprentices (mainly located in the north, where direct labour is more common and there is therefore a ready supply of mentors) who are recruited at the age of 16 for a three-and-a-half-year course. Most of these are now classified as Modern Apprenticeships and the apprentices are of employed status (they are also paid at National Agreement rates of pay). These apprentices are studying towards NVQ Levels 2 and 3. The training is a mix of on-the-job training and block release. The appraisal of operatives at site level is used to plan development for such staff, and the company has issued a guide to operative training for site managers. Training is also available for technicians, who take four-year courses in such qualifications as HNC/D quantity surveying, planning, and site management. Most of these students progress on to professional qualifications, and some are sponsored for degree courses.

Shepherd provides industrial placements for undergraduates studying relevant degrees, usually for one year. The training plans for such students are agreed with the universities before the start of the training, and jointly monitored. Such placements may lead to company sponsorship of the student during the final year of study. The company jointly sponsors degree courses and individual students. Courses include Commercial Management and Quantity Surveying at Loughborough University and UMIST, and Construction Management at Salford University. These are four-year sandwich courses with a guaranteed one-year attachment to the company. There is also a two-year graduate training programme for university graduates in relevant disciplines. The aim is to widen rapidly their knowledge and competence, and they are also encouraged to gain their appropriate professional qualification.

There are both site supervision and site management courses. Some 15 years ago the firm started in-company site supervision and site management courses which are CIOB-accredited. These courses are run in-house in block-release mode, and are now being revamped to update and focus them towards the new NVQ Levels 3 and 4. Shepherd Construction was the first company to register as an assessment centre for the new CIOB/CITB NVQ 3 site supervisory and NVQ 4 site management programmes in 1994. An in-house NVQ 4 pilot undertaken in 1994 indicated that the NVQ led to a new emphasis on managers' responsibilities for expenditure and recovery, encouraged the pursuit of information, and helped managers reconsider the development of teams, individuals and themselves.

In conjunction with Leeds Metropolitan University, a postgraduate development programme has been developed by the company, which leads to the award of an advanced professional diploma. The core course is jointly delivered by both the company's own staff and external specialists. Reflective learning assignments are managed and assessed by the University.

Finally, a Management Development Programme for middle managers was developed with Leeds Metropolitan University; it was first run in 1992. The programme leads to a post-graduate diploma and allows participants to progress to an MSc in Construction Management. This course includes accreditation of prior learning, work-based learning as well as seven short block modules taught by university staff, company staff and external specialists. Participants have included staff from a variety of backgrounds. Indeed some members of staff started with Shepherd as craft apprentices at the age of 16. Nine trainees gained the diploma in 1994, and three have since been promoted to construction manager and three to project manager. This programme has won a national training award.

The training and development manager has his own budget to cover courses and the cost of graduate sponsorship. In addition, each region has its own budget to cover apprentice training, external courses and building students' fees. The figures are collated centrally. Including the cost of administration, courses, time and travel expenses for those attending courses, as well as the full cost of young trainees (apprentices, students and graduate trainees), Shepherd's expenditure on training is around 7 per cent of payroll and salary bill. The company estimates that two-thirds of the cost of training is directly recovered from the work of young trainees and the CITB grants. Moreover, the company believes that the payback on its training investment is considerably more than this sum in terms of improved company performance.

Shepherd Training and Development Services was formed in 1996 to market and deliver Shepherd expertise externally. This includes short courses linked to post-graduate qualifications.

Total excellence programme

The development of the Investors in People programme within the company was initiated in tandem with a total quality management programme – 'Shepherd's Total Excellence Programme'. The Total Excellence Programme was prompted by increasing competition within the industry and the possibility of a recession after the building boom of the late 1980s. The programme was designed as a means of achieving constant improvement in the quality of the company's services and in the building process and products. It was adopted at board level in 1990, and has been worked down through the organization with target dates for implementation of the various stages. At present the programme is confined to salaried staff.

One of the main elements of the programme is the encouragement of the personal involvement of employees in raising standards and understanding the company's objectives. Communication, involvement and training opportunities are seen as key elements in the process. The programme also concerns the selection of sub-contractors and suppliers on the grounds of their ability to meet the company's excellent standards of performance as well as price.

The Total Excellence Programme was launched in 1991 with a workshop for senior managers; it was followed by a half-day workshop for team leaders and all staff in 1992. Shepherd produced its own video to sell the programme to employees.

Parts of the Shepherd Group are working towards the quality standard ISO 9000, but the company says that this only audits the company's systems and procedures. In its view, people are as important as systems and a successful company needs strength in both areas. Investors in People was therefore seen as a useful adjunct to the total quality programme in that it provided an audit of the quality of the employees.

The commitment to IIP

The company became aware of IIP in 1991 and IIP commitment was made in January 1992. The full standard was achieved within six months in June 1992. This rapid success demonstrated the degree to which Shepherd had already achieved high levels of investment in training and development before committing itself to IIP.

The company decided to commit itself to IIP for a number of reasons:

- the training plan was directly linked to the business plan
- identification of individual training needs was improved
- simple messages were communicated across the company
- consistency was achieved in carrying out appraisals
- company-wide communication from the chairman on the need to develop all employees to achieve business objectives was achieved
- more vigorous evaluation of training was possible, including the monitoring of training's contribution to general business objectives
- a manager guide to operative training gave a new focus to the importance of this level of training
- it encouraged a 'right first time' approach
- it encouraged the further development of site supervision and management training
- it linked management and supervisory training to continuous improvement through projects
- training was linked to NVQ standards
- it encouraged a quality culture within the company.

The evidence for the IIP assessment was completed almost at the same time that the company committed itself to the standard. The assessment was undertaken by a consultant on behalf of the then National Training Task Force, who visited all the regional offices and a number of construction sites. Altogether some 120 interviews were conducted at all levels of employee, starting with the chief executive. Each region provided a list of all employees, from which the assessor could select interviewees. The process of assessment took two weeks and cost the company £2175. The company was successfully reassessed in 1995.

The outcomes of IIP

The main advantage for the company in going through the IIP assessment was that it led to critical review of the training being undertaken and its usefulness. This meant examining in detail how the training being undertaken related to the company's needs, and led to more focus on particular areas. The company is not spending more money on training as a result of gaining IIP but is getting better value for money. The three-year review of IIP status is also seen as a useful device for keeping the company on its toes and looking for continuous improvement. This fits in with the long-term approach adopted by Shepherd.

Linked to the Total Excellence Programme, IIP is seen as providing important benefits for both the company and employees. Together they have contributed toward a number of outcomes:

- market share has been increased
- the objective of completing contracts on time and to the required quality has been reinforced, thereby improving the company's image with clients
- the business has weathered the recent recession in the industry well and with relatively strong order-books
- the high level of repeat business has been improved
- accidents at work have been reduced
- the policy of concentrating on seeking widespread incremental improvements has yielded consistent cost savings
- staff turnover is very low in relation to the norm in the construction industry
- the average length of service is well above the average for the industry
- the company has few problems recruiting and retaining staff because of its reputation for fair dealing and good career development opportunities
- employees are motivated and committed to the company.

The benefits for employees are:

- there is relatively good job security in an industry known for its insecurity, especially among operatives
- there are good opportunities for progression within the company – the majority of Shepherd's middle and senior managers started their careers with the company
- there are good opportunities for achieving vocational, professional and academic qualifications
- the training budget is secure, irrespective of the state of the industry, so employees know that there is a long-term commitment to their development

- there have been improved employment opportunities with the company for apprentices, graduates and technicians, thereby benefiting the local economy
- the culture is friendly and supportive of employees in a tough industry.

A major benefit of IIP is that it demonstrated that Shepherd's training and development was audited against a national standard which applied to all sectors of industry and commerce. The process helps to highlight areas for improvements to be undertaken before assessment. According to the company, 'Perhaps the single most important contribution which IIP can make towards business success is that it provides a clear focus on the value of training within the context of strategic business planning.' It means that managers concentrate on whether the training programmes meet the company's medium- and long-term needs. The achievement of IIP has also sent a message to all employees that the company values their contribution and their involvement in improving the business.

Note: Sources for this case study include both Investors In People UK and IDS Study 530/May 1993, 'Investors In People'. Special thanks go to John Foreman, chief personnel services manager, and Peter Blackburn, training and development manager at Shepherd Construction.

Index

Page numbers in *italics* refer to illustrations

Learning Resources
Centre